(Vampires)

(Vampires)
An Uneasy Essay on the Undead in Film

Jalal Toufic

Station Hill

Copyright © 1993 by Jalal Toufic.

Published by Station Hill Literary Editions, under the Institute for Publishing Arts, Inc., Barrytown, New York 12507. Station Hill Literary Editions is supported in part by grants from the National Endowment for the Arts, a Federal Agency in Washington, D.C., and by the New York State Council on the Arts.

Distributed by the Talman Company, 131 Spring Street, Suite 201E-N, New York, New York 10012.

Cover painting by Ruan Jie. Cover design by Susan Quasha.

Library of Congress Cataloging-in-Publication Data

Toufic, Jalal.
    Vampires, an uneasy essay on the undead in film / Jalal Toufic.
      p. cm.
    ISBN 0-88268-146-X : $12.95
    1. Vampire films—History and criticism.   I. Title.
PN1995.9.V3T68 1993
791.43' 675—dc20   93-23052
                                                                CIP

Manufactured in the United States of America.

Contents

Introduction	1
Who will warn us about the warning?	4
Thresholds and *imaginary lines*	5
Letters	8
Parenthesis	11
Lapses	12
Counterfeiting	22
Through a Glass to encounter the already-there double (in-the-mind)	28
Secrets	30
Ruins	31
Vision and its absence	36
Immobilization and Tunneling	48
Gaps	62
Circles	64
Labyrinth	65
Ci-gît and the virtual	70
Reference	71
The absence of ether, the vacillation of dimensions and excessive presence	73
Silence	77
Fear	79
Some physical characteristics of what has no image	85
Broken Mirrors/glass	85
The off-screen and/or the set	86
Close-Up	93
Extras	94
Out-of-sync	95
Voice-over/Sound-over/Image-over	97
The mourner and the dead/undead	98

Composites	102
Reception and its absence	103
Asceticism and proliferation, or is the iris a halo or a matte?	106
Presence	108
Haunting	108
Telepathy	109
Coincidences(?)	116
Faith	119
Coexistence of tenses	120
Backward Movement	121
Time idiosyncrasies	122
Memory, amnesia and flashback	123
Dissolves	127
Acting	129
In the *you* mode	130
Gutless	132
Masters	133
Vampire Sexuality	134
Absence of breathing	135
Absence of sitting (exception: sleeping in a sitting position)	136
Different Spectra	136
Hibernation	138
The doubling between the vampire and the mad	139
Sensitivity to initial/final conditions	141
Beyond supersaturation (contributing factors: off-film—), *precipitately*	142
Accidents	145
Animals	147
Pain	148

It [the altered state] happened and is over with, and it is still unfolding in a bifurcation branch. And it [resurrection] did not happen	150
Bifurcation	152
Over-turns, or the discrete way in which an angle can widen toward the obtuse	156
Counterfeiting	162
Unfinished Business	167
Death	169
Guilt	177
Matte	178
Parallel Montage	183
The undead has no mirror image	186
At no point did their [many, if not most, non-posed photographs] referent really exist	187
What does not resemble me looks exactly like me/what looks exactly like me does not resemble me	188
Non-embodiment/Indefinite embodiment	189
Bifurcation versions/filiation/remakes	191
Why make another version of *Nosferatu*?	192
Re-creation and period	196
Am I dreaming?	197
Reality-as-filmic	198
Aphorisms	202

Author's Acknowledgements

The author wishes to acknowledge Casey O'Conner and gallery Show N' Tell, San Francisco, for permission to use *Basic* (1989); Ted Julian Arnold and Gallery Morphos, San Francisco, for permission to use *Second Child I, II,* and *III, The Dismay of Mr. Boulager,* and *21*; Susan Morrissey for permission to use *Fear of Flying, Turn-a-bout, Have a Ball Sw'theart*.

The author wishes to thank Annette Barbier, Jim Calabrese, John Corbett, Albert Saikaly (for taking the photographs at the *Aswaq*, Beirut), and Jason Watts.

*In memory of the amnesiac Jalal Toufic
(not that he no longer exists,
but that he was/is undead then/now).*

Introduction:

Writing the introduction after finishing the rest of the book, my memory is coming back to me, and so at present I can give some indication in what context to place it.

Why write on vampires now? It is precisely because vampire films and novels are back in fashion (new version of *Dark Shadows*, Coppola's *Dracula*—) that we should ask: why on vampires now, by what coincidence? How come what functions in the too-late and too-early mode is being written about now, when it has become fashionable? But isn't it characteristic of telepathy that it reaches the present of fashion by a too late of the too early or a too early of the too late (that other version of the subliminal that has to do not with a speed that is beyond the threshold of processing, but with a speed that is due to the too early and the too late)?

Why write on vampires now, at this stage of my life, or rather, to be more precise, at this stage of the amalgam Toufic-*Distracted*? Did the liberty of association allowed by the aphoristic necessarily determine or at least facilitate the future clinamen toward the telepathic, toward what establishes the reign of free association? The aphoristic is what may lead one to the telepathic, but it is also what will allow one to resist the latter, since the aphoristic is what subsists—with the non-aphoristic, any state is a transition toward what follows it, disappears, is sublated in what it leads to; but with the aphoristic the state is not a phase, not a transition. Hence *Distracted* is simultaneous with, not over-turned by *(Vampires)*, by what is, at least in certain instances, outside of time, or that belongs to the absence of time. It is because it already resists itself that it can resist what has no self. But *(Vampires)* is being resisted in another way also, a bad way, a cheap way: why has *Distracted*, nine months after its publication, yet to receive its first review? Why is it that several months after its publication one could find only two copies of it in Chicago, at Barbara's Bookstore? Is it also because the telepathic action at a distance between it and *(Vampires)* can be lessened (for certainly *Distracted* must have been read by at least one person by now) the closer the *coincidence* of the two books? In which case, it will be reviewed and be more widely distributed only by the time *(Vampires)* gets published.

Why write on vampires at this stage in history? If humanity can conquer death (and certainly we are moving in that direction, whether or not only in an asymptotic way), it would suddenly dawn on us that the same facets of death, or pastiches/parodies of them, as unearthed from vampire films and novels and those of the undead in general, will have become salient facets of life:

— Cryopreservation hence lapses.

— The virtual body in virtual worlds hence a sort of astral body; affect/hurt the virtual body (an image) and you affect/hurt the material body, equipped with sensors, in another locality—a reversion to image magic.

— Smart houses where things move on their own, smart weapons that home in on their targets on their own, etc., echo the doors that open on their own in vampire films. Will we then be in a hypnagogic world?

— Already one kind of idiosyncratic time, the fast-forward, is no longer only made possible by immobilization, which is an aspect of the realm of undeath, but has already become a facet of the world: in 1987 Chinese scientists inserted genes for human growth hormone into goldfish and loach, with the result that they grew four times faster to the adult size[1].... Hence the subject of vampires and the undead is of relevance even to those who believe in nothing beyond biological death, to those who believe in death-as-extinction.

The less rigid organization of the contents of *(Vampires)* was to permit a non-restricting of the freer, more wide-ranging association which takes place in reaction to subliminal stimuli or to stimuli directed to a suppressed sensory channel (as in binocular rivalry): «in an experiment by J. Allison, subjects were to report changes in a neutral face when the words "sad" and "happy" were subliminally superimposed on it: some subjects were to do this under the condition that they should try to write as organized a description as possible ... try to include only things which are related and fit together ... while another group was asked to be quite free and impressionistic ... do it in a free associative way ... The experiment showed that a cognitive structure which allows less logical, less differentiated elements can better permit the incorporation of new stimuli»[2]. But then why not try to organize *(Vampires)* more tightly once the spoils from the freer organization have been gained? The reason is that the maintenance of the aphoristic, disjointed, fragmented ensures that the stranger, less probable ideas and connections are not canceled out: the consequence of using large time intervals is that most, if not all of the fluctuations in images and perceptions cancel out, one ending up having the gross approximation that normal perception is. It remains to be ascertained whether these fluctuations are merely hallucinations, or are real effects, as both the shrinking of objects in the direction of motion and the dilation of time are real effects of motion. One of the dangers of the editing stage is that as one gets more and more permeated by the normal state, one increasingly has the temptation to get rid of all the errors/projections/mistakes, whereas what should ideally happen is that one get rid of many illusions, since they reinforce the necessity of the unreal, while substituting in their place projections/errors/mistakes that break the necessity of the real and the unreal; hence editing should stop before the end set to it by the normal state. It is a *(Vampires)* law that one must interrupt processes, end them prematurely, until one reaches the stage when it becomes manifest that there is no unfinished business, the stage where one feels that what others consider to be an interruption does not interrupt anything. This is to be mistaken neither with impatience (impatience must cease, for when it does it points to the interrupted), nor with the state of being in a hurried time (*Distracted*); it rather echoes and responds to the fact that many altered states give one the certainty that they will go on indefinitely but then cease abruptly. To continue till the book is totally done is to already be addressing oneself exclusively to the living, to those in normal states[3]; this shows that one is forgetting that this not only oppresses but is a fatal danger to the undead or to the one in an altered state. In this sense there is a deadline (set by nobody); and in this sense one must always be late. This sudden cessation is different from the aphoristic interruption we find for instance in Toufic's *Distracted* («[an aphorism] is interrupted by its own conciseness»); but the two abruptnesses echo each other, for both are related to death: the aphoristic to the suicidal, to death-as-extinction and disappearance; the other interruption to death-as-undeath and the attempt to do away with the indefinite cycle of redeath-rebirth.

The book could have been written in terms of chapters, the following ones:
Chapter 1: *Night and Day* [Through matting]
Chapter 2: *Night and Night* [Through matting]
Chapter 3: *Night for Day* [as in *Day for Night*]
Chapter 4: *Neither Day nor Night* [Through excessive closeness (as in Van Gogh's *Road with Cypresses*)]—with each chapter joining sections at different locations of the book, the links happening by tunneling. For instance, one chapter would link sections that deal with space: The absence of ether, the vacillation of dimensions and excessive presence (p. 73); The off-screen and/or the set (p. 86); Labyrinth (p. 65); Circles (p. 64). Another chapter would be linking sections that deal with sound: Silence (p. 77); Out-of-sync (p. 95); Voice-over/Sound-over/Image-over (p. 97), etc.

Who will warn us about the warning?
Renfield says to Harker concerning the latter's forthcoming trip to Transylvania: «And, young as you are, what matters if it costs you some pain—or even a little blood?» A warning that occults the real danger, even when it seems a prophesy revealing the worst that can/will happen. It is exactly when the character has a hint that something so terrible that it goes beyond anything he could have expected (or can expect) may soon happen to him that he tells himself *if only I had listened then*, precisely not to listen to what the present situation should disclose to him: that the warning was misleading since it says that the worst that can happen is that he will lose a little blood, and since one can negotiate how little is little, that the worst is that he will die from losing too much blood. The warning hides that the danger is not the cessation of life but madness and undeath; hence it was an exaggeration hiding from him that no exaggeration could disclose the danger facing him. Murnau's handling of the theme of the warning in *Nosferatu* is disappointing since in that film the worst that can happen to Harker is that he would die (he does not die in the film), for those who are bitten by the vampire do not become vampires/undead in Murnau's film (the analogy the professor makes between the carnivorous plants he shows to his students and

vampires stresses the sucking facet of the vampire rather than the fact that he is undead).

Thresholds and *imaginary lines*:
One must be cautioned, *fore*warned (*cautioned*: «forewarned»), since fear inhibits that part of preconscious perception which maintains a certain aura around one (aura: person walking while reading, suddenly stops and looks up: just in front of him was a rope stretching across the street). That is why one is surprised by almost everything when one is fearful (no margins. We are not even dealing with a topological space—which admits of no distance—for a topological space still admits sets, hence separation). The iris' black in Murnau's *Nosferatu* can be seen as an added margin to counteract the margin that no longer exists because of fear.

But that is not enough: people who walk down stairs (stairs, in vampire films, are there to lessen the floating movement of the vampire and of the somnambulist[4] (Somnambulist Descending a Staircase)) without looking and yet do not fall (for instance the old Lord Hidetora whom the enormity of the disasters that have befallen him puts in a trance as he walks down the steps in Kurosawa's *Ran*), or move around while conversing without looking at each other and yet do not bump into each other, trip for no apparent reason on the smoothest spaces. These trips are the sign that a threshold has been reached: the threshold of the vampire's lair in Dreyer's *Vampyr* is not at the door, but at the spot where Allan Gray trips; the threshold of the house of Maria is where Alexander, in Tarkovsky's *The Sacrifice*, falls off his bicycle. Hence caution is *pre*caution[5] (in altered states the same is the case with: *disposed* and *predisposed*, *occupied* and *preoccupied*, *monition* and *premonition*. Maybe one becomes a sage only when one no longer needs presages), in the sense that one must pre-forewarn (the *fore* is to recreate the aura that has been neutralized by fear) by *guessing* where the *false threshold* is and warning both about it and about being fooled by the apparent threshold[6]. Guessing taken here in the way it manifests itself in the experiments conducted by Larry Weiskrantz on *blindsight*: patients who have lesions in the striate cortex or first visual cortical area were thought to be totally blind in the part of the visual field that corresponds to the damaged section, but it turned out that they could still discriminate in that part visual events, when these began and ended, and their orientations; the patients say that they were guessing for they saw nothing[7].

These presentiments must be coupled to postponement. The two are found in Maya Deren's *Meshes of the Afternoon*: she moves toward a record player and before she removes the needle, the sound stops; then we see her moving the needle away. In a later shot the music continues playing even after she removes the needle from the record; then, after a lag, the music stops. They are also found in Herzog's *Nosferatu*: the long delay before Harker moves to his wife's bed following her scream caused by the premonitional nightmare she has.

What then about these postponements? It is not a matter of experimenting until one trespasses beyond a threshold of no return; that can be achieved more or less easily (death, madness). One has to go beyond a threshold of no return, but only with the help of strategies of postponement, otherwise one may be moving into the worst of prisons. Hence the absolute importance of *critical point*[8] (or near critical point) states and *super-/under-* (as in supersaturation and undercooling[9]) states, such as yoga (the continuity of karma, karma as continuity has to be disrupted by yoga (suicide is not a solution, since it is itself a karmic force, a *desire* for annihilation), which must not itself be disrupted, must not be interrupted by lapses (the passage from life to death, or from the waking state to the dream state, must not happen in a lapse)—an interruption that works through continuity (the yogi has to penetrate lucidly states of consciousness that are inaccessible normally in the waking condition: for instance sleep). Any impurities, in the form of distractions, are proscribed: purity is necessary not on moral grounds but, as in supersaturation and undercooling, so as to delay the catastrophic phase transition, to have continuity where normally one would have a discontinuous jump (the extreme irritability one suffers from as an after-affect of the altered state is the double of the heightened sensitivity to the world and to what does not belong to the world during the altered state. Not to mistake this extreme irritability with an increased sensitivity. Rather, to view it as a form of impurity that endangers the metastable state that is allowing one to cross the threshold without a phase transition). *Precipitously* renders the abruptness, the in the *bat of an eye* manner with which the *precipitation* occurs in a metastable, supersaturated solution due to introduction of impurities. He knew that a threshold has been crossed and that an undercooling is going on, because he suddenly began to act with the utmost prudence (the slowing down of thinking due to fear has nothing to do with prudence, though it can very easily be mistaken for it, for prudence is what one fights the fear with), although nothing noticeable has changed externally or internally (no extension of spectra and sensibility (as happens in far from equilibrium dissipative structures)), except precisely for the sense that the utmost prudence (the danger of surprises) is mandatory now), which by permitting one state to go into another (it is said in Zen: when you reach the top of the mountain continue climbing), explore it (is the realm of no return a prison? Can, if not oneself, at least what one changed into (not stolen/replaced by) go beyond it?), without a sudden phase transition, maintain the possibility of coming back (the metastable memory we have then, rather than being the possibility of the evocation of what has been lived already (this, by the mere crossing of the point of no return, has been forgotten), consists in this reversibility). *Super-* and *under-* forms of maintaining a state beyond itself must not be mistaken with phenomena of *after-*, for instance *after-image, after taste*.

There is another possibility of maintaining an ability, not to return, but to turn up back on this side of the point of no return—through an idiosyncratic form of reincarnation: the points of bifurcations (at each transition threshold in far from equilibrium dissipative non-linear systems two new stable structures become spontaneously available from which the system takes one) in the past are a possibility that can be taken again by another version of the one who crossed the threshold of no return.

Without the help of phenomena that permit one to postpone the phase transition and/or without bifurcation, one will not be able to go back to or turn up back at the other side—not only do doors close behind the person who enters the vampire's castle, the crossed bridge has swung 90° from horizontal to vertical (this other form of crossing the *imaginary line*) and now is a sign of the bifurcation without which one cannot turn up on the other side of the point of no return.

Harker can no longer pass on a bridge, only under it (*under*passes (vaults) everywhere); the bridge-become-underpass is a secret passage (the castle of the historical Prince Dracula the impaler and the castles of vampires in vampire films and novels are perforated by secret passages) through space to its secret, the labyrinth (so that by retracing one's steps one will not be back at the place at which one was before the crossing of the bridge). If Herzog's Harker can return, it is because he loses his memory, becomes amnesiac, arrives in Wismar as another, as the vampire.

That's one sense of the importance of the bridge in *Nosferatu*. But bridges are important also because a bridge is needed—not to cross water or an abyss, for in such cases horizontal mattes have rendered bridges outmoded, supplanting them: Nam June Paik made Allan Kaprow walk on water in his video *Allan and Allen's Complaint*, 1982—to cross the ground on which the back-and-forth of the coach transporting Jonathan to the castle in Stoker's *Dracula* took place («The carriage went at a hard pace along, then we made a complete turn and went along another straight road. It seemed to me that we were simply going over and over the same ground again; and so I took note of some salient point, and found that this was so»)[10]. This back-and-forth movement contrasts with a movement forth, then, without turning, a movement back over one's steps, especially when a somnambulant person or a dancer does it. In the latter movement one disappears (our pursuers still following our footsteps reach a dead end), while the former movement makes space and time themselves somnambulist, makes them get lost («a lost part of Transylvania»): the traveler and the space covered disappear.

Weakening is only a projective going back below a threshold of no return (where is the elusive point between weakening and going too far?).

Letters:
Mina establishes a unifying chronology from the journals and letters of the different characters. The incorporation of separate accounts into one narrative is an act of confession: Jonathan's desire for Dracula's brides and Seward's desire for Lucy are disclosed. Van Helsing: «We have told our secrets». These confessions, though, hide that a bigger

secret is being hidden, for the different fragments, like different shots from different angles, are being used to edit around all the objective inconsistencies in the chronology and space. This remains a secret to them, that they confessed their secrets precisely to hide the secret(s): the inconsistencies in reality. If only the community, rather than any one individual, can conquer Dracula, it is not because each can enlist his specialty in the fight[11], but because the differing points of view permit the intercutting of a smooth story that does away with the inconsistencies to be otherwise met in the world. Gregory Waller writes that by divulging the letters and diaries, «the limitations of each individual perspective are exposed»[12]. But this only in order to replace them by the limitation of the community's perspective (the community can extend its power precisely because it maintains its limitations). The danger of a certain kind of telepathy is that it can extend the frame of what each person can perceive so far beyond its usual limits that the inconsistencies that are part of the world (or rather that are not part of the world, since they appear when one withdraws from the world or when the world withdraws from one) show up. The other forms of instantaneous communication (television, telephone, computer) are an occulted form of telepathy, precisely because they remain below this threshold, hence occult the occult.

The use of the letter/diary/journal/log device also makes it possible for the author to avoid showing us what the vampire thinks (or if he thinks at all) and what he perceives (or if he perceives at all): we are shown the others' point of view of the vampire (intriguing, since those who encounter the vampire, at least in vampire films and novels that underscore hypnosis, do not have a personal view during the encounter because they are entranced by the vampire). Yet in vampire films the person who encounters the vampire writes a diary and sends letters *and* we see the vampire without the mediation of a living person's gaze, directly, getting the vampire's povs. The directors of vampire films that do not underscore the theme of hypnosis—in these, due to posthypnotic amnesia, the encounter with the vampire cannot be remembered, hence portrayed to us indirectly—should, perhaps, have resorted to the flashback, for in the flashback we are shown the undead or the one who died before he died or the withdrawn not directly but through the mind of another person (the dead who were once alive hence present should in no way be remembered (otherwise the living are at risk of ending up, as in Truffaut's *The Green Room*, with a *life on hold* (phone operators say: "please stay on hold")—*life on hold* would not though make him/her any the closer to the dead/undead, for *life on hold* is not at all the same as the immobilizations the undead/dead or schizophrenics undergo); only those who were not present should be remembered: one remembers an event that never happened or to be more precise that can happen only as remembered (hence, the fact that those who encounter the undead/vampire most often become amnesiac—one cannot go back to the other side of the point of no return even in memory—is not an obstacle to the occurrence of such memories), and yet *it is* not *only a memory* (as in *it is only a dream*). Memory here does not do what memory otherwise often does: falsify, beautify, interpret; it does not even fool one into believing/feeling that the event happened an original time and that one is just remembering it (it is the reverse feeling from déjà vu, where an event seems to have already happened; here the person feels that he is remembering an event that never occurred. True, sometimes when dealing with such memories one has felt that they did occur an original time, but always simultaneously feeling that one is having a déjà vu experience). Do not misunderstand me when I write: *I will be remembered*).

Another solution would be that in the film's first scene the camera be identified with the character who will encounter the vampire: this indicates that what may seem to be an objective shot can still be considered the pov of the character with whom the camera was at one point totally identified. In the beginning scene of Rouben Mamoulian's *Dr. Jekyll and Mr. Hyde* the camera is identified with Jekyll: people speaking to him look at it. When we revert to the traditional system where the camera is at times objective, at times subjective, the camera remains, even when in the objective mode, contaminated by Jekyll-Hyde, who therefore can know about events that he did not see but the camera saw (that should have been the reason why and the manner by which Hyde knows about the visit Ivy Pearson renders to Jekyll. Unlike Stevenson's book, in which the two personalities, Jekyll and Hyde, «had memory in common»,

Mamoulian's film should have been about multiple personalities with an amnesiac barrier between them, for this would have made it very clear that the formal identification of the character with the camera in the first scene is *the* origin and cause of the memory they have in common in the diegesis. Unfortunately, this is not the case in Mamoulian's film).

Parenthesis:
Eric Auerbach wrote on the Homeric impulse of never leaving anything obscure. He gave as example the interruption of the narration of Ulysses' encounter with Euryclea by the account of how the old scar on his neck, which she recognizes, was inflicted: «all is narrated... with such complete externalization of all the elements of the story... not until then... does Euryclea... let Odysseus' foot fall back into the basin.» In vampire films the parentheses in the form of Euryclea-like immobilizations are literal ones that belong to the diegesis itself rather than being merely a narrative device; that is, this absence of time, rather than being an interjection of the author/filmmaker, takes time in the film diegesis. Vampire films contain many other kinds of parentheses:
— The parenthesis of light in *Vampyr*: just before Gisele's father enters Gray's room, a non-motivated light appears on the wall adjacent to the door and fades just after he leaves the room. The parenthesis of light in *Nosferatu*, the vampire coming out of the non-motivated light behind him to suck Harker's blood then dissolving back into the light. These parentheses are a sort of *vacuum diagram*.
— This situation recurs in vampire films and books: someone is writing a letter or reading a book: the manservant reading in Dreyer's *Vampyr*; Harker writing letters in Bram Stoker's *Dracula*[13]. Harker writes his diary in order to keep in the present, or as close to the present as possible, a record of what is happening. Yet, the frequent writing of letters, diaries or *journal de bord* envelops the person in question in a strange parenthesis/*temps mort*: these persons can give a date, in their diary and in their letters, only to what comes outside of time, hence the shot of them writing is quickly replaced by an intertitle of what they wrote. Since we are dealing with films that underscore the theme of telepathy, letters do not so much serve to

give information to others (others would telepathically have a hint of what is happening (and if what is received telepathically is ambiguous, open to interpretation, and hence uncertain, we must remember that the character encountering the vampire is himself suffering from uncertainty (Todorov) and an inflammation of interpretation, and hence receiving a letter from him would in no way have produced a clearer version of what was happening)) as to create a distance between the letter writer and where/when he is: the distance achieved by letters is no longer the distance between the one who is writing the letter and the one who will receive it (in works that deal with telepathy, letters are used to fight telepathy, to create an off-screen and a delay. But telepathy subverts this: in Murnau's *Nosferatu* Harker sends, from Nosferatu's castle, a letter to Ellen telling her that he is leaving immediately for Bremen. But he soon discovers that he is imprisoned in the castle; when he manages to make a rope out of the bed cover, it is not long enough to reach the ground from the high room where he is imprisoned, so having reached the end of his rope he has to let go, injures his leg and faints. But, despite the objection of the doctor, Harker *leaves* the hospital—to which he was transported by some peasants—to Bremen *immediately* upon regaining consciousness, *just after* Ellen receives his letter, as if the letter did not take any time to get there), but rather the distance between the one writing the letter and the space-time where he is located[14]—as if the one writing a letter could be reached only by a letter.

Lapses:
In Murnau's *Nosferatu*, Harker loses consciousness while leaving the vampire's castle; the entry into and exit from the realm of the undead occurs in a lapse (hence is missed; with the exception of the yogi/Zen master, one is always already undead). The frontier, the place of entry is inaccessible since hidden by the trance that seizes one there (*entrance*: 1) «the place of entry»; 2) «to put into a trance»). On a map, a labyrinth would be formed of one line that meanders on and on, twists and involutes, forming a fractal object with a dimension between one and two, with the consequence that the labyrinth, though a surface, is all border—hence one cannot be fully

inside it—and that lapses are sure to occur to one in it since it doesn't have a dimension of 2, is not a full surface.

There can be no understanding of primitive cultures without undergoing possession, for if understanding is a form of possession in the normal sense of the word, they in turn must possess us, in their way, or rather what possesses them must also possess us. We can include them in history and memory only if they can possess us, that is include us in amnesia, in lapses, in that which maintains outside. A true relation presupposes this unbalanced, equivocal (since it maintains the two meanings of *possession*) exchange. It is not accidental that the records (and in the case of Armand Schwerner's *The Tablets*, the false records) we have of ancient cultures are full of holes, lapses, are in the form of fragments, for what is primitive is more akin to primary processes, closest to the unconscious, itself full of lapses (a schizophrenic: «I turned around and did something and looked at my watch, and it jumped an hour and a half»[15]). In the case of the primitive, though, these lapses, holes, do not create ambiguities but an absolute necessity for the one who undergoes them, which is not the case in Schwerner's *The Tablets*, where they induce a proliferation of interpretations.

Films about lapses in consciousness and disorientation are very important in cinema since cinema is itself largely (exceptions: primitive cinema, Hitchcock's *Rope* (1948), many of Warhol's films, etc.) made of changes of place and focus (Walter Benjamin: «the work of art of the dadaists... hit the spectator like a bullet... It promoted a demand for film, the distracting element of which is primarily tactile, being based on changes of place and focus which periodically assail the spectator»[16])—something classical cinema tries to occult through smooth editing. These changes of focus and location and lighting should be foregrounded not merely in a structuralist, modernist investigation of the medium (as was the case with the modernist stress in painting on the flatness of the canvas (Jasper Johns' painted targets and flags), the shape of the support, the properties of the pigment) and specific art form that film is, but through a highlighting of films that deal on the level of content with reality-as-filmic. One would not forget to say *en passant* (but not too quickly) that bullets (or things with their speed: what causes amnesia in concussions is not so much the material that traverses the brain as its acceleration) have been the cause of many concussions that resulted in amnesias, and hence in the creation in real life, and outside of all cinemas, of «changes in place and focus which periodically assail» the amnesiac.

Marguerite Duras criticizes most filmmakers for a condescending attitude toward the spectator, which reveals itself for instance in their showing him/her all the successive stages of an action, as if the spectator were a dolt who could not otherwise understand what was happening. Duras is only partially right in her insistence that the continuity in the portrayal of actions be dispensed with; for a generalized habit of letting the spectator piece up what happened by projecting what was skipped makes it extremely difficult for the filmmaker to thwart such a projection, and thwarted it often must be for in many cases nothing happened between the two shots forming the jump cut. It is only the aphoristic and those who suffer lapses who neither project nor feel any shock when, in *Potemkin*, Eisenstein joins «without transition» a shot of a woman wearing a pince-nez to a shot of the same woman pince-nez shattered and eye wounded, because for them nothing happened between the two shots, no ellipsis occurred. To the normal spectator there was the ellipsis of the ultra rapid but gradual wounding of the nurse's eye by the bullet, creating a jump cut between the shot that precedes the hitting and the shot that follows it. The spectator must not be able to project, must have the slow-wit of those who are scared (this slow-wit is different from the one Marguerite Duras is speaking about). Robbe-Grillet writes: «the duration of the modern work is in no way a summary, a condensed version, of a more extended and more "real" duration which would be that of the anecdote, of the narrated story. There is, on the contrary, an absolute identity between the two durations. The entire story of Marienbad happens neither in two years nor in three days, but exactly in one hour and a half»[17], i.e. the existence of the man and the woman in Marienbad «lasts only as long as the film lasts»[18] (this contrasts with Bazin's viewing the screen to be a mask: «The screen is not a frame like that of a picture but a mask which allows a part of the action to be seen. When a character moves off-screen, we accept the fact that he is out of sight, but he continues to exist in his own capacity at some other place in the decor which is hidden from us»[19]). Robbe-Grillet's general characterization is correct; nonetheless, I do not think that it is fully exemplified by *Last Year at Marienbad* (1961), since the latter is still structured in terms of scenes. That implies that between two scenes—a scene being « a unified action ... that normally takes place in a single location and in a single period of time»—there is a narrative, extra-diegetic ellipsis, with the consequence that the spectator is not inhibited from filling it with a duration. This projection can be inhibited in various ways: in case the characters can still be surprised, feel the lapses within a given scene, it suffices to make them surprised and disoriented at the beginning of each scene, at each different location-time, alerting the spectator that no time has passed between the two locations-times, and hence inhibiting him from projecting any transition time between the two scenes, the diegetic world presented by the work lasting then only the time of the projection of the latter. In case the characters are not surprised by diegetic jump cuts (the jump cuts in Godard's *A bout de souffle* are not diegetic; it is tacitly understood by the spectator that the action continues in a temporal off-screen), the transition from one sequence of shots full of jump cuts to another at a different location and time should happen by means of either a cut on movement (a paradoxical continuity at the level of the image), as in Maya Deren's *Meshes of the Afternoon*, or a cut on the two consecutive parts of a continuous phrase, with the words said in sync (a paradoxical continuity at the level of sound), hence with the characters filmed in close, medium or medium long shots, sync being mandatory in this case to ensure that the continuation of what was being said is not construed as a fade out of the previous sequence or a fade in of the following sequence (as indeed happens in Robbe-Grillet's *L'Immortelle* in the transition from shot 44 to shot 45, from shot 45 to shot 46 and from shot 46 to shot 47, all of which take place, at the level of the image, by a rapid fade): for instance, although shot 24 in *L'Immortelle* (1963) shows the woman and the man starting toward Beyköy and shot 25 shows them arriving there, Leila, who was saying in sync "Vous êtes étranger ... Vous vous êtes perdu ..." in shot 24, continues her phrase in sync in shot 25 (the script is explicit here: «continuant sa phrase»): "Vous venez d'arriver dans une Turquie de légende ..."—this making it impossible for the spectator to project that any time had actually transpired between heading toward the more or less remote city of Beyköy and arriving there (tunneling). One particularity of such a situation is that the outside is no longer what belongs to a different location-time, since, through the cuts on movement and/or on consecutive parts of the same phrase, the diverse locations-times are no longer separated, but form one ensemble; rather, the outside is now inside the same location-time interval, for instance a room or a hall (in one shot in *L'Immortelle* the man standing next to the window starts walking toward Leila who is standing, her back to him, in the middle of the room, and almost reaches her. In the next shot, he is in the middle of the room while she stands next to the door)—it is at the start of the second shot of each jump cut that one again says *hello* to the other person(s) in the same location (while one never greets as one changes locations-times), with the three or so *hello*s in a sequence of such jump cuts echoing the character's impression that the place is empty and that no meeting happened ("I met you last year at Marienbad." "No")—a sort of amnesia.

Build up: «Dramatic cutting leading to a climax in the action; the insertion of frames to designate a missing section or shot in the work print». Everything after these blanks, lapses is experienced as a climax, as a surprise (one should have *sang froid*, though not during these hibernation-like lapses, but as one is suddenly out of them; how to start [begin] without starting [being surprised]?)(*epilepsy*: *surprise* in Greek). Only when the outstanding (the surprising, the uncanny) is abolished is the other outstanding (the unaccomplished, overdue) in the same movement also abolished; only those who no longer ever get surprised can definitively short-circuit. With people who both undergo lapses and continue to be surprised, the absences they undergo (which may last no longer than the span of one of the refractory periods of the body) may be inhabited virtually by all the events that connect the two sides of the jump-cut: between «Les vers de la doublure dans la pièce du Forban Talon Rouge» and «Les vers de la doublure de la pièce du fort pantalon rouge», all the events of Raymond Roussel's *Chiquenande*; between «Les lettres du blanc sur les bandes du vieux billard» and «Les lettres du blanc sur les bandes du vieux pillard», all the events of *Parmi les Noirs* or *Impressions d'Afrique*. Unlike the examples from Roussel, such events are never lived in the present, not even by a multiple personality; nonetheless, they can become a memory.

Stoker's *Dracula* begins with Harker's stress on timing (making him stressful: «*3 May. Bistritz.*—Left Munich at 8:35 P.M., on 1st May, arriving at Vienna early next morning; should have arrived at 6:46, but train was an hour late. Buda-Pesth seems a wonderful place ... I feared to go very far from the station, as we had arrived late and would start as near the correct time as possible»)(having passed the bridge, (Murnau's) Harker is from then on always late, not reaching the door in time to open it himself: it opens by itself—he turns into a witness), and continues with an emphasis on chronological time (what is chronology but timing, so that events that belong to the past should not arrive too late, that is in the future, and events that should occur in the present would not occur too late, in the future, or too early, in the past), with Mina preparing a history: the multiplicity of letters and journals, which are different angles on and fragments of what happened, makes possible cutting around the jump cuts, around the eternities and lapses of some characters, around the intervals that were missed-stolen, to produce a smooth narrative. Yet, by covering up the inexistent jump cuts between the different sections, the inserts/cut-aways in the form of shots of nature between the narrative sections in Murnau's *Nosferatu* reveal the existence of the displaced inexistent jump cuts between the shots of the smooth scene at the end or beginning of which these landscape shots occur, an existence which otherwise we would not have suspected. These landscape shots show us that where we see smoothness, there are jump cuts (on the contrary, the ones in Ozu's films show us that underlying the jump cuts is smoothness). While both the transition from chapter III to chapter IV («Jonathan Harker's Journal—*continued*») and from chapter I to chapter II («Jonathan Harker's Journal—*continued*») in Bram Stoker's *Dracula* each occur after an explicit lapse—chapter III begins with «and I sank down unconscious» and chapter II starts with «I must have been asleep, for certainly if I had been fully awake I must have noticed the approach of such a remarkable place»—the underlined transitions (*continued*) from chapter II to chapter III, from chapter XIV to chapter XV, from chapter XV to chapter XVI, and from chapter XVI to chapter

17

XVII, don't occur after a lapse. «Chapter XV, Dr. Seward's Diary—*continued*», «Chapter XVI, Dr. Seward's Diary—*continued*», «Chapter XVII, Dr. Seward's Diary—*continued*», «Chapter III, Jonathan Harker's Journal—*continued*», as well as «Chapter IV» (the beginning of chapter IV continues the diary entry from the previous chapter) are inserts/cut-aways (does the *continued* function as a dissolve?) that function in the same manner as the shots of nature in Murnau's *Nosferatu*, pointing to the existence of lapses that would not otherwise have been sensed. Similarly, films about the mad that use abbreviation to discard and cover-up the lapses/absences, and hence the suddenness with which events occur to the character, secrete, as a symptom, the abruptness of the transition from the first, and longer, part of the film when the character behaves in a more or less traditional way to the latter, much shorter part of the film when he begins to behave in a bizarre manner.

Dans le temps one was always in time. No more; this *from time to time* is experienced literally by schizophrenics, epileptics, and people on LSD. Only occasionally do they return to *c'est le temps*, that is to the appearance of time, but *entre-temps* where are they? An epileptic: «It was about eleven o'clock when I put down my pen, feeling suddenly tired... I made the tea, looked up at the clock—a strange chance—and saw that it was ten minutes past eleven. The next moment I was still looking up at the clock and the hands stood at five and twenty minutes past midnight. I had fallen through Time, Continuity and Being»[20]. When she tries to go to her bedroom, she realizes that she does not know which way it is. With the epileptic, the two meanings of *fit* exclude each other. Coming back to consciousness, the familiar is no longer so: the first degree of being lost is not yet recognizing a familiar place immediately after a period of epileptic *petit mal* (*lost **and** found*, simultaneously). While the unfamiliar becomes familiar (this often induces as much apprehension as when the familiar becomes unfamiliar): with many epileptics the aura that announces a fit/black-out takes the form of a déjà vu sensation (naming *aura* an "I've been here [or witnessed or done this] before" or a smell that is there without an object that would exude it (like a reproduction that is divested from both the painting and its location), i.e. what does away with the aura, would have interested Walter Benjamin).

«It [cinema] makes a molding of the object as it exists in time and, furthermore, makes an imprint of the duration of the object»[21]. Hence cinema preserves also the absence of time. Both by documenting such instances as epileptic fits (*petit mal* or *grand mal*) and trance, allowing the one who underwent them to see what his body did when he was absent (Jean Rouch's *Les maîtres fous* (1955); Herzog's *Heart of Glass*, during the filming of which all the actors except one were hypnotized); and by portraying in fiction films states where there is an absence of time during which the person is not unconscious (as for instance in Robbe-Grillet's films (*Last Year of Marienbad*—)). Cinema has to do much more with preserving this absence of time than with preserving time.

If by the end of one refractory period (for instance the closing of the camera's shutter) the spoke pattern of the wheels of the coach driving Harker to the vampire's castle is in the same position, the wheels will appear stationary; if the spokes have moved less than a complete turn, the wheels will appear to revolve backward; if the spokes have moved more than a complete turn, the wheels will appear to turn forward at a slower speed. Due to refractory periods and lapses of all sorts, and the stroboscopic effects they allow, events can *seem* to be moving in a reverse direction. Intermittences are very important not because of these and other stroboscopic illusions they permit but because lapses allow the deployment of many quantum effects. In films manifesting quantum effects, we are to expect intermittences forming interference patterns, and vice versa: the copresence, in Kubrick's *The Shining* (1980), of the alternation of the silence and the sound of the wheels on the marble as the child's tricycle repeatedly passes over the alternating carpeted and bare sections of the corridors of the Overlook Hotel and of Torrance's tunneling through the locked larder door of the kitchen; the quantum world of Robbe-Grillet is permeated by these intermittences: the window blinds behind which Robbe-Grillet stands on the cover of the 1965 Grove Press edition of the two novels *Jealousy* and *In the Labyrinth* and which recur in *L'Immortelle*; the soldier in *In the Labyrinth* passes repeatedly out of the darkness and into the stretches of light under the street lamps, the darkness and the light forming the zones of an interference pattern; in *La Maison de Rendez-vous* the woman's «skin gleams ... when the young woman passes under the ... sconces, which one after the other illuminate the successive flights of the staircase»[22]; one telling difference between *Last Year at Marienbad*, the film directed by Alain Resnais, and *Last Year at Marienbad*, the elaborate and precise script by Robbe-Grillet, is that the interference pattern in the opening section of the script («at regular intervals, a lighter area, opposite each invisible window, shows more distinctly the moldings that cover the wall») is not in the opening section of the film.

Lapses make the existence of persons who suffer from them aphoristic only if things/events are received.

Sometimes he got drunk to experience the *continuous* sending in his direction of the light by the lamp.

In Bertolucci's *The Spider's Stratagem*, Athos asks two conversing men directions to get to the hotel; they begin arguing about which direction it is, pointing in opposite directions. "When you settle [which direction is the hotel] I'll pass by again." What if you passed them again and they were still arguing? Or have you passed them the second time? The second time Athos walks in the direction of the two arguing men, *there is a crossing of the imaginary line* before he reaches them, so that we see him walking, in the exact same scenery, away from them, with the two still-arguing men having now exchanged positions, so that the one who was standing screen left is now screen right and vice versa. *This indicates that a cut/lapse occurred* and therefore that Athos did not pass the two arguing men a second time.

1/15 of children experience epilepsy during their first seven years, mostly of the *petit mal* variety. The many *petit mal* episodes he had daily resulted in his seeing the world in time-lapse cinematography (time-lapse cinematography, for example that of the decomposition of an animal, reproduces both the absence (skip-frame) and the convulsion (jerkiness) of epilepsy), so that everything was speeded up and he could follow more easily what was usually too slow to be perceived (intermittent absolute slowness, blocking, makes us see what is otherwise too slow to be perceived). When he became older and the *petit mal* episodes stopped, the world became slower.

The painter Andrew Wyeth portrays Helga in so many works—246 works: 4 temperas, 12 drybrush paintings, 63 watercolors, 164 pencil sketches and drawings, etc.—in so many attitudes, positions, surroundings, moods, that in the situations that have not been portrayed she is absent from herself.

His talk is occasionally interrupted by a black screen then resumed at the same point with "as I was saying." At other times, although the shot is not interrupted and none of those present interrupt him, he keeps interjecting his talk with: "as I was saying."

Cryopreservation followed by successful restitution to life (another form of time travel, hence a new form of exile) will certainly some day become possible, precisely because it actualizes the temporal cuts/lapses that we encounter in schizophrenia and in Robbe-Grillet's books («Henri de Corinthe est donc resté tout ce temps-là—près d'un an—la plume relevée, en attente d'on ne sait quelle apparition, de quel fantôme»[23]) while divesting them of the character of disorientation, since the one who is preserved by cryobiology would still have as part of his memory upon awaking from his hibernation/coma the sequence of events that led to his cryopreservation, to his extended lapse, and that explains it.

Both Dracula and the Isma'ilis are related to *ghayba* (hidden, absence): Dracula is in the grave for more than half his undeath; the concealment of Isma'il, the first hidden Imam, began in 767 (as a schizophrenic put it: «I am in disguise and one might say a blessing in disguise»). The law of hibernation, of *ghayba*, which we find in vampirism, applies to *Nosferatu*: past the first few months after its premiere, it was not shown for the next nine years. Not that the world is not *in part* (one of the overdetermined reasons for *Nosferatu*'s absence was its banning for infringement of the copyright for *Dracula* held by Stoker's widow) to fault for that: assassins should be sent against it. This *ghayba* has as its flip side the manifestation of the esoteric: the psychotic world of *Nosferatu*, where the unconscious has come to the surface; in 1164, two and a half years after his accession to the leadership of the Assassins, Hasan II, the grandson of Hassan i Sabbah (who initiated the Nizari Ismaili order of the Assassins), announced, in the middle of the fasting month of Ramadan, the *qiyama*, the Great Resurrection, proclaiming the millennium: «then he set a table and seated the people to break the fast». People were relieved of the duties imposed by *sharî'a* (religious law) and Hasan was proclaimed the imam (for the imam can no longer remain hidden once the esoteric has become manifest).

Counterfeiting:
One must keep reality or unreality from becoming the necessary, through both:
— an indistinguishability of reality and acting (indistinguishability in *Lightning Over Water* between the real illness of Nick and his acting sick (Nick is relieved by his ability to act from getting stuck to the real, so that the spectator remains uncertain whether a certain cough was a real cough or an acted one (or whether there is a point where the cough that began as acting ended up becoming a real cough, or vice versa))). Hence the necessity of counterfeiting. This is the counterfeiting that Nick must have had in mind when he conceived of making a film where an old painter counterfeits his old works and substitutes the original paintings in museums with the counterfeits. Unfortunately, Wenders says to him: «Why say he's a painter and not a filmmaker since everybody knows it is you?» (Why not a filmmaker? Maybe because in cinema counterfeiting is often mutilating (not always: in *Tokyo-Ga* Wenders frames an alley first with a normal lens, then using a 50 mm lens (the one Ozu used for all his shots), counterfeiting an Ozu shot; in Wenders' *Until the End of the World* one shot counterfeits a Vermeer. The counterfeiting here is not only legitimate but also sublime: a person is to bring back to a lab a camera supposed to allow, when coupled to a computer, blind people to see the images it has recorded; while flying toward the laboratory, situated in a more or less deserted area of Australia, a series of nuclear explosions seems to have occurred causing the end of the (rest of the) world; this end of the world coincides with the arrival of the camera at the lab and the resumption of the experiments, which this time succeed, and we hear the blind person initially saying in reference to the shot that is Wenders' forgery of Vermeer: «I see a red, a blue—». It is this *creation*, from the inchoate state, that is simultaneous with the end of the world (in the U.S., copyright protection extends for the life of the author plus fifty years according

to the 1977 Copyright rule, after which the work is no longer subject to copyright but has fallen into the public domain. After the end of the world, there is no longer any ban not merely on the reproduction but even on the creation of what was there before. Is this why many schizophrenics, who experience the end of the world, feel that thoughts, accomplishments, songs signed by others have been stolen from them, the real creators, by these famous artists (some of whom composed their songs or wrote their books prior to the birth of the schizophrenic or when s/he was still a small child)?) that affirms the forgery, makes it not an imitation; in special cases not only is counterfeiting not mutilating, it is even mandatory: following the appearance of Robert Zemeckis' *Back to the Future 2* (1989), there should have occurred a retroactive changing of the events of *Back to the Future* (1985) so that at one point in the modified version of the original film we would have two copies of the Michael Fox character in the 1955 section. In the absence of the modified version of *Back to the Future*, either replacing the original *Back to the Future* or coexisting with it, the latter becomes a counterfeit film): the second version of Wenders' *Nick's Movie* (1980), edited by Wenders, could be viewed as a mutilated forgery of the first version (edited by Peter Przygodda), which itself, a film about an American friend that starts with a remake of the beginning shot of *The American Friend* (1977), hence with a forged shot, is a mutilated forgery of *The American Friend* (in which a painter thought to be dead (played by Ray) counterfeits his paintings); the second version of many a film, especially in the silent era, the original film shortened or even thoroughly reedited: in 1935, Greta Garbo having become a star, G.W. Pabst's *The Joyless Street* (1925) was reedited to promote her, the studio cutting out all of Asta Nielsen's role, ≈40% of the original film). How does one change reality into a forged fiction? And if money is involved, it is not that one counterfeits to gain money, but because poverty glues us to reality (utter poverty often glues us to unreality). This counterfeiting has nothing to do with the creation of the *false self* R. D. Laing writes about in the case of schizophrenics[24], for the false self is either what precedes the attempt at forging or its failure. One forges to elude also the false self.

— the presence of a minimal amount of projection/shit as a vaccination against the fiction gaining unmitigated necessity: for even if Nick acts that he is ill, his acting forms a fictional world that has its own necessary laws and logic (in Brian De Palma's *Body Double*, the main character, who plays the vampire in a film, is suddenly frozen still, unable to raise the coffin lid. The reason? Claustrophobia (yes, the fact that he is claustrophobic will be used later in the film). But the crucial thing is that he was playing the vampire, an undead, one who often either is himself immobilized or sees others immobilized[25], when he could equally well have been playing the role of a war prisoner). The freedom the spectator gains at the level of one act (is the cough real or simulated?) ends up reinforcing both the necessity of the fiction and of the real world. So now within the film we have to have *false acting* (not in the form of Wenders' blocking, his being stuck to the real; unfortunately, Wenders thought that he could counter this blocking, his being stuck to reality, simply by his ability to distance himself through the editing), a performance that is not true to life but true to death, or rather untrue to undeath, a forged performance. To *utter*: «to circulate (as a counterfeit note) as if legal or genuine». One has to add this projection, this shit, in order to be able to speak, to utter. There can be no style (*utterance*: «style») after an initiatic experience through an altered state without a modicum of projection/error/shit. The gutless, or the one who was for a time gutless, can have a style only if he sprinkles with shit, becoming someone who has guts (in both senses). It is only in this sense that we shit on writing («Don't write on the shitters, shit on writing»[26]).

In Bergman's *Persona*, Elizabeth implodes into a black hole due to the precipitation of all the roles she played on each other (without the distance of the forger), this sucking the other person toward her. The pros and cons of acting can be argued, but in this case Alma had no other alternative but to act to maintain a warp between her and what was otherwise certain to suck her (vampiricly obliterating any of her individual markers), the other sucking the role (a virtual person to be swallowed by the black hole) rather than her. There is no false self here since it is being sucked and hence obliterated as soon as it is being produced. Alma should have acted being Elizabeth

(Alma: «That evening when I had been to see your film, I stood in front of the mirror ... I think I could turn myself into you»[27]. But if the film proves anything, it is that Alma couldn't: she was not actress enough) or any other character, i.e. she shouldn't have talked about her past but about that of another character or of an invented, fictional Alma. She could not deploy a healthy forging against the impending bad, nihilistic forging, so the two faces forged each other, became forged faces (there is no jealousy in the indistinguishability of faces; the shot in which Elizabeth faces the camera while *behind her back* Alma and Elizabeth's husband have a conversation and kiss, a shot that reproduces the spatial positioning of the protagonists in Munch's *Jealousy*, is a bad forgery of the latter). During a harsh crisis Leonard Lowe undergoes in Penny Marshall's *Awakenings* (1990), he addresses the doctor thus: "Film me to learn". It is not so much the character saying this as the actor Robert De Niro: that particular section of the fiction film should have been inserted in the documentary film of *Awakenings* shot with actual patients in 1973 and incorporating documentary Super-8 film footage of the patients filmed by Oliver Sacks in 1969. A forging by a film actor playing a patient that answers to the forging by the patients—for aren't they forging reality as filmic when, for instance, they have kinematic vision, seeing in stills, with the occurrence of divergences from the chronologically-proper order of the stills? In Lubitsch's *To Be or Not To Be* (1942) Joseph Tura, an actor, disguises himself as Colonel Ehrhardt. This is not to viewed as an imitation (not even as an imitation that precedes what it imitates, a simulation), but as a forging, for what it "imitates" does not already exist, not even in the sense that it can be projected from what Tura already knows about Colonel Ehrhardt; hence when Tura disguised as Professor Siletsky says, in response to Colonel Ehrhardt's "so they call me Concentration Camp Ehrhardt!," "that's how I thought you would react," one should in no way take that to be a double entendre by Tura through which he indicates that he was right in his projection, but as Siletsky's condescending reaction to both Ehrhardt's vain words and the silly laugh that accompanies them. This temporal inversion is not to be viewed as an external narrative device that could otherwise be changed into some other one, but is required by the content since forging presupposes the potentialization/non-actualization/blankness of what is to be forged, i.e. the inversion in the order of events pertains not only to the order of narrative (Gerard Genette, *Figures III*) but also to that of story; it is only after Tura disguised as Ehrhardt conducts himself in a definite manner during his meeting with Siletsky that that same manner becomes that of Ehrhardt in his meeting with Siletsky.

There is a radical difference between the secrets and lies that are part of every person's history, especially that of a star (the beautiful disjunction, in *Singing in the Rain*, between the flashback images and Kelly's narration), and the forging that is not dealing with history, with the past, but with the late, the dead, yet is in a way no less objective. First way of interpreting *Fedora*: we see the corpse of the ageless Fedora in the casket circled by the people who came to see her for the last time, the ceremony organized and presided over by Countess Sobryanski and her son, who used to love Fedora. The producer Barry Detweiller is present there and looks for the truth of the late Fedora, this leading to forgery (with the dead we are dealing with forgery since to them applies not only *from dust to dust* but also from blank to blank, from superimpositions to superimpositions. The forgery is inflected by the personality of the one doing the search (the same way the kind of measuring device inflects the result in quantum mechanics)): Fedora no longer looks like herself or how she would have looked when old, this in turn making her place blank for her daughter not to impersonate her (one can impersonate another without this forcing a divergence of the latter's identity) but to counterfeit her, which forces Fedora to counterfeit Countess Sobryanski, who is dead (it is only once Antonia-become-Fedora forges another, Anna Karenina (the former's face was deformed when the train hit her body), that Fedora can re-claim herself—not within history but within the forgery). Wilder at one point entertained the thought of calling his film *Fedora II*: beside and beyond the irony or humor implied in relation to sequels, what thus becomes clear is that the films where one encounters the motif of impersonation, for instance *Double Indemnity* (1944), where the insurance agent impersonates the husband on the train, and *Some Like it Hot* (1959), where the two male protagonists impersonate two females, were overdetermined as to the reason for their making: one of their functions was to occult the virtual *Fedora* that made the first filmed *Fedora* (1978) already *Fedora II*. We are not dealing with a progression from a more straightforward, less threatening motif, impersonation, to a more intriguing one, forgery; rather, the former is already there to occult the latter, it impersonates the latter—one more instance where the bad, cheap interpretation is provided by the artist/filmmaker. Second way of interpreting *Fedora*: Barry Detweiller is interested in history, i.e. in the past of Fedora (history is always that of and for the living), and dis-covers that the corpse in the casket is not Fedora's but that of Fedora's daughter, Antonia, who looks exactly like her mother, and that Fedora, after a disastrous surgical operation, looked totally different and, Countess Sobryanski having just died, took on the latter's name, impersonated her. In Wilder's *Sunset Boulevard*, on seeing the silent era films that the old actress watches with her young guest and in which she is the star, one has the unsettling feeling that one is watching forged films; it is a feeling that remains without a justification until the scene in which the actress having come to visit De Mille directing a film, the camera moves to the extras and one of them says, makes explicit an impression common to most of those present on the set: "I thought she was dead." In Thomas Tyron's story "Fedora" (on which Wilder's *Fedora* was based) in his book *Crowned Heads*, there is a remake of the scene: Fedora and her daughter Antonia watch Fedora's old films. While substantiating the aforementioned impression, Tyron's story and Wilder's adaptation undercut it since they limit the forgery to a specific number of times: Fedora's daughter counterfeits her mother in three films in Wilder's film, and in nine films—one of them, *Ophelie*, being a 1963 remake of a silent feature made by her mother in 1927—one cameo role and one uncompleted film in Thomas Tyron's "Fedora".

I have to remain blank in order to forge (no self-consciousness). Every time I forge I either create a blankness in the other, in which case the latter goes through a successful forgery, or I fail to do so, in which case the other undergoes a compulsion/obsession.

What can be achieved by time travel can be achieved by other means, for instance by forgery.

Through a Glass to encounter the already-there double (in-the-mind):
Whether suddenly as in Cocteau's *Orpheus* (1950) or gradually as in the dissolve in Carroll's *Through the Looking-Glass* («the glass was beginning to melt away, just like a bright silvery mist. / In another moment Alice was through the glass»[28]), to pass through the mirror is not to be immaculately oneself to the other side, but rather to find oneself either a) observing one's-double-who-was-already-in-the-mirror, as in both *Duck Soup*[29]—near the end of the shot in which Groucho stands in front of a mirror-frame trying to ascertain whether the person he sees there is his reflection or an impersonator imitating him, at one point momentarily and inattentively crossing to the other side, he sees two duplicates of himself in the mirror. This shot (simultaneously one of the scariest and one of the funniest, i.e. one of the most uncanny, in film) deploys in a comic mode an array of features that pertain to the undead and schizophrenics: diegetic silence-over (which did not occur during the rest of the film); *thought broadcasting*: it is not accidental that Chico, who in that scene impersonates Groucho and knows every improvised movement the latter does, is a spy; if we consider the match between the movements of the ones to either side of the mirror from the perspective of the one inside the mirror, the most plausible accounting for it would be that his impulses and actions are controlled by an external force, Groucho—and Rouben Mamoulian's *Dr. Jekyll and Mr. Hyde*, where in the beginning scene, in which the camera is identified with Jekyll, the latter stands in front of a mirror and sees himself: this shot must have been filmed with a frame devoid of a mirror, and hence with the actor playing Jekyll coming to stand in front of the camera to the other side of the frame. Unfortunately, the rest of the film is a double of the film that one would have expected to unfold from the opening scene, namely a film about the double, usurping the latter film's existence, for in both Stevenson's *Dr. Jekyll and Mr. Hyde* and Mamoulian's film, Hyde is a freeing of Jekyll's own evil impulses[30]. *Dr. Jekyll and Mr. Hyde* could still have been a just double story (that is unjust) if Jekyll was destroyed or punished for a crime neither he nor Hyde committed. He should have been *the wrong man*: not on moral grounds of justice, for the moral grounds apply to Jekyll and

Hyde (who is not the former's double precisely because he is merely the precipitate of Jekyll's bad impulses), but on grounds of injustice, the injustice of the double. «Like a man restored from death—there stood Henry Jekyll!»[31] remains a mere metaphor; or b) having been replaced by or inhabiting the same mind with him/her as both in *Alice's Adventures in Wonderland*—once Alice crosses to the other side she is no longer sure she is the same person: «But if I am not the same, the next question is "who in the world am I? ... I must have been changed for Mabel!"»[32]—and in experiments Helmut Schmidt conducted to check for psychokinesis: the results showed «a negative scoring tendency: if the subjects tried to superimpose an overall clockwise motion on the random walk of the light, then the light tended to move in a counter clockwise direction»[33]—for example when parapsychology researcher R.R. tried to affect the lights only «47.75% of the 6400 light jumps went in the desired clockwise direction»[34].

Freud writes: «Whenever my own ego does not appear in the content of the dream, but only some extraneous person, I may safely assume that my own ego lies concealed, by identification, behind this other person ... On other occasions, when my own ego *does* appear in the dream, the situation in which it occurs may teach me that some other person lies concealed, by identification, behind my ego. In that case the dream should warn me to transfer on to myself, *when I am interpreting the dream* [the dead cannot do this, they don't wake up from that world], the concealed common element attached to this other person. There are also dreams in which my ego appears along with other people who, *when the identification is resolved*, are revealed once again as my ego.»[35] In many dreams this is exactly the case, but in some dreams (and in modes of the unconscious more transpersonal than dreams) it may be the other's desire that functions in the dream (or in the altered state), in which case censorship by an agency pertaining to my psychic apparatus does not explain the identification. In many a dream I have been objectively replaced by the other, to whose desire can be applied, if s/he is a living other, the interpretation mechanisms mentioned in the quote: the censorship by an agency of the other's psychic apparatus may apply to his representation in my dream so that in dreams where the other and other persons appear, I have to uncover the common element between the other and them, this common element uncovering or being itself the wish of the other; in other dreams in which my ego appears in conjunction with other egos, I will have discovered, when the identification is resolved, which other person among those appearing in the dream is the one whom the others, including my ego, represent.

Freud, a Jew, writes concerning a dream he had: «In mishandling my two learned and eminent colleagues because they were Jews ... I had put myself [this active, in-control perspective, when it is the other way round!] in the Minister's place ... He had refused to appoint me professor extraordinarius and I had retaliated in the dream by stepping into his shoes.»[36] Be careful, he lets you step into his shoes only because, like a Loa, he has stepped into you. And when you either leave the shoes behind intentionally (your intention is his lapsus) as incriminating evidence and the authorities imprison the other, either this indicates that it is the other, not you, who committed the act, or you will discover that you killed someone whom the other wanted killed, that you made a mistake and killed *the wrong man* (the attack on the Jewish colleagues); or forget, in a lapsus, the other's shoes in a lecture or, like Cinderella, in a party, people will come looking for him, not you: for he will always give you what will lead to him, whether that be his shoes, your speaking a language you don't know, or having powers you do not normally have (Brakhage saw an angry Maya Deren pick up a standard-sized kitchen refrigerator and hurl it from one corner of the kitchen to the other[37]).

Secrets:
If light is what is inimical to the vampire, what destroys him, this is not because it is what renders manifest, for if it did only this, it would not be able to destroy the secretive, the one who does not appear in mirrors, who has no image, and hence the one who turns those who have seen him into hypnotized people who had a *positive hallucination* of him (if the vampire does not appear in the mirror, neither would he appear on the retina, that other, latent, mirror). Light, what renders visible, manifest, can destroy the vampire, the secretive only because light is simultaneously the paradigm of the

secret (and not just in the case when it comes in excess, blinding, hence maintaining in the secret).

The first version of this secretiveness was Lorentz-FitzGerald's theory of contraction. Trying to save the ether wind theory, George Francis FitzGerald explained the negative results of the Michelson-Morley experiment, 1887—the light speed is constant—by postulating that the ether wind puts pressure on a moving object, causing it to shrink a little in the direction of the motion, the contraction increasing as the object's speed approaches the speed of light. The contraction would be just enough to keep the speed of light constant: the ether wind contracts the arm of the interferometer pointing into the ether wind, so the reduction of the velocity of the light traveling into the ether wind and back cannot be detected (a secret). This theory cannot be tested by measuring the length of the apparatus to see if it shortens in the direction of the earth's motion, since the ruler would also shorten in the same proportion. Lorentz also postulated that clocks would be slowed down by the ether wind, and in just such a way as to make the velocity of light always the same[38]. The theory became known as the FitzGerald-Lorentz contraction theory[39].

The contemporary version is the double slit experiment: a very weak coherent light—one photon at a time—moves from source to detector, between which is a screen with two very tiny slits, at A and B. If B is closed the photon goes through the open slit. The same if A is closed. When both are open and we do not know through which slit the photon passed, there is interference. If we put detectors at A and B to be able to tell through which hole the photon goes when both holes are open, interference no longer occurs. We can have interference only if the path the photon took remains a secret to us.

Zeno's paradox in quantum theory: an unstable particle, which has a known half-life when we apply intermittent observation to it, does not decay when a continuous observation is postulated (a refractory period is needed; change happens in the secret).

Ruins:
All the mirages he saw in a desert like the one in Herzog's *Fata Morgana* were of ruins.

The houses deserted by inhabitants trying to preserve their lives threatened by the probable imminent explosion of the volcano (Herzog's *La Soufrière*, 1977) turn into ruins by the mere fact of having been deserted even if for a short period. Did the inhabitants return to ruins? Jalal Toufic and his family deserted their house during the Israeli invasion of Lebanon. Did this make the house a ruin? Yes, and not because the house was severely damaged and burned during the last days of the invasion, for even after it was remodeled and restored, it remained a ruin. And that is why what is damaged during the continuing civil war (as of 1990) is most often not fixed or replaced (the usual explanation is that one wouldn't want to spend much money on what could any moment be damaged again or totally destroyed. But shouldn't we invert the way we consider what is taking place? It is because these houses have become ruins by being deserted that the war gets extended until they begin to turn explicitly into ruins, to manifest their being already ruins). Maybe the refusal of the Bustros family to sell their house (Jennifer Fox's *Beirut, the last home movie*) is due less to their obstinacy to never part with it, and much more to an apprehension that were they to sell the house it may be more readily deserted in a situation of intensive bombing by those who bought it, this ushering and completing its becoming a ruin.

The vampire in *Carmilla* calls herself Millarca when she gets introduced to the first family on which she preys, and Carmilla in the second family. The vampire, who does not dissolve-disintegrate (Millarca is the anagram of Carmilla), has an affinity with ruins (Renfield's weedlike eyebrows in Murnau's *Nosferatu*), with what disintegrates. As we clearly see in vampire films, the remains in the sense of unfinished business (those who died of an unnatural death (murder, suicide—) were at risk of becoming vampires) are connected to the remains as ruins.

Things happen so quickly in vampire films, in time-lapse cinematography (hair that suddenly turns white from fright), that only the turning into ruins, or the transformation of ruins into ruins, the ruining of ruins gives the feel of a gradual change, of growing old. In undead films only ruins disintegrate continuously and slowly, into ruins, more ruinous ruins.

«The places I showed in *India Song* were on the verge of ruin, they were unconvincing, people said that they weren't habitable. But in fact if one looked closely at them, they were not so uninhabitable ... In *Son nom de Venise* these places are definitely uninhabitable»[40]. True? False?

False, since in Beirut many people live in houses even more destroyed than those shown in *Son nom de Venise*; and in the desert of *Fata Morgana* some people live in the left-overs of smashed airplanes, cars and trucks. The real, utter ruins are those unfinished, interrupted buildings found everywhere in Beirut (the rise of the dollar in relation to the Lebanese pound occurring in the middle of the construction process, making it too costly to continue building): nobody inhabits them. Ruins that don't decompose, hence that don't even have the life of degeneration. Beirut full of photographs (someone is sitting in a moving car, looking. His pov: moving shots of the scenery, mostly showing destroyed areas, intercut with static shots of these unfinished buildings).

True, since the actors who move in the places of *India Song* do not inhabit the characters who inhabit these places. «In *India Song* the actors proposed characters but didn't embody them. Delphine Seyrig's fantastic performance in *India Song* came about because she never presents herself as someone named Ann-Marie Stretter but as her far-off, contestable double, as if uninhabited, and as if she never regarded this role as an emptiness to be enacted»[41]. A risk, for by introducing the double, it is now the film itself that has to be double, that has a double: *Son nom de Venise dans Calcutta Desert*. And if the appearance of the double signals death, then the latter film is not so much the portrayal of the death of the people and places of *India Song* («The swallowing up by death of places and people is filmed in *Son nom de Venise dans Calcutta Desert*»[42]), as the death of the previous film itself, of *India Song*. And «let the cinema go to its ruins».

One has to see the disintegration of organized matter, of all these statues, walls, ornamentation, to know that it is precisely because it contains its memory in itself that organized matter cannot recreate the present. And that on the contrary it is voices which disappear, which are over (voices-over in this sense also) almost instantly and hence have no memory (of their dissolution) that can recreate the present. From *India Song* to *Son Nom de Venise*, while the images (true, shot in another palace) became older, the voices did not.

The house that has been demolished has left its marks on the walls of the adjoining building[43]. In these houseprints, one witnesses the inside turned into an outside. One can imagine a Cronenberg character living in an apartment facing such a wall who one day, on coming home from work, sees that the building with such a wall, separate from the other houses and facing him, has been demolished, that it is no more; that same day symptoms revealing the presence in him of the drive to turn the inside outside begin to manifest themselves.

Ruins: places haunted by the living who inhabit them.

One is somewhat surprised when one remembers one of those mushrooming private communities in Orange County, California, behind their gates, with both the houses and the streets built by private contractors; except, one very soon remembers that California is an earthquake region, and therefore that both houses and streets would be equally damaged by the catastrophe most likely to hit California. In parts of the world where such a form of catastrophe is very unlikely, a joining of street and house as an architectural unit seems strange, forced. It is in ruined areas that the disjunction between the street and the building becomes the clearest. The cars passing by in the vicinity of the ruined buildings in the *Aswaq* area, Beirut, give one the same impression one has on seeing the character in the Van Gogh section of Kurosawa's *Dreams* walking and running *in* the paintings.

If there is a link, it is between the ruined buildings of *Aswaq* and any road where the jam produces the current Lebanese "solution"— one lane in one direction becomes first three lanes in the same direction, then, by totally blocking the original lane in the opposite direction, five lanes in the same direction. The excess cars totally blocking the other lane are the same phenomenon as the excess stones that have fallen from a destroyed building. It is hence the excess cars rather than the holes in the roads, and in the case of the *Aswaq* area, rather than the burned, turned upside-down cars, that both are a ruin and indicate a ruined road (hence one must not be fooled by the presence of burned, turned upside-down cars on the streets next to the ruined buildings into thinking that buildings and streets are destroyed conjointly by the fighting)—yes, roads too get destroyed. Maybe the aforementioned behavior on the part of a large percentage of Lebanese drivers is the latter's intuitive way of defending themselves against the disjunction of the streets from the buildings-become-ruins.

Except in ruined areas, the placards with street names and building numbers indicate the nearby street. In ruins, the perforated-with-bullets-and-shrapnel blue placards with street names and building numbers imply a virtual road rather than the adjacent road on which the cars and the pedestrians pass, this giving the impression that the area is a set, with the "off-screen" to these placards being at variance with the surrounding streets on the "set".

Suddenly one sees a design, a motif, for instance vases, in what is a destroyed facade, and it is as if one has made an archaeological find. But it is not really an *as if*: these are truly archaeological, ancient sites, and what are found are archaeological artifacts. For the ruins function in an idiosyncratic time, often in time-lapse (in vampire films, which highlight the theme of ruins, the vampire decomposes on exposure to the light, or ages (*The Hunger*), in time-lapse. A more interesting example of this time-lapse temporality can be discerned in the shot in Godard's *Nouvelle Vague* (1990) where the hand of the man who has just died rises up with the temporality and movement of the time-lapse growth of a flower (the woman's words addressed to him, "c'est une merveille que de pouvoir donner ce qu'on n'a pas," also mean that by giving her his hand with that temporality and kind of movement he is giving her a flower he does not have (maybe the one resurrected in Godard's *King Lear*, 1987). Not a man who magically conjures up a flower from nothing or from an empty hat, but a man whose hand has become a sort of flower. The hand has not decomposed, yet is, by a miracle, already ascending with the temporality of the time-lapse growth of a flower). The *Aswaq* are part of the archaeological sites of Lebanon—as much a part of it as Baalback. Though still, years-wise, a youth, one has become the contemporary of what is much older than one. Another tradition, one that has to do not with memory, but with amnesia.

Dima El-Husseini, currently a fifth-year architecture student at the American University of Beirut, went, as part of an excursion by her class, to the destroyed *Aswaq*, before the sand blockages were cleared and the area officially opened. The duty to look at the buildings from an architectural, hence technical perspective, and to position them within a mental map while the different regions were being mentioned ("this was Suq El-Tawileh; this was Bab Idriss, etc.") entered in conflict with the emotional reverberation, or rather onslaught that these names presented, and the second-generation memories—imbibed from her parents—they elicited. The too-many stimuli she had to deal with, the confusion of so many elements during the excursion left the whole episode in suspension, in abeyance, making it very difficult to take stock of what occurred. Later, in her home, she tried to re-call what she saw. Instead of the destroyed, deserted *Aswaq*, it was the *Aswaq* of the memories of her parents, the colorful, populated *Aswaq* that sprang to her mind. It was with difficulty that she could re-call the destroyed *Aswaq* and superimpose them on the pre-war *Aswaq*. This corroborates that there is a very old past that the present itself secretes, for indeed in that case it is natural that it would be more difficult to remember the destroyed *Aswaq*, which are maybe as old as Baalback, in any case older than the 1940s, than to remember the *Aswaq* imbibed through the memories of the parents, hence which belong to the 1960s, '50s, '40s. It was only by the third or fourth visit to the *Aswaq* that she really felt that the destroyed *Aswaq* were the reality. What facilitated this realization was her noticing the presence of refugees in some of the destroyed buildings.

It strikes one how provincial 1992 Beirut would be were it not for its ruins (the *Aswaq*, etc.), which imbue it with another temporality.

The demolition of the ruined buildings of *Aswaq* (by implosions), which is yet to happen, is war by other means. The war on the traces of the war is part of the traces of the war, hence signals that the war is continuing.

Vision and its absence:
While Dreyer's *Passion of Joan of Arc* is constructed through gazes and eye directions, the film that followed it, *Vampyr*, is about the

impossibility of looking and/or the undecidability of whether someone is looking:

In the fourth shot Gray moves a few steps away from the glass door of the inn and looks up. The next shot is a pan of the roof that continues with a tilt down and ends with Gray entering the frame that was supposedly showing his pov. Hence, as early as the sequence formed of the fourth and fifth shots, one is witnessing either:

— Gray looking at himself (an exacerbation of vision), one knowing, without having to wait until later in the film, that an explicit dissociation/out of the body experience/hypnagogic state will be undergone by Gray. Dissociation/out of the body experiences[44]/ hypnagogia makes it possible for someone to see what otherwise he could not see (from a hypnagogic episode reported by Andreas Mavromatis: «View of a tree from under the ground—seen as if I were lying under the tree looking up through its roots»[45]; we notice here the actualization at the level of experience of what is sometimes criticized by many as a gratuitous cinematic mannerism: placing the camera in a position where in the diegetic world it could not have been placed); hearing strange voices outside his room, Gray walks up the stairs leading to the room from which he thinks they are coming: what begins as his pov, showing a low angle view of the ceiling at the top of the stairs, continues with a tilt down into a room at right angles to the stairs, hence seen from an angle different from that of someone standing on the stairs.

— or an impossibility of vision, the fifth shot revealing itself to be an objective shot rather than a pov. Gray's being undead means he has no possibility of seeing: his open eyes, like those of any corpse, have no pov. Hearing strange voices outside his room, Gray walks up the stairs leading to the room from which he thinks they are coming: what begins as what we think is his pov, showing a low view of the ceiling at the top of the stairs, reveals itself to have been from the beginning an objective shot as we see a man walking toward the camera out of a room at right angle to the stairs.

In vampire films we see the undead/dead looking and we are given their povs. Dreyer must have filmed the scene in which we have a shot of Gray in the coffin followed by his pov to drive the point that we already have accepted the paradoxical thing that the

vampire Chopin, who is doubly prevented from seeing since she is not only dead but also blind, can have a pov: after sucking the blood of Leon in the garden, «the figure turns its head irritably and stares at the newcomers with the dead eyes of a blind person»[46], and we are shown her pov, a shot of Gray and Gisele, who have come to rescue Leone. That Chopin should at all have a pov is much more paradoxical than that Gray laying in the coffin should have one, for what is taking place in the latter case could be something similar to what occurs in zombie and tetrodotoxin poisoning cases: paralysis of motor functions while the person retains consciousness. There is at least one confirmed case of a Haitian zombie, reported in Wade Davis' *Passage of Darkness*: Clairvius Narcisse. Although completely immobilized, he remained conscious and could hear his sister's weeping when he was pronounced dead in the hospital. He felt the cover being pulled over his face. Narcisse does not recall how long he remained in the grave before the zombie makers came and took him out. Houngans say that a zombie may be raised from the grave up to three days after the burial [for three days and three nights did Jonah remain in the belly of the Whale, Lazarus in the grave]. According to Wade Davis, the houngan's poison contains tetrodotoxin. Tetrodotoxin poisoning results in:
— pallor
— paresthesias of lips, tongue and throat which spread gradually until the whole body is numb, this making the person feel his body is floating. The paresthesias cause respiratory difficulty, the body becoming cyanotic.
— paralysis beginning in the throat and larynx resulting in aphonia.
— subnormal temperature
— the eyes becoming fixed and the pupillary and corneal reflexes lost[47], this resulting in glassy eyes.
— the patients feeling ants crawling over them or beneath their skin and biting them.
— a peeling of the skin.
— the person becoming comatose while retaining consciousness until shortly before death. Akashi: «The patient's comprehension is not impaired even in serious cases. When asked about his experiences, he can describe everything in detail after recovery». He reports the

case of a gambler who was thought dead after eating puffer fish (which contains tetrodotoxin) and put in storage until an official from the region to which he belonged could examine him. A week later he regained consciousness and recovered from all the symptoms; he was able to recall what he went through, his major fear all along being that he would be buried alive[48]. That (the out-of-the-body component of) Gray in the coffin can still have a pov is not such a paradoxical thing, since similar occurrences have happened many times in reality.

Article 249 of the Haitian penal code prohibits substances which induce a coma indistinguishable from death. If a victim of such poisons is buried, the act is considered murder whatever the end result. The prohibition occults more than it sheds light on the phenomenon of the zombie, for it is not enough to induce a deathlike stupor in the person who is to become a zombie, making others, including doctors, believe he is dead. He must be abruptly thrown into a death of the mind: zombies are given datura after they are retrieved from the grave (Haitians call Datura stramonium, *concombre zombi* (the zombi's cucumber)); the plant induces stupor, hallucinations and delusions, followed by confusion, disorientation, and amnesia (Datura is associated with initiation rites among the Luisena Indians of Southern California and the Jivaro of South America. At puberty, adolescent boys of the Algonquin of northeastern North America were separated from the rest of the tribe for up to three weeks during which they ate only Datura. In parts of Highland Peru datura is called *huaca*, the Quechua name for grave). Spending up to three days in the grave completely paralyzed yet conscious does not create a zombie: witness the many cases of blower fish poisoning, where the person who was believed to be dead and spent several days in stupor recovered completely after that; hence, the section in *Vampyr* where we see the pov of the Gray in the coffin, a low-angle shot of the landscape traversed by the coffin on its way to the cemetery, rather than being the part of *Vampyr* that most exemplifies death is rather the part in which Gray, who is undead throughout the rest of film, is no more dead than the person suffering from a tetrodotoxin poisoning. It is both the fact that the potion the houngan prepares is a mixture of bones, of parts of animals and plants (many have no psychopharmacological or pharmacological characteristics)[49] etc., this symbolizing the mixing that takes place during the decomposition of the corpse, and that the victim is made to ingest datura that signal that the person who was on hold, taken hostage in the grave, died and was then resurrected.

Why the bandages/covers over the eyes of those under experiment in *La Jetée*, if not because it is only the dead, those who don't have a pov, who can experiment with time?

Gray enters a cluttered, dust-covered room. The camera tracks laterally to an empty coffin and beyond it to a placard with the inscription "Doctor of medicine". The camera swish pans from the latter to Gray moving away. It is not only the spectator who is unsure whether Gray saw the placard before he moved away; the uncertainty extends to Gray himself: it is a secret even to him whether or not he saw the placard and the inscription. *What was I saying?* is replaced with or rather joined to *what was I seeing?*

What was I saying? has been replaced or rather joined by *what was I seeing?* in another sense as well. After showing what might be the person's pov, there is no return to the person looking. The cycle of person looking/pov/person looking has been short-circuited: one shot of Gray looking up is followed by a shot of hands (supposedly of the vampire) moving down the handrails, then, instead of going back to the shot of Gray looking, to allow him to (re)claim the second shot as his pov, there is a shot of someone walking quickly down the stairs. We witness the same phenomenon in the first sequence of *Vampyr*: in the first shot, Gray enters frame, walks from right to left, and looks up; almost instantly there is a cut; the next shot begins on a statue, the camera then tracking down to an inn sign; the third shot is from the inside of the inn: the camera tracks toward David Gray who stands outside peering in the window. Vision remains uncertain without the *re* of re-claiming, without return. This non-return introduces also a temporal indecision: whether what we are seeing is in the future or in the present: the camera pans from Gray looking to a diminutive skeleton, books, a skull, then he enters what seemed up to then to be his pov. Does the shot of Gray at the end of the room signal a dissociation he underwent so that he sees himself in his pov, in which case the two shots are in the present?

Or does it rather show a clairvoyance on the part of Gray, who while looking from one end of the room sees himself walking at the other end in the future?

The inability of the spectator (and of the other characters) to know whether a character in *Vampyr*, in specific Gray, is looking and if so at what—one can add to the aforementioned reasons for this inability and to the means deployed to implement it: the diegetic mist and the extra-diegetic flare Dreyer obtained by directing a light at the camera lens in most of the shots; the surfaces of varying degrees of opacity (thick glazed windows, doors with shutters, etc.) interposed between Gray and the camera; the frequent shots of Gray peering in a window or in a glass door, the camera filming him from inside, the outside overexposed (it is undecidable whether the excess light is an extra-diegetic phenomenon due to a slow speed of the film stock and a large difference between the brightness outside and inside, or whether it is rather a diegetic phenomenon, since we are dealing with a vampire film)—subsists in *Ordet* and *Gertrud* despite the frontality of the characters, since the characters in the latter two films rarely look at each other, even during the long conversations—during the section of the first scene that precedes the mother's visit, a section that lasts around eight minutes, Gertrud looks at her husband only four times, each time for a few seconds, i.e. for a total of less than fifteen seconds—and hence the spectator does not know where they are looking, or indeed if they are looking at all since for most of the time the look is without an object inside or outside the frame (there are no cuts to povs)—they are close to the dead, who have no povs (Gertrud, "Have I lived? No"; hence, Have I looked? No).

In José Larraz's *Vampyres* (1974), the two female vampires, having sucked the blood of one man until he died, kiss under the shower (while another man with whom one of them had sex earlier sleeps in a different section of the house). The two vampires are shot with a jerky hand-held movement from behind a clearing in a trellis with climbing plants. Here telepathy is due neither to the kind of floating, overdetermined montage in Murnau's *Nosferatu* (the link created by the juxtaposition of the shot of Nosferatu in Transylvania walking from screen left to right with the shot of Ellen in Bremen hands outstretched toward the right[50]), nor to dissociation by means of superimposition or matte shots, but to the presence of shots filmed as subjective but that should have been shot as objective. Let us consider the following sequence of shots. First shot: close-up of a face with open eyes; second shot: medium or close shot of what is in front of the eyes; third shot: long shot of the corpse, whose face we saw in the first shot, surrounded by mourners. The second shot, which is an objective shot, will at first be mistaken for a subjective shot, the spectators correcting their error when they see the third shot of the sequence. The presence of the dead with open eyes (whether or not we actually see a medium shot of what is in front of the dead's face and mistake the objective shot for a subjective shot) is countered by the presence, either within the same film or in other films, of shots that are paradoxically subjective when they should be objective (the famous ambiguous shot in *L'Avventura* which may be construed to be a pov of the woman who had disappeared is possibly such a shot). It may be that the number of shots of deads' faces with open eyes in films equals the number of shots that look subjective but should have been objective. What remains of subtracting one from the other is not zero, but *presence*.

The corpse's eye is a fixed film/video camera. To mourn the dead is to experience this paralysis (the first shot in Bruce Baillie's *Roslyn Romance*): is visible to the mourner only what is brought within the shot's fixed frames (any space equivalent to a shot filmed with a fixed camera and that both lasts indefinitely and has no off-screen is the grave). Light itself has to be brought inside the fixed frame, as if space there had a 5 ASA sensitivity. Light and everything else that is being brought inside the frame is like sand being thrown back on the pit where the corpse has been deposited, until the frame protrudes (corpses become bloated, so do graves). Crying is a non-Steadycam hand-held film/video camera moving up and down in a slight hitting on space (like Shiites hitting the tops of their heads in Ashoura), hence is not part of the aforementioned state of mourning.

The suspended movement of people in Edward Hopper's paintings, for instance in *The Lee Shore* (1941), has nothing to do with a photographic arrest of movement, but is the effect of a gravity-induced slowing down of time (this slowing down caused by gravity often induces a feeling of lightness, since the heavy object is *suspended* by its extremely slow movement). It is the same in Dreyer's universe. This gravity can also be discerned in the skewed, at an angle looks that signal that light, and hence these looks, are being strongly bent by gravity (in many cases these skewed looks have to do also with matting: «It [*Cape Cod Evening*] is no exact transcription of a place, but pieced together from sketches... The grove of locust trees was done from sketches of trees nearby. The doorway of the house comes from Orleans about twenty miles from here»[51]. Only the clear light that joins everything in Hopper's paintings can and does join the man, woman and dog in *Cape Cod Evening*); *Western Hotel* (1957) is one of the few of Hopper's paintings where the person looks toward the viewer, but the viewer's gaze is askew, awry, having been formed by viewing Hopper's earlier paintings. Paintings empty of any human presence such as *Early Sunday Morning* (1930), *Sun in an Empty Room* (1963), etc., seem to be the povs of the persons looking off-frame in the paintings in which people are shown. If, nonetheless, there is a strong sense of the absence of the look in these povs, it is due to the slowing down of the look of Hopper's characters, up to its suspension. If there is a virginity in Hopper's work, it is not to be found in nature, but in this delay that suspends the look so that the painted view as a pov is nonetheless seen first by the viewer of the painting. There is another virginity in Hopper's work: the interiors are virginal due to the awry looks of the characters that never look inside; in Hopper's world, it is not in nature but in people's houses that the virginal resides.

In most vampire films the vampire preys only on virgins. This is because, like the vampire, and like the quantum wave, they have either not brought forth something to observation, or, as in the case of the Virgin Mary, what they brought forth managed paradoxically to remain, though embodied, unmanifested. For Mary is a virgin not because her hymen was not penetrated, but because what she later brought to the world remained unmanifested, i.e. because she remained the site of the possible (indeed Mary says in Godard's *Hail Mary*, and Godard quotes: «To be chaste is to know every possibility—»). «They have eyes and do not see, ears and do not hear» should be understood within this context and not as a criticism Christ is directing at the people: Christ remained the site of the possible because he remained, although begotten, although incarnated, unmanifested. The vampire becomes dead (and those he contaminated regain life) only when a measurement (and not a positive hallucination of a measurement («Of these 19 [hypnotized] subjects, 10 were able to tell which light was real, because the hallucinated one... failed to be reflected in the metal box»): the doctor looks in the mirror at Mina speaking to the vampire in Browning's *Dracula* and sees her alone[52] (Coppola missed a beautiful opportunity in the scene in *Dracula* where Mina tells Dracula that "it [Dracula's voice] comforts me when I am alone»: the camera should have panned to a mirror where we would have seen Mina *alone* while hearing Dracula's voice speaking to her); it is unfortunate that no vampire film shows, as the light of the day strikes the vampire, if he has then a picture/reflection in the mirror) collapses all the possibilities (the plague, the companion of the vampire, is another version of this proliferation of possibilities through the inversions it brings about) except one, actualizing it alone.

As an undead, his ability to see through things meant that he could no longer *suddenly* behold, as he turned a corner, behind a skyscraper «a colonial architecture, apparently whisked from some distant savannah of Louisiana or Alabama»[53]. The undead cannot be surprised by what is behind the corner. The coexistence of widely diverse architectural styles, which is a facet of the realm of the undead due to visual tunneling (and to idiosyncrasies of time), is increasingly becoming a facet of the world in general in postmodern culture, where the late modern can coexist in the same building with the ancient Egyptian and/or the Roman and/or the baroque, all lined up on the same plane, so that one does not even have to turn a corner to see them. Tunneling abolishes the *secret beyond the door* (the title of a 1948 Fritz Lang film in which, incidentally, a number of rooms are «whisked» from their original space-time coordinates to the house of the main male character), establishing instead secrets below the *joiner* pieces that overlap, blocking each other, and through whose intersections one cannot tunnel. Is the disappearance behind the corner in *Meshes of the Afternoon* due to an accidental coincidence of the corner with the frame of a joiner's section?

In Wenders' *The Wrong Move* (1985), a medium shot of a young girl sitting in a train looking is followed by a shot of a train seat stained with blood, then by a medium shot of Rüdiger Vogler sitting at the opposite window looking in the direction of the seat. Whose pov was the shot of the two blood stains on the seat? Not children in common, but povs[54]. That is also what happens in the case of the person and his guide/master, even/especially when the person is dead.

One pan in Pasolini's *Medea* begins on a person looking past the camera and moves slowly across several others standing next to one another, all looking in the same direction. The next shot is the pov— of all of them! It is not merely that all are looking at the same thing and seeing it in the same way: all have exactly one and the same pov. Shooting a large number of people looking in the same direction creates a collective single pov, whereas shooting a pan which shows one person at a time as it moves creates the same exact pov for each one of them (which is not the same as a collective single pov). One expects possession/haunting and telepathy to appear in such films— two persons who had even once the same pov remain correlated— and in films where the exact same pov is repeated (one can be possessed by oneself): the same panning shot of the inside of a room is seen at different points in *Meshes of the Afternoon* by all three of the woman's multiple personalities.

There are many ways of preventing the formation of a collective single pov in situations where many people are looking in the same direction. For instance, after showing many people looking in the same direction, one may cut to a wide shot that includes them with the person or animal or thing that they are looking at. Or else one can make certain that in the shot showing many people looking in the same direction there is at least one person not looking in that direction, because s/he is looking somewhere else or talking to the person next to her/him, or sleeping, or writing, etc.; one can then safely cut to a shot of the person or animal or thing in whose direction they are looking without this shot becoming a collective single pov.

In *Last Year at Marienbad* a shot of five people looking in different directions is followed by a pov, which is followed in turn by the same shot of the five people still looking in the same directions. This induces a strange memory since it is not clear which of the five characters saw the pov. The uncertainty is not merely that of the spectator but belongs to the diegetic world, with the consequence that any of the five can remember the pov if not in actuality then de jure. Thus, even those who could later have affirmed that they were looking at something else then (perhaps this will apply to all five) will nonetheless probably have the impression that they are amnesiac about something.

In one scene in Fritz Lang's *The Testament of Dr. Mabuse* (1932) Baum gets hypnotized by (the already dead) Mabuse: the shot of Baum reading at the beginning of the scene is intercut with shots of masks, skulls, and a painting with distorted faces; these are looking at Baum (from the same point of view, since the reverse shot, showing Baum, is from the same angle irrespective of the fact that the direction of the virtual gaze of these objects, located in different sections of the room, is not the same). *Ça vous regarde*: 1) it concerns you; 2) it looks at you. The expression is misleading, for it is only when something qui ne vous regarde pas [which does not concern you] intrudes on you that ça vous regarde [it looks at you], you simultaneously losing the possibility of looking: the vision of Baum becomes impossible as the objects in the room look at him going deeper and deeper into hypnosis. The indifference of what is seen to the direction of the look indicates that in Baum's altered state it is not the eyes that look but the whole face, indeed the whole body. Without this indifference of what is seen to the direction of the look, the spectator would have thought that it is the eyes of the masks and painted faces that are looking.

By looking at what the vampire is looking at, or to be more precise, at what would have been his pov if the dead could see, one is sucked in an absence of an image. This absence of an image is hypnotic. Looking in the mirror in front of which oneself and the vampire are and seeing only oneself, one is driven to look at the emptiness in the mirror (a black hole is not visible, but it can be detected since it exerts a gravitational force: Cygnus X-1 consists of a visible, normal star orbiting around a black hole; similarly, the vampire is not visible in the mirror, but his presence can be detected by the attraction, fascination this absence of an image exerts on the look of the other person, who is visible in the mirror. Adjani and Kinski stand in front of a mirror in Herzog's *Nosferatu*: the gaze of

Adjani, who is standing to the left, is attracted to the right side of the mirror despite the fact that there is no image there, while the vampire's gaze, since he has no mirror image and since the camera has been positioned in place of the mirror, seems to be and is in fact directed at the film spectator. It turns out that the aforementioned film shot of Adjani and Nosferatu does not exist (in the film) but is a production still!). This emptiness is a blind spot in the mirror, turning the latter into a sort of eye; therefore, like the eye, the mirror has a refractory period: hence the *persistence of reflection* in Magritte's *Le Soir qui tombe*.

We are moving toward a telepathic era, one that deals with matting and overlay, which means that we are turning blind to the surrounding immediate environment, over a section of which is superimposed the blank monochromatic matte. In Bunuel's *The Phantom of Liberty* (1974) the parents, who have been asked to come at once to the school because their daughter was kidnapped from her classroom, stand in the classroom with the school superintendent and the teacher reviewing the circumstances in which the kidnapping occurred, while the daughter, standing in the same room, is chided by her mother for interrupting the adults' conversation. The parents *and their daughter* then go to the police to report on the continuing disappearance of the daughter and to ask that the police find her. These two scenes show a response that will be, with the mounting use of mattes, much more frequently encountered: the person one is perceiving in the same space-time with one is treated as overlaid, hence not really present there.

Dreyer: «Why must a dialogue scene be bound to the idea that one either sees the people in profile or sees one actor with his back turned around? ... In a dialogue scene, both faces are important.» The frontality of the figure in *Gertrud* (the most exemplary shot in this vein: we see the mirror reflection of Gertrud entering the room. To see her and not her image in the mirror Gabriel must turn toward her, that is facing in the direction of the camera, while we see her face on in the mirror, so that both are facing us while facing each other), the face-to-camera postures can, unfortunately, divest the characters of that other *hidden observer*, the detachment manifest on the visible part of the faces of actors who are seen from the back in over the shoulder shots.

Wenders: "Do you think it's wise to have two guys work on a film who are both blind in their right eye." Nick Ray: "Start again". Wenders: "I just don't think two one-eyed jacks would be a good cast." The fact that a person's two eyes show him *almost the same view* is given a furtive misleading analogy, a line that repeats the same meaning by *almost the same wording*. But this analogy disregards situations in which *binocular rivalry* occurs, where, although information from only the dominant eye achieves conscious representation at any one time, the sensory inflow from the suppressed eye continues to be registered. The second eye must remain there, even if it hurts (one should not follow Christ's injunction to extract the eye that hurts one), even if, due to amblyopia or cortical lesions, one can no longer see with it (it is above all laconic persons who maintain the suppressed eye even when it hurts), to be submitted to suppression as in binocular rivalry (suppression is at work in Murnau's *Nosferatu*: the iris reproduces the effect of looking with one eye)—the monocular vision of Fritz Lang, of Buster Keaton in Beckett's *Film*, and of Nicholas Ray in *Lightning Over Water*. This allows for the extension of the number and range of associates elicited by a stimulus (presenting a supraliminal stimulus to a suppressed channel is equivalent to presenting a subliminal stimulus to a non-suppressed channel. Since subliminal stimulus operates at a preconscious level, the restrictive/filtering effects of awareness are neutralized).

Immobilization and Tunneling:

Stanislavsky: «This moment is what we in actor's jargon call the state of "I am" ... in the course of my fruitless [imaginary] walk through Famusov's house there had been one instant when I really felt that I was there and believed in my own feelings. This was when I opened the door into the antechamber and pushed aside a large armchair; I really felt the physical effort entailed in this act. It lasted for several seconds; I felt the truth of my being there. It was dissipated as soon as I walked away from the armchair and I was again walking in space, amid undefined objects.»[55]

In the case of Virginia Woolf, it is, on the contrary, an object, a puddle, that makes her—and later Rhoda—unable to move (a photographer should succeed in showing whether a person normally walks back-and-forth (and not by means of superimposition or by shooting with very slow shutter speed, creating a blurred path). Not in the case of these immobilizations), creating a sense of unreality and taking away from her the ability to say or feel "I am." Sartre's Roquentin writes: «I saw a piece of paper lying beside a puddle ... the rain had drenched it and twisted it ... I bent down, already rejoicing at the touch of this pulp ...

«I was unable.

«I stayed bent down for a second, I read "Dictation: The white owl," then I straightened up, empty-handed. I am no longer free, I can no longer do what I will.»[56]

Ça va? How can things be fine when one is *stopped dead* in one's tracks, when these immobilizations are happening. *Muscle* comes from the Latin *musculus*, which means little mouse. There is a proliferation of mice and rats in the infamous plagues of vampire films, as if people's muscles had slipped from them and were moving around, leaving them to an immobilization/paralysis due to fear and death.

With Stanislavsky it is an object, a chair he is able to move, that permits him to feel *I am* (the ultra-cold Jalal Toufic is unable to perform some manners: he cannot move chairs for women (let alone men). But through the absence of friction of superfluidity (in the two-fluid model), he is always performing the *after you*). How can the undead feel and say *I am* when objects either cannot be moved at all (he saw the objects on the table; they could never be moved (was he looking at the past?). At most a layer, a superimposition, a geometrical surface could be detached (as in Wenders' *Wings of Desire*, 1987) and manipulated. In Hollis Frampton's *Poetic Justice* (1972) the cup of coffee and the vase with flowers remain next to pages of the script describing what happens to them. In Robert Wiene's *The Cabinet of Dr. Caligari* (1920) this freezing takes the form of painted light and shadow patterns) or, more deleterious still, if they move on their own before him, if they have become automobile: coffin lids that open on their own and ships that steer their way on their own («The ship [transporting Dracula] ... found the harbor unsteered save by the hand of a dead man!» (Stoker's *Dracula*)). That is why we often see in vampire films and films of the undead in general someone quickly stretching his hand to *hold fast* static objects, for these can at any moment move on their own (in the rare photographs Jalal Toufic took, all shot with the camera resting on a fixed tripod rather than from a moving vehicle, it is not the persons who are blurred due to slow shutter speed, but the objects—a pencil sharpener, a shoe): the knife that slides on its own from the bread and the key that falls after coming to a stop on one of the steps of the stairs in Maya Deren's *Meshes of the Afternoon*. The resulting absence of obstacles is very detrimental to the unembodied or dissociated, for obstacles permitted them to become in-focus: «When this sensation of dereality occurs while walking, I try to move over against a building or doorway until I become one again»[57]—a non-narcissistic hug of oneself.

When the object or movement is left on its own it has the quality of not being stoppable, hence both the absence of the one who let go of it (it is this ability at non-interference/-obstruction that helps one later to deal with these unstoppable objects/states of thinking and behavior, allowing one not to be enslaved to the latter as compulsions and obsessions), and the fascination, hypnosis of the one who is observing it or against whom it is directed.

In the somnambulistic walk, there is a doubling in the walker—one part walking, going through motor movements, the other part immobile, just looking (every movement is perceived by the latter to be a wipe, s/he feeling s/he has no way of stopping the moving people, even in the sense of accompanying them (if one accompanies the other, one can say, because of the relativity of motion, that oneself and the other person are immobile and it is the world that is moving)) while being transported by the other part, feeling it has no control on the walk (*to stand on one's own feet*: to think or act independently): it is as if one were in the seat next to the driver. Inside the shadowlike Dyer shown in profile in Francis Bacon's *Portrait of George Dyer Riding a Bicycle* is another Dyer. This is not due to a cubist simultaneity of different angles of view, but to somnambulism: being transported by the double (cubist simultaneity applies to the three positions of the bicycle's front wheel; the other direction of Dyer's face does not confirm to any one of these). Hence the mannerism connected with somnambulism—let us consider a somnambulist wanting to drink from a well: one component of the somnambulist holds the rope attached to the bucket, neutralizing the weight of the water filling the latter, while the second component pulls the bucket out of the well, exerting just enough force and effort to raise an empty bucket. A separation of the two components occurs in Dreyer's *Vampyr* as Gray trips at the *false threshold*, one of the selves/components spilling.

Being an undead, when he did not tunnel through space but covered it in a gradual, continuous way, he did so in a somnambulistic manner, did not move while moving (strangely enough, it is when the somnambulist sits that s/he gives the impression s/he is moving: the four people sitting outside the house staring at the landscape in Hopper's *People in the Sun* look as if they are in a moving train).

In Fritz Lang's *M* (1931), a hand gesture during a meeting of the police chiefs gets continued, through an edit on movement, by the hand movement of a criminal at a meeting of underground chiefs taking place at the same time at a different section of the city. This problematic editing is also found in Maya Deren's films; in Bruce Baillie's *Castro Street* (1966), where the train passing in one shot makes the grass sway in another shot on which the first is superimposed (there is no wind in the second shot—even were there a moving train off-screen (behind the camera) in the second shot, producing the air current swaying the grass, this would signal an overdetermination in the causation of one effect); in Murnau's *Nosferatu*: a shot of Mina with hands outstretched from right to left in Bremen is followed by a shot of Nosferatu looking from left to right in Transylvania (telepathy does not apply at the level of content only (Mina is telepathic) in Murnau's film but also at the formal level)— the edit as lapsus; in *Un Chien andalou* (1929), where a character opening the door of a room and stepping out in a first shot puts down his foot on the beach in the next shot. Normal continuous movement (walking—) ends very quickly in a fall and death (all the armed men in the beginning section of *L'Age d'or* (1930) end up falling and dying), or, as in Maya Deren's *At Land* (1944), introduces, soon enough, a lag between the persons strolling together. To avoid that, transportation is accomplished by cutting on movement shots of the person in different locations and/or times. *One no longer moves in an unbroken manner*, since one can be at a certain place and the next moment at another location hundreds of miles away, *but one's movement/ gesture/words is/are continuous, smooth.* It is no longer the shots that are cut on movement but the scenes, while jump cuts proliferate within the same scene. This tunneling is the only manner of avoiding the lag, the fall and/or death: when problematic editing stops in *Un Chien Andalou* and the couple walks on the beach, the result is that they end up half-buried in the sand (the undead, like infants, have to learn how to walk (Lyne's *Jacob's Ladder*, 1990). In *The Discreet Charm of the Bourgeoisie* (1972) this has already been accomplished).

The pervasiveness of teleportation or tunneling through space-time would drastically increase the blockage of normal walking or running (Virginia Woolf and Rhoda immobilized in front of a puddle; the heroine of *Meshes of the Afternoon* can run but always within the same frame of the joiner, never reaching the walking figure she is pursuing: a mobile immobilization, an immobile mobility). Maybe in years to come people will come to think that teleportation was created to make transportation possible in a world plagued by very frequent blockings of walking or running (I did this in the previous paragraph!): the cause viewed as the remedy. One of the prices that will be paid for tunneling, by means of which one moves through (perceptible) walls/barriers, is that unexpected, invisible barriers will spring up everywhere: immobilizations where there is no perceivable barrier. Many of these barriers will be objects that for no apparent reason cannot be removed, objects that put one into a trance[58] (is tunneling's induction of a trance state surprising at all since we know that one of the special effects of hypnosis is visual tunneling: the hypnotized person may have no difficulty in deciding which of two persons is the hallucinated double because in the case of one of them the object behind him is visible "through him"[59]?), depriving one of one's motor ability, as with Roquentin: «this morning ... I wanted to and could not pick up a paper lying on the ground»[60]. In a shot filmed with a telephoto lens in Jalal Toufic's *Night for Day* one can see a person out-of-focus in the foreground while the background is in-focus—an arrangement which almost always ends with a rack-focus. Not in this case, for the in-focus plane is inhabited by an absence of a figure, by a *presence* (the out-of-focus shots in Antonioni's *Red Desert* (1964) that remain out-of-focus presage/lead to the invisible ball in *Blow Up*, 1967). One cannot dismiss this *presence* since it has the effect of paralyzing any rack-focus: the person in the foreground remains out-of-focus (this unfocus resembles that of the images one sees in Herzog's *Fata Morgana*, shot in the desert. A warning against a mirage?).

Doors either open by themselves like sleepwalkers or the vampire tunnels through them in dissolves (Browning's *Dracula*) or cuts. The dissolve or cut between two shots of the vampire, in the first of which s/he is far away, for instance at the end of a long corridor (according to the mirror, s/he is not at that location), and in the second of which s/he is next to the victim (according to the mirror, s/he is not at that location either[61]), or vice-versa, may either indicate that the future victim of the vampire has just undergone a lapse or that the vampire has tunneled through the intervening space[62] (« I saw a female figure standing at the foot of the bed... A block of stone could not have been stiller... As I stared at it, the figure appeared to have changed its place, and was now nearer the door» (*Carmilla*)[63]; in *Meshes of the Afternoon*, Maya Deren changes location on the stairs without covering the intermediate space; Dracula tunnels through the spider's web without tearing it in Browning's *Dracula*). Tunneling in vampire films, made possible by the uncertainty of the momentum (is the vampire moving or still?) or the position of the undead, applies not only in the case of doors (*Carmilla*), but also to the space-time between two shots or between the planes of one shot. In the case of tunneling due to uncertainty of position, the pov of the person looking at the vampire should be from the beginning a dissolve, rather than, as in Murnau's *Nosferatu*, beginning with one shot of the vampire in one position then dissolving to him having become closer or further away.

Tunneling is related to doubles. In Tarkovsky's *Nostalgia*, the pan from the wife to the daughter to the mother in the background to the wife again now holding the son in the distant background is an instance of tunneling. While Josephson opens a door to either side of which are not walls but empty space and crosses to the other side, the poet passes through the empty space to the side, that is he tunnels through that space—the door being there largely to alert us to the tunneling that would have otherwise probably eluded us. Having encountered tunneling, we are quick to encounter doubling: the reflection of Josephson in the mirror in front of which stands the poet alone, and the former's doubling by the mime, who imitates him in a mocking, stylized way. In *Solaris*, there is the doubling of the dead wife by all her replicas, who seem to think that one can tunnel through a locked door, each time getting shredded (the cessation of replications coinciding with learning not to try to tunnel through the door). In Antonioni's *The Passenger*, a film that deals with (the) doubling (between Robertson and Locke), there is tunneling both in the form of the pan from Robertson and Locke standing still talking on the balcony to them continuing their discussion in the adjoining room, Locke now without a shirt and sweating profusely; and in the form of the tracking shot through the window bars. In Dreyer's *Vampyr* the tunneling of Gray, for instance in the shot where the camera pans from him standing still looking to a diminutive skeleton, books, a skull, then to him now at the other end of the room, is concomitant with his doubling/dissociation.

The black of the iris (Murnau's *Nosferatu*) functions in the manner of the barrier in a Josephson Junction.

The clearest index, in *Citizen Kane*, of the extremity of withdrawal Kane has reached behind the "No Trespassing" sign and the bars that close his *self-sufficient* palace, Xanadu, to others is that the camera—which, elsewhere in the film, in the scene where the reporter goes to see Kane's wife in the bar, can tunnel through a glass roof in a continuous movement from the outside of a nightclub to its interior[64]—can enter his room only by simultaneously remaining outside: on the shot of the inside of the room is superimposed the snow of the outside (an outside that belongs to the section in Kane's past when he was playing on his sled Rosebud).

In *Vampire Lovers*, a shot of a shrouded vampire walking in a cemetery is followed by a close-up of her face, although she did not lift the shroud. This successful tunneling of vision through a veil (and in other instances through space, the vampire/undead experiencing a cut in his pov from a long shot to a close-up) is sometimes accompanied by the presence/*presence* of a curtain that extends from the background to the foreground, tunneling through the figure, imprisoning it, as in Francis Bacon's paintings *Study after Velazquez's Portrait of Pope Innocent X*, *Study for a Portrait*, *Study for Crouching Nude*, and *Head IV*. This is the real shroud of the revenant: one is hidden by/inside what is behind one (another form of the crossing of the *imaginary line*). In some cases the presence of these peculiar shrouds-curtains presages the advent of one's ability to tunnel (or, to be more precise, one's inability not to tunnel), in other cases it follows it, in still others one occurs without the other.

"I hit him on the fist with my cheek." This sort of comic inversion is often encountered in tunneling: it is not the heroine's leg that tunnels through Carmilla's body when she kicks the latter, but Carmilla's immobile body that tunnels through the heroine's leg.

Her face, with its excessively oval shape, gives the impression she has a scarf around it. Had she put a scarf around her neck, this would not have deterred the vampire from attacking her, since his teeth can tunnel through the scarf. It is the aforementioned impression that deterred him.

One needs a leap (Kierkegaard's, or Eisenstein's *pathetic leap*) to go from tunneling (a subatomic particle can have an extra amount of energy as credit out of Heisenberg's uncertainty principle and *jump* over the energy barrier) to the normal state, that of being stopped by obstacles too high to leap over in the traditional sense.

On leaving Mecca to Yathrib, the prophet Mohammad was pursued by a band of Meccans. He took cover within a cave, and prayed to God. A spider weaved its web at the cave's entrance. In fast-forward or in time-lapse? Or was it that Mohammad had tunneled through an already existent web. The sight of the web stopped his enemies from searching for him in the cave, saving the life of the person who *died before he died*. It may be that he died before he died there (or in another cave, the cave of Hira, where he had his first revelation).

The two immobilities, the one in Duras' *India Song* and the one in both Robbe-Grillet's *L'Immortelle* (also in *Last Year in Marienbad*, his joint film with Alain Resnais) and Roman Polanski's *The Tenant* (1976) are different; the former is merely a way to negotiate hot weather, while the latter is a feature of the realm of the undead.

Unlike Roland Barthes, we are not concerned with the still,[65] but with the immobilization of characters or of film images *in* the motion picture. It is the frozen frames (the stuffed animals, humans, and things specific to cinema) in Vertov's *The Man with a Movie Camera*, 1929 (Vertov's negative of time is not, as Annette Michelson writes, reverse motion, but the frozen frame) that render possible fastforward, slow motion, auto-motion (the camera comes out of its case, mounts the tripod, which performs a series of movements on its own, while the camera's winding mechanism revolves by itself, signaling that the camera is filming), vibrational movement (the alternating fast cuts between two images), backward movement (already in *Kino-Glaz* (1924) a bull whose meat had been sold is resurrected), simultaneity (multiple exposures), and animation (the move from freeze-framing to normal motion). The shots of dead Lenin in Vertov's *Three Songs of Lenin* (1934) are differentiated from photograms by the presence of a moving element in the frame, for example a shadow moving on the face of Lenin, or someone moving at the edge of the frame. The intertitle «If only Lenin could see our country now!» recurs three times in the film. Indeed Lenin could not see the future because his immobility as corpse is not one that allows for idiosyncrasies of time; hence Vertov had to revert in this film also to freeze framing in order to be able to have fastforward ....

The immobilizations schizophrenics perceive and/or undergo make possible backward movement (Mark Vonnegut saw the water of a cascade going up (*The Eden Express*)). Immobilization/freezing permits the fast forward in René Clair's *The Crazy Ray*; the prophecies of the shepherd in *Heart of Glass*; and the one-lapse time-lapse of the grass over the train tracks in the last scene of Bertolucci's *The Spider's Stratagem*. Similarly, it is the immobilizations we encounter in Dreyer's script of *Vampyr*—hearing approaching footsteps from the other side of the door, «Nikolas stands rooted to the spot ... [he] has hardly dared to draw a breath for fear of giving himself away»; elsewhere in the script, «Nikolas stops too ... [he] waits as quiet as a mouse»[66]— that allow the reverse motion in the film's diegesis: the sand that rises from the ground to the grave digger's shovel ...

The shot of the woman opening her eyes in Chris Marker's film *La Jetée* indicates that the spectator is not supposed to project from the stills to their animation, but must accept them as (diegetic) immobilizations (hence *La Jetée* is not a filmed photo-roman). Which means that the film shows the male character's actual going back to and reliving of part of the cycle of events shown in the film rather than merely a rescanning of the cycle; a finite recurrence, the actual number determined by the number of times each frame was printed.

In the sequence of the raising of the bridge in *October* (1928) the shots of the dead young woman on the bridge are chronologically out of order (other instances where a movement will unfold and come to an end only to take place again from a further point than where it began in the previous shot: in *October*, Kerensky's meeting with one of the Tsar's servants on the staircase; in *Potemkin*, the walk up the Odessa steps by the woman holding her dead child in her arms). These time idiosyncrasies are most probably consequences of Eisenstein's use of montage to occasionally create «an artificially produced image of motion»: in *October* a close shot showing the face of a soldier holding a machine gun of which only the rear part appears in the shot is followed by a medium shot of the gun, with the quick alternation of the two shots creating the illusion that the gun is firing bullets; in *Potemkin*, three shots of three statues of a lion, in the first of which he is lying down dozing, in the second of which he is awake and ready to rise up, and in the third of which he is already risen, are edited together, giving the paradoxical impression that the marble lion has risen in response to the massacre of the Odessa Steps.

Even objects, if they become really frozen and not just immobile because inanimate, can permit time idiosyncrasies. And they can become frozen, since at one point they did become auto-mobile.

Hence idiosyncrasies of time, such as fast-forward or backward movement, were to be for me the criterion by which to decide whether patients suffering from *encephalitis lethargica* were really frozen, in which case the common name for that disease, "the sleeping sickness," would be a misnomer (as is the French title of Rene Clair's film *Paris Qui Dort*. The American title, *The Crazy Ray*, is more appropriate). It turned out that, at least in some cases, those suffering from *encephalitis lethargica* are truly frozen: Hester Y. and other patients discussed in Oliver Sacks' *Awakenings* told him that sometimes, when having *kinematic vision* (during which they perceive (in) *stills* («sometimes these stills form a flickering vision, like a movie-film which is running too slow»)), they experienced «the displacement of a "still" either backwards or forwards, so that a given "moment" may occur too soon or too late»[67]. Probably the reason the woman in *Last Year in Marienbad* finds it so difficult to remember is that the immobilizations of the other people make possible an actual movement backward in time, which means that gradually events are happening at the year before at Marienbad. Hence her awkward, difficult position: she is asked by the man to remember their first meeting at Marienbad, when both she and him have been transported back to that first time (this implies that even the first time they met he was already asking her to remember their previous meeting at Marienbad).

In those vampire films where a *nature morte* appears (the food laid out for Harker in *Nosferatu*), it would be nice to see at least once the latter coexist in the same shot with *still life*s, i.e. frozen people, or else—if we take into consideration that there is a superposition of a walker-mover and a still life/frozen person in the somnambulist—with somnambulists.

The fixity, frozen quality of persons in films and books about the undead (*Last Year at Marienbad*; *Carmilla*: «and I saw a female figure standing at the foot of the bed... A block of stone could not have been stiller...»[68]) is conjoined to an excessive fluidity: Nosferatu, who feeds on blood (for vampires animal flesh is chewing gum; vampires dislike gum-chewing), goes from his castle to England by river and sea. The blood of vampires, like that of the corpses of saints, does not coagulate, but remains liquid. Blood continues to seep from the victim because of the anticoagulant contained in the vampire's saliva. The slow motion encountered in many films about the undead renders movements fluid (*At Land*).

The eternal—where immobilization reigns—can be reached by a total continuous observation (the Zeno's paradox in quantum theory), hence by yoga, which allows the psychomental stream not to be invaded by distraction, automatisms, and memory, so that a continual observation through concentration can happen, an observation that takes place only once *pratyahara* («withdrawal of the senses») is realized, since all the senses function with refractory periods.

The guard must be intermittent in his guarding/observation, otherwise he would immobilize those he is guarding (the Zeno's paradox in quantum theory—the contemporary version of Medusa's gaze).

"Buried by the dust." How long has he stood still in his room?

Defending oneself against the anxiety-/panic-induced sudden immobilization and discrete about-face by a surprise and since the latter, being the unexpected, cannot be counted upon to happen at the right time, by this jumpiness, exaggerated startle response, autonomic hyperactivity, and generalized starting (free-floating anxiety as vaccination against a more threatening anxiety?). The latter surprise, or the jumpiness, is to withhold one from the former, to place one elsewhere at the time the other one happens. A first way of viewing Susan Morrissey's triptych *Fear of Flying*: the woman starts, drops a cup of coffee before a paper airplane suddenly tunnels from the right panel (where a boy is standing with a paper plane waiting for the one in the air to fall in the same location, i.e. in the same panel) into the middle panel, where she is. It is not clear whether the former surprise, induced by the jumpiness, has managed to transport the woman in the middle panel elsewhere by the time the other surprise, that of the sudden eruption of the tunneling plane, which functions in the too-early mode (it is always too early for the impossible, for the never), took place, in which case, the four different positions of the face as it turns from one side to the other at the eruption of the airplane should be considered an awkward attempt to represent movement in painting (a rendition that is revealing precisely because of its awkwardness, since movement is not a trajectory but a tunneling; while the line of trajectory tracing the cup's fall is both awkward and falsifying), hence extra-diegetic, or whether the former surprise happened too late and hence these are freezings and discrete turns. A second way of viewing *Fear of Flying*: it is unclear whether a surprise that happened too-early, the eruption of a tunneling plane (the fall of the cup is then merely an effect of this surprise) into the space-time of the woman, managed to place her elsewhere by the time an imperceptible surprise, deducible from the immobilization, took place (or did it *take place*? for nothing really happened to elicit the precipitation of the freezing (*Last Year at Marienbad*)—the absence of time does not reside only in the freezing but also in the absence of cause for the freezing). There are at least twelve balls in *Have a Ball Sw'theart*, 1987. The two balls in the hands of the juggler, a green ball and a yellow one (we see a decomposition of the movement of the former on its way from the juggler's right hand to his left hand, where it firmly lodges), plus the red one he threw to the woman, referred to in the ironic title of the painting, the ten red ones she received. There is a discrepancy between the number of faces of the woman, two, and the number of red balls in front of her, ten. This discrepancy signals that we are not dealing with a representation of movement in painting but with immobilizations/freezings of the red ball, which multiply it, in this instance into ten balls. Beyond the ironic sexual and gender overtones to the title, the humor in the Lugosi-like juggler throwing a ball to a woman who will receive ten—a koan: "how to juggle one ball without letting ten fall?" In Patrick Bokanowski's *L'Ange*, the maid probably brought to the table in addition to the five vases that we see immobilized in the vase's fall, the number of vases we see crash on the floor (about ten; so she brought to the table around fifteen vases). In this scene it becomes quite manifest that an actual immobilization of the five vases (another version of the double and doubling) is taking place, since the woman continues her walk within the same frame where the five vases, three of which are in mid-air, are immobilized. It is clear then that in the case of the vases we are not at all dealing with a Marey-like decomposition of a movement. Another form/version of the multiplication of an item, the other one being Christ's miracle of the multiplication of the five loaves of bread and the two fishes to feed over five thousand people, here in relation to a gutless person whose absence of hands denotes that he cannot eat. We can already detect the apprehension of catatonic immobilization in Morrissey's Table-lady series, with pieces falling whenever the table-lady—whose skirt is a table on which various items can be found in the different paintings: a child, plates, knives, glasses filled with water and other liquids, etc.—moves. In *Turn-a-bout*, a woman who is holding a glass of wine is surprised by the sudden intrusion of a boy and drops the glass; her surprise would not have saved her from a too-early surprise, for the boy, who suddenly appears at the door, unlike the vampire, has a shadow and hence a reflection in the mirror, i.e. announces himself (it does not matter if the other person actually perceives the shadow/reflection or not), lags behind himself. *Turn-a-bout* can be considered the control sample in a triptych formed of itself, *Have a Ball Sw'theart* and *Fear of Flying*, at the level of both the kind of surprise and the sort of immobilization, and because in that painting we are not dealing with a person undergoing anxiety since although we have an ineffectual preventive surprise we do not get diegetic freezings. In Ted Julian Arnold's *The Dismay of Mr. Boulager* (1992), two ways of viewing the left figure must be maintained conjointly. 1) The figure has just appeared at an opening (the right foot is already within the room onto which the opening gives). 2) If one follows the contours of the thick lavender line that delineates the thigh and delimits the leg within the space of the opening, what looked like a schematically painted foot in the section adjoining the space were the figure is and occupying a lower part of the painting becomes a blotch of color having a purely painterly effect, with the consequence that the space below the figure is no longer horizontal, receding, but frontal (hence does not function as the floor of a room), this producing the double effect of making it a sort of pedestal (an impression reinforced by having the figure's head and inscrutable eyes tilted up) and of flattening the figure (a flattening *under*scored by the perceivable patches of drapery linen within the face, i.e. by the background and the figure in the foreground seeming to be on the same plane, a plane that is affected with an idiosyncratic depth since it covers the unlocalizable space between the foreground and the background (one can certainly consider the drapery linen appearing in parts of the figure as having also a modernist function: drawing attention to the flatness of the canvas). The quasi-sculptural figure was at the opening for an indefinite period; yet, since it has patches of the background, it gives the feeling that it has prematurely detached from the background (this is another effect, the first being imprisonment, of the tunneling of the background/backdrop through the figure): its arrival surprises one. The left figure has nonchalantly (since it announces itself) and accidentally appeared at a door *and* been already there for an indefinite time, and it is in this second role that it really and essentially surprises Mr. Boulager.

We witness a superimposition of two radically different ways of interpreting what is going on (why did I use the expression *going on*? Am I, is something favoring one of the two interpretations?) in one of Munch's paintings: it could either be showing a woman become three women through immobilization, this answering the original of the two titles, *The Sphinx*, or it could be showing the gradual change of one woman that corresponds to its second title, *The Three Stages of Woman*, or, if we take the *Woman* of the title as the generic term, three different women standing for the three archetypes of Woman according to Munch. In the case that the three are produced by the multiplication that immobilization can cause, all three, rather than only the third, will have the same affective state: anxiety. We see a gradual moving away from a similar affective expression, anxiety, for the three women in the 1893/94[69] version toward the differing states in both the 1894[70] and the 1895[71] versions.

Gaps:
The amnesia of Herzog's Harker may have the function of occulting that there is no continuous trajectory between Transylvania and Wismar. Instead of the continuous connection in a homogeneous space and time between the local and the global, we have either an alternation between or a simultaneity of the immobilization/blocking (Leila, in close-up, in *L'Immortelle*; catatonic stupor and rigidity; the freezing of the vampire in the coffin during the day) and (Bell's/ David Bohm's) non-locality. It is as if this freezing (which is not merely non-movement, but the coming of the non-movement to a violent, furtive stop) has liberated/exiled a double that can travel faster than light beyond the light cone, hence open to the influences of what is off-screen (the light cone is otherwise a screen with no off-screen). In the aftermath of World War II reality was in the image of the street in the Florence section of Rossellini's *Paisa* (1946): between its two sides is a space emptied by the snipers' bullets and that nothing can cross except a primitive dolly. But such gaps in reality and the similar ones that Bazin writes about («The technique of Rossellini undoubtedly maintains an intelligible succession of events, but these do not mesh like a chain with the sprockets of a wheel. The mind has to leap from one event to the other as one leaps from stone

to stone in crossing a river. It may happen that one's foot hesitates between two rocks, or that one misses one's footing and slips. The mind does likewise. Actually it is not of the essence of a stone to allow people to cross rivers without wetting their feet ... »[72]) do not allow us to understand the gaps in vampire films: the undead can tunnel through the former gaps (in Maya Deren's *Meshes of the Afternoon*, the woman, who passes from the house to the more or less distant beach by taking one step, cannot be stopped by the stones in Bazin's river being too far apart for a normal person to safely attempt crossing the river. The undead standing on one bank can find himself/herself on the other bank without having any notion how s/he not so much crossed the river (for s/he did not spend any time doing that) as found himself/herself on the other bank (*tunneling*: the passage of a system from one authorized state to another through prohibited intermediary states. These intermediary states don't exist as real states since the time of passage is null (one can say that the speed is infinite)), but s/he is stopped by the blockages specific to the undead, the schizophrenics and the hypnotized. If tunneling can succeed in covering the river, can a *pathetic leap*? Eisenstein defined pathos as a going out of oneself. Yet Eisenstein's *pathetic leaps* occur within the confines of a model of dialectical organic progression, so that the leap would fail if we removed the next shot: «the smallest part must be to the largest what the largest is to the set ... It is in that sense that *the set is reflected in each part*»[73]. This saves Eisenstein from the eventuality that the gaps between shots be, like the ones between the rocks in Bazin's river, too wide (the gaps Bazin is dealing with are closer to the leap for they make gaining momentum impossible).

If Eisenstein's pathetic leaps are unable to cover the gaps we are dealing with, maybe Vertov's Kino-eye can. Indeed, how stale is Eisenstein's «pathetic leap» compared to Vertov's Kino-eye: «Now I, a camera ... free of the limits of time and space, I put together any given points in the universe, no matter where I've recorded them»[74] (the arrogance of everything local, provincial: the news in Oshkosh began with over ten minutes of interviews with *Packers* fans about their team's win, followed by over five minutes of interviews with Christmas shoppers; only then was the news about the in-hiding Noreiga seeking that day asylum in the Vatican embassy, and the capture of Cessaueco, mentioned. Death is cosmopolitan). The freedom that the camera movement conjoined to the editing creates induces a fundamental immobility, the photogram—hence gaps—which in turn permits all sorts of idiosyncrasies of time.

Bazin's homogeneity, «la robe sans couture de la réalité,» cannot exist except where death has been reduced to the cessation of life, to an absolute framing of life that admits of no off-screen (most of the examples Bazin gives of prohibited montage are those where an animal or a child, rather than an adult human being, are in danger of being eaten or killed («it is inconceivable that the famous seal-hunt scene in *Nanook* should not show us hunter, hole, and seal all in the same shot. It is simply a question of respect for the spatial unity of an event at the moment when to split it up would change it from something real into something imaginary... [the scene in *Louisiana Story*] of an alligator catching a heron, photographed in a single panning shot, is admirable...»[75]). This is most probably because they don't *seem* to go through undeath: death seems to be their final abolition (in archaic societies, the death of an infant gets a very weak funerary reaction. This is because the child is still close to an almost total non mastery of the world and hence can better deal with the non mastery that awaits him/her in undeath and because the loss of time is not felt as a radical surprise during undeath, since it was almost never there even in life (Piaget))). But in the realm of death-as-undeath (Robbe-Grillet, Ruiz) homogeneity is undone. The closest one can get to homogeneity then is as in Godard's *King Lear*, the film pieces of two shots having to be stitched.

Circles:

The circle shows up in many guises in altered states, among which are the following two:

— the constitution of a circle where there was none: in Maupassant's *La Horla*, «all at once it seemed to me that I was followed... I turned abruptly. I was alone. I saw behind me only the straight, broad path... horrifyingly empty; and in the other direction, too, it stretched away as far as the eye could see, just the same... I closed my eyes. Why? And I began to twirl about on one heel, very rapidly... I opened my eyes... Then, ah me! I did not know which way I had come!»[76]. The hero of *La Horla* is as if doing a Sufi whirling dance, this resulting, as in mysticism, in the suppression of opposites or their indistinguishability.

— the circle is undone when midway in a circular path, one suddenly feels that there is a big distinction between the left and right paths, one direction becoming the good direction (at the threshold of his apprenticeship, Castaneda was asked by don Juan to find his good spot). This undoing of the circle may permit one to fight the first way in which the circle is encountered, where instead of the two directions, there is one direction with a double.

Labyrinth:
Duras considers the houses, hotels, drawing rooms in which her films take place, «echo-chambers». Echo-chambers of silence. This provides a link with the blindness that we find in her films (in *Hiroshima Mon Amour* the French woman says she saw the effects of the atomic bomb dropped on Hiroshima; the Japanese man replies that she saw nothing. The majority of people in Hiroshima who did not die were blinded; how can one take photographs of Hiroshima, how can one take a photograph at Hiroshima of someone who was blinded by the atomic explosion? At most a photograph can be taken and subjected to an Arnulf Rainer overpainting), where people find things through echolocation, where the voice is sent, bumps or does not bump against something (be it the *yes* or *no* in *India Song*, their utterance taking the smallest amount of time possible) and comes back to give «direction on how to get lost». For echoes, a form of mise-en-abyme, often figure in labyrinths.

The labyrinth is elsewhere: in *The Shining*, the physical maze in the grounds of the hotel is not the real labyrinth; rather it is the book Jack Torrance is writing, made out of the same phrase *occurring* on and on, a writing in circles, a returning to the same point (would the book's title be the same phrase?). There are two forms of the labyrinthine moving in circles: I keep coming back to the same impasse (*The Shining*); I go through a lapse and the trajectory rescans itself (Renny Harlin's *Nightmare on Elm Street IV*, 1988)—the latter is the much more dangerous state.

In the physical maze, Danny, fleeing his father (who wants to murder him), retraces his steps backward, at one point jumping to the side and hiding behind one of the hedges, so that his father, following his steps, sees the steps cease—beyond is virgin snow. Danny is not dealing with a labyrinth, since at no point while retracing his steps backward does he either see or have the apprehension that he would see them end abruptly. In the case of Danny, who is telepathic and clairvoyant, we are still dealing with a linear, although reversible, time: Danny sees the linear future and the linear past, whereas the labyrinth undoes linear time (when the person in bandages screams near the beginning of Polanski's *The Tenant* this is already the last shot of the film, and it is not Choule who screams in the former shot (witness the fact that the person in bandages does not recognize Stella, who is a very close friend of Choule), but, already hidden behind the bandages, Tralkovsky-become-Choule (is it the scream of the one who sees in dread his double?); the middle-aged Jack Torrance who arrives at the Overlook Hotel presumably sometime in the nineteen seventies was there as a middle-aged undertaker in 1920). It is precisely because he is already lost in the labyrinth of the book that Jack Torrance is unable to find the exit of the physical maze.

The closed door of room 237, and the locked larder door of the kitchen, where Jack Torrance is imprisoned by his wife, are found open, though none of the living occupants of the hotel performed the act of opening either. This does not necessitate resorting to the hypothesis that someone dead opened the door, but can be accounted for by the fact that we are dealing with a labyrinthine structure, a structure where the inside is outside—and vice-versa: it is easy to overlook the fact that the *overlooking* shots of the credits sequence that begins *The Shining*, showing Jack Torrance's drive up to the Overlook Hotel, are part of the hotel.

The following structure recurs in Hopper's work: the people who appear inside a room or a house do not look at the objects or people inside the room or at the room itself, nor at the visible outside, but rather at the off-frame outside. The result is that the visible outside—in *Morning in a City*, it consists of two windows with their blinds half-closed, the roof above them and a stretch of sky—becomes part of the room. One more similarity—the first is that the light in the painting is at times incongruent with the time of day, for instance daylight in night landscapes, as in Magritte's *L'Empire des Lumières* (1950) and Hopper's *Conference at Night* (1949)—between Hopper's work (*Morning Sun* (1952), *Hotel by a Railroad* (1952), *Morning in a City* (1944)) and that of Magritte (*L'éloge de la dialectique*, 1936).

As in hypnosis, where one cannot hypnotize someone if s/he wants to resist, Nosferatu has to wait till Mina invites him to enter. Yet it is not so simple: one of Milton Erickson's induction techniques, the *confusion technique*, which he uses when faced with the conscious interference or resistance of the subject, entails confusing the subject so much («to get there now... I take a combination of three *right* turns and three *left* turns... but I don't know which is the *right* series of *rights* and *lefts*... all *right*, pay attention very closely, because we've got to make it *right* or we'll be *left* behind... I'll take a *right* here (I think that's *right*), and then a *left* and now I'm *left* with two *lefts* and two *rights*. So all *right*, I'll take another *left*, which means I am now *left* with a *left* and a *right* and a *right*...»)[77] that he ends up complying with any leading statement ("drop into trance") that would take him/her out of the confusion/uncertainty. In Stoker's *Dracula* the coach taking Harker to the castle keeps going back and forth on the same path (amid the howling wolves), only then does it proceed to the castle. Nosferatu says to Harker, "enter of your own free will," only after the back-and-forth episode and after Harker had undergone a lapse and no longer knows where he is, where is the outside and where is the inside (Magritte's *Le Noctambule* and *L'éloge de la dialectique*).

The running person being pursued by the vampire cannot evade him even though the latter is walking nonchalantly. This inability reveals the normal space to be a labyrinth (or else is to be ascribed to the vampire's ability to tunnel («For the dead travel fast»), hence to his ability to be in different places during the chase without covering the trajectory between them[78], this producing on the victim the effect of being in a labyrinth, hence of going in circles (the aura of the labyrinth)). Yet the circularity of time may save us from the result of the circularity of space: we are still fleeing the vampire who had already caught us. Except that this would be tantamount to being fully inside the labyrinth. Those who suffer a trauma upon discovering the circularity of time, and hence have a post-traumatic amnesia, have confronted only amnesia as an accidental facet of the labyrinth (accidental both because other kinds of events can inflict trauma and post-traumatic amnesia, and because the discovery of the circularity of time does not necessarily induce a trauma). Those who both can confront this discovery without trauma and discover that the circularity of time can save them, in a way, from the circularity of space, are struck by the labyrinth's essential amnesia, an amnesia that has no other reason than the abstract one which says: one cannot be fully in the labyrinth (a cause that is the effect of its effect. Circularity again). An amnesia that maintains one outside (only the labyrinthine has aura because even the one inside it cannot penetrate it, but remains on the outside).

If the labyrinth is what does not let us enter it (we have crossed it without having entered it), it is the intermediary prohibited state that cannot be penetrated, only tunneled through (no time passing during the passage). Rare are those who can withstand the absence of time (when people speak of wanting immortality they still mean a realm where time still exists, but where it and their life are extended indefinitely), for time is what saves us from the labyrinth that is the absence of time. The vampire deals with the absence of time.

It is in the labyrinth that one can hide, and not because one is inside the labyrinth for the labyrinth maintains one on the outside, but because it is in the labyrinth that one is lost.

Omens and warnings almost always refer to the apparent threshold. There is a *false threshold* to the labyrinth: prior to it one is outside the labyrinth, *past* it one has always been in the realm that undoes all borders but maintains one outside.

When lost, not only in space and time, but also in one's mind, one should stop following signs and landmarks, above all disregard the subliminal, what one glimpsed fleetingly at the edge of one's vision, or had a presentiment of, or vaguely sensed—stop any reliance on meaning. An eclipse of meaning should occur, one treating one's mind as an image track on the sound track. This should replace the attitude one has when one still thinks one is not yet in the labyrinth, and which resides in noticing, so as not fall into the labyrinth, all kinds of foreshadowings in the guise of jokes, parapraxes, metaphors: near the beginning of Roman Polanski's *The Fearless Vampire Killers* the professor puts the skïs on in the wrong direction (a crossing the *imaginary line*); in Zemeckis' black comedy *Death Becomes Her*, the undead Madeline Ashton momentarily wanders with a 180°-dislocated neck (a crossing of the *imaginary line*), and her rival, an undead who was fired at, has for a short while a gaping hole in her stomach: our vision tunnels through her as she moves about. Warning that concerns the reader or spectator and not only the character (the spectator may notice the lapsus in Bertolucci's *The Spider's Stratagem*: "— Dead?— Dead. No, they're alive", and the even slyer phrase: "He doesn't live... he rules", which marks the labyrinthine realm of the dead/ undead; the reader may notice the sly usage of the metaphorical to hide the literal in Dostoevsky's *The Double*: «more dead than alive,»[79] «He had no more life in him»[80]): be cautious about the fact that you are noticing these warnings, announcements of the labyrinth, since, unfortunately, these cryptic announcements of the labyrinth continue to occur even after you are already in the labyrinth (one encounters here yet another figure of the impossibility of being fully in the labyrinth: alongside memory, a kind of forgetfulness of what happened, since the warnings against an eventuality that already happened continue), seducing you into both thinking that you are not yet in the labyrinth and into continuing to interpret them, notice them, rather than revert to an eclipse of meaning. In the case of a labyrinth, the only time when you don't need the warnings is when you don't notice them, since one notices these warnings only in the labyrinth.

The labyrinth changes the tele- unto itself. The tele- mode truly comes into its own only when the separation between receptor and sender is a labyrinth, since the message can then reach the receptor, rather than be lost in the labyrinth, only by tunneling (the phone call that reaches the person in the labyrinthine Zone in Tarkovsky's *Stalker*, 1979) —uncertainty of position to either side of the labyrinth against the uncertainty of position of the one in the labyrinth; the message reached the recipient although the messenger was lost and will remain lost in the labyrinth.

***Ci-gît* and the virtual:**
The traces of death are very important as signs of placement. «Au lieu même de la référence gît la mort, qui fait de l'espace autre chose qu'un vide homogène. Être-là se traduit aisément dans la langue française: ci-gît, antique formule funéraire... Ci-gît: cela veut dire ici repose tel ou tel, mais signifie au fond: par la vertu de tel ou tel mort, le gisement d'ici paraît... La mort fait naître l'ici ou le là, je suis né non loin du lieu où l'aïeul se dissout. Je me situe par gisement et distance donc par écart à la mort.»[81] But the ability of the dead to create reference and location is at the price of his/her being lost in the world of the dead, a world that undoes any map, any topography.

This turning of the dead into the homeless (or better still of the worldless) can be seen in *Weegee's New York, 335 photographien, 1935-1960*, where photographs (in the section «Crime») of dead in the streets, whether these were killed in car accidents or murdered by gangsters (*Corpse with revolver; Dead man in a restaurant; Dead man in a bar; Murdered while playing boccia*), become (almost) indistinguishable from the photographs of the homeless (the charcoal/chalk outline on the ground of the scene of the crime reproduces the matte outline, indicating that the ones killed already belong to the absence of context, to the radical ubiquity, the homelessness that the matte institutes). The only difference is that the dead are recycled.[82] The last sentence is not always true, for *ci-gît* (here lies) is taken literally by many a schizophrenic: a curse that prohibits dissolution (the body does not dissolve into elements that move away); and applies literally, as a curse, to vampires, and, as a blessing, to saints (of the forty-two saints who lived between 1400-1900, at least twenty-two are said to have remained non-decayed after their deaths): «Beginning with the thirteenth century... we again find the funeral inscriptions which had all but disappeared during the previous eight or nine hundred years.

«They reappeared first on the tombs of the illustrious personages— that is to say of saints or those associated with saints.»[83] It seems natural and logical that the reintroduction of individual tombs should happen in the case of those corpses that don't undergo dissolution into everything else.

While a real photon can leave an electron indefinitely, a virtual photon can only exist, according to the uncertainty principle, for $\Delta t = h/\Delta E = v^{-1}$, after which it is absorbed back by the electron. Δt permits the photon to travel at most a distance c/v away from the electron. If the virtual particle has a rest mass, then $\Delta t = h/mc^2$. The restriction on the movement of the vampire away from his tomb is not to be understood in terms of sedentariness (*ci-gît*), but in terms of his being virtual. The problem with uncertainty, Heisenberg's and Todorov's, is that though it creates out of the blue, out of emptiness, it does not free what it creates (neither the vampire nor the virtual photon are amnesiac: the former has to go back to and be reabsorbed by the grave in which he was buried, the latter by the electron).

Reference:
Frederic Jameson: «highs and lows really don't imply anything about the world, you can feel them on whatever occasion.»[84] Really? What about set (expectations and attitudes) and setting (physical and psychological environments)? Imprudence of Jameson, but he can allow himself this imprudence since he is still this side of the threshold. If there is anything that can permit us to feel something, or better still, nothing «on whatever occasion», it is yoga (which stresses so much the role of the guru as reference). Lows induce paranoia, hence *ideas of reference*, and hence recreate a reference that was, according to Baudrillard, on the wane or non-existent. Lows may be countered by maintaining a non-local correlation with a master/benefactor/guru/sheik. The non-local is connected to reference, as can be seen very clearly in holography: since two waves are needed to create the interference pattern, the beam is split/*dissociated* into two waves one of which is a reference wave (the witness), a control sample, since it does not interact with the object off of which the first wave is reflected (Bohm's hologramatic universe can bypass locality and hence reference points only because the hologram itself cannot be created without the presence of a reference beam). Masters and guides do not need the reference, guidance of a master for they are their own reference (the electron beam intensity in a field-emission electron microscope is so low that one electron occupies the microscope at any one time, so that the interference needed to create a hologram

is a single-electron phenomenon), their own guides (what about their disciples? Can't they be at times the reference of the master/guide/guard? No, disciples always sleep when needed: in Shakespeare's *Julius Caesar*, Lucius responds to Brutus' offer that he sleep: «I have slept, my Lord, already.» Brutus: «and though shall sleep again; / I will not hold thee long...» Lucius plays music for a very short time and falls asleep and it is then that the threatening Ghost of Caesar appears to Brutus;[85] Jesus leaves his other disciples at Gethsemane, and goes, in the company of Peter, James and John, to pray. He asks the latter, «stay here and watch with Me». He moves *a stone's throw*[86] and prays. When he comes back, the three are sleeping: «What? Could you not watch with Me one hour?» Three times he leaves them, to pray, each time, upon returning, finding them sleeping. «Are *you* still sleeping and resting? Behold, the hour is at hand, and the Son of Man is being betrayed...» and finishing his words he sees Judas coming toward him and is betrayed[87]): Castaneda's sorcerer don Juan, as well as many a yogi and Sufi master, can be at two places at the same time, this allowing them to have interference, and therefore not to become lost in an interconnectedness that does away with space and time. In the case of normal people in altered states, neither they nor their double plays the role of a reference, hence the fact that the appearance of the double is almost always viewed as the sign of imminent death.

We find reference also in such a non-local phenomenon as hypnosis—where the hypnotized person is often overlaid on a set/context other than the one in which the induction began—in the figure of the hypnotist, but also in the phenomenon of the *hidden observer*: a highly hypnotizable subject was hypnotized and told to feel no pain when one of her hands was put in ice-circulating water, while the other hand, kept out of awareness, was to report, at five-second intervals, through automatic writing on the pain the first hand was feeling (scale 0-10). She orally reported feeling no pain, while in automatic writing she was reporting 2,5,7,8,9...[88]

The absence of ether, the vacillation of dimensions and excessive presence:
In the absence of ether, the whole horse (the same can happen in the case of larger objects: the whole sky, a whole crowd) can be perceived/felt as a close-up.[89] The whole horse in close-up becomes bigger than itself and closer than itself and largely divested from the background. The whole horse as close-up can act as the switch between two settings (the close-up can also be reached in hypnosis and in meditation: «see the vase as it exists in itself, without any connections to other things. Exclude all other thoughts or feelings or sounds or body sensations... Let the perception of the vase fill your entire mind»[90]; in these instances too it often acts as a switch between two settings). We are no longer confronted with the close-up of the terrifying object or dealing with the close-up that changes the normal into the terrifying (Eisenstein: «a cockroach filmed in close-up appears as fearsome on the screen as a hundred elephants in long-shot»[91]), but are submerged by the terrifying becoming-a-close-up of the long shot.

One knows that it is no accident that the creation of a space-time continuum where time does not pass was dependent on abolishing the ether, for the same happens when one no longer experiences any time passage: one feels there is no air/ether covering/permeating everything. Passing through Pennsylvania at night, on the way from Milwaukee to New York, the windows of the car closed and the ventilation on, looking at the stars in the darkness he had the very clear sensation that there is no envelope of air covering the earth, but that one is in direct relation with the interstellar space, which now extends down to the ground, conjoined with the very clear feeling that the earth is a small (compared to the entirety of space) sphere floating (like an astral body) in space.

We are in the large hall of the Milwaukee Public Library, some sitting, others walking. Once again this feeling I had already experienced at *Woodland Pattern Bookstore* in Milwaukee while listening to improvised music by Tom Cora: we're in a detached space capsule, beyond the walls of the hall is interstellar space or nothing.

Michael Snow's *The Central Region* (1971): by the same movement whereby one frees oneself from gravity, one frees the sky from its gravitational attraction to the earth, so that it becomes cosmic, the only earthly thing about it being its blue color and the clouds, the former possibly added through filters, the latter through matte (glass shots with cloud plates). Once we connect the small patch of earth seen on the screen to the sky (while creating a disorientation as to what is up or down), that small patch becomes the whole earth, an earth before or after man existed (nothing but the circles of flare in the camera lens landing on this alien earth). That small patch is much bigger than itself joined to its background (hills and lake), for in the latter case it is merely one recognizable, localized deserted part of the much larger Earth. The freedom outside of gravity is counteracted/balanced with a structuralism that insures that one gets reterritoralized on recurrent movements, from some stones up to the sky and then back to the stones on and on. Once we lose the normal perspective of someone glued to gravity, then the sky is an abyss. Every time the camera points at the sky, there is much air that evades the earth's atmosphere: the frame-as-hole (increasing ozone depletion?). Were Snow's camera for *The Central Region* to continue pointing at the sky for a long time, we would end with no sky, just the cosmic interstellar space.

Simulated distance: Wim and Nick speak to each other from across the house in *Lightning Over Water*, the same way that the son and the father sitting in the small truck in *Paris, Texas* talk to each other in walkie talkies. True distance is experienced whenever diegetic silence-over falls or when, as happened once to Jalal Toufic, things are seen as if separated from one by glass (Gray in the coffin in Dreyer's *Vampyr*; the broken glass in both Maya Deren's *Meshes of the Afternoon* and Magritte's *Le Soir qui tombe*—in the latter two cases the landscape we see through the broken glass is itself *vitré*), or by nothing(?!): he was feeling disoriented, looked at the servant and asked her to do something. She could not move. He turned to do it himself, but as he tried to move he suddenly felt a strong shock and fell to the ground—he had hit against nothing/space! He stood up and tried to move again and once again he hit against space, and looking at the servant he saw her staring with terror in a certain direction. Dread filled him. He looked and he knew he was seeing death: an old man, but not extremely old (somewhat leaning to one side in a mannerist pose), holding a child by the hand. True distance: during an LSD trip one felt that people standing twenty feet away were so distant one could send them letters or receive letters from them. This latter radical distance caused by the absence of ether alternates, or rather, since we are dealing with a temporality full of lapses of consciousness, is at times an absolute proximity since there is no air/ether between one and the object, no spatial, metrical division (no other experience gives one such a verification that gravity is a warp in *space*-time, for here the sense of fall comes from a feeling of an absence of space, as if no warp which would have sustained the object existed), a proximity that is not near, and that is at the same time not far (the fact that it can be so proximate and yet still outside one's face, outside one (he looked at her setting the alarm. Closing his eyes he saw a hologram of her face smiling, from a different angle than the one from which he saw her face with his eyes open. Her saying with great joy in reaction to his telling this to her, "You feel that close to me?!", felt extremely foreign to him. There is no to**gether**ness in the absence of the ether. He said: "It is not proximity in a metrically divisible space." She repeated: "You feel that close to me?!"), makes it not far but beyond). Two peasants plowing the field, and up in the sky blue clouds in vortices that are plowing/ turning the sky. A very tall cypress cuts the frame of the painting in two: one is day, the other night; in the foreground two men belonging to neither day nor night, too close, outside both (Van Gogh's *Road with Cypresses*)—the woman who managed to maintain the vampire with her till sunrise discovered what she had sensed the moment she encountered him: he is too close, outside both night and day. This is the truer **fall**, rather than the one which happens in a divisible, metrical, breathable space and which still admits of a ground at which to stop (whereas the former carries the fall through and past every ground (answering to tunneling)). Though, the latter kind of fall makes perceptible what otherwise remains imperceptible, that the gravitational pull is, in however infinitesimal a way, different on different parts of the body; in situations where the gravity becomes extremely strong (the limit case would be a black hole), the difference between the gravitational force on the lower body (e.g. the feet) and that on the upper parts (e.g. the head (or rather, since the head no longer acts as one single region but is itself affected differentially by gravity, the chin and the forehead)) is not only felt but tears one apart. This differential attraction can be seen/felt in the falling bodies of Vladimir Velickovic; one can imagine a Velickovic subject offered, between one run and spring and another, part of a puffer fish cooked by a Japanese chef, since one of the symptoms of puffer poisoning is, as James Cook, who ate part of a puffer fish, reported in his journal, an inability «to distinguish between light and heavy objects, a quart pot full of water and a feather was the same in my hand». Back to the more radical fall: Francis Bacon's *Study for a self portrait* (1982) is not so much the portrayal of a man sitting in a precarious position at the edge of a tilted chair, as it is a rendering of the extreme closeness, created by an absence of ether, of this man to the one looking at the painting, this necessitating that he appears at the verge of falling although he is sitting balanced on a chair in no danger of falling.[92]

The fact that vampires are burnt by the sun has also to do with a spatial disorientation (how close or far they are from the sun (Badham's *Dracula*)) that does not remain subjective but becomes objective. Vampires' corpses that have been exhumed even from shallow graves are found to have shed their old skin and grown new white skin[93]—tanned by a closeness to the burning core of the earth.

A loss of the ability to distinguish dimensions. The cat is no longer seen as of a definite size. Sometimes the cat is perceived as being maybe as small as a cockroach or a rat; sometimes as being maybe as big as a lion. The cat makes an electric-like sound with her mouth when she discovers a fly and is ready to spring on it. Entering the room I heard the cat make the same sound while looking in my direction. For a moment the uncertainty of whether she saw me as very small or whether she had already seen a small fly where I stood.

All objects get closer to one, except that the distance they lose in relation to one they gain in relation to each other: in relation to one they are seen in a telephoto mode (this haptic feel to objects), but in relation to each other they have a wide-lens separation.

Due to the absence of divisible distance, of background/foreground, though a person still sees that of two objects one is closer to a third object than the other, all are as close to the person. Seeing someone walking in the remote background without hearing the sound of his footsteps does not indicate that the sound of his footsteps existed but had gradually become fainter due to the distance separating one from him, until it became inaudible, but that, since there is no separation of background/foreground, the background no more distant from one than the foreground, his footsteps make no sound.

Silence:
He no longer had conversations with people: what they said when addressing him reached him too late or too early (telepathy), by then they were doing something else. He no longer heard, only overheard—always as if through headphones. He was sitting in the back seat of the car during a drive from Milwaukee to Oshkosh. He could not clearly hear the voices of the two women having a conversation in the front seats. It wasn't that they were whispering; nor that their talk was submerged by the sound of the wind against the speeding car or by the noise of cars and trucks overtaking their car. It was as if the volume had been lowered on a radio. No, not *as if* (to be precise, it was *as if as if*): the volume of their talk was lowered.

He was a corpse disintegrated by their laughs and endless talk, anticoagulants of time. Simultaneously, he was over-hearing a silence-over, heard as through earphones. Then suddenly as the "endless" talk subsided, the silence, like a sound one hears coming from far away. Two silences superimposed.

Frozen/preserved under silence, under a sound vacuum. But what preserves one from what can preserve only by freezing/immobilizing? Music-over (heard telepathically)—music that the character would play to evade the silence cannot do away with the diegetic silence-over. Then silence is no longer static-immobilized as in a photograph but floating on the music.

One must become immobilized to listen to the silence (Eric Rohmer's *Quatre Aventures de Reinette et Mirabelle* (1986); Antonioni's *The Eclipse*, 1962). But reciprocally the emergence of silence immobilizes one (Robbe-Grillet's *Last Year at Marienbad*; in Tarkovsky's *Nostalgia* (1983), a pan moves from a mime, who can be legitimately taken in this instance to be a symptom of silence, to people frozen on the stairs).

There are two sorts of silence-over: a diegetic silence-over and an extra-diegetic silence-over. If the silence is an extra-diegetic silence-over then it would be there in spite of the movements, not interfering with them. A diegetic silence-over freezes the person into a sort of tableau vivant (rather than, as in Maya Deren's dance film *Ritual in Transfigured Time* (1946) or Cocteau's *Le Sang d'un poète* (1930), into a statue), or gives a floating somnambulistic feel to the moving people, who appear not to be touching the floor on which they are moving or the objects they are handling (unlike the case of turning into a statue, where the floating is annulled since the pedestal, however thin, represents the ground moving up, doing away with the floating feel (though some statues (mostly Buddhist ones) manage to float over their pedestals)), so that Robbe-Grillet's recourse to soft earth («The soft earth here makes no sound, fortunately, when anyone walks on it»[94]) or thick carpets («silent halls where the sound of footsteps is absorbed by carpets so heavy, so thick that nothing reaches the ear... as if the floor were still sand or gravel...»)[95] or gravel, and Dreyer's recourse to dust in his script of *Vampyr* («La poussière s'y trouve si épaisse, qu'elle étouffe le bruit de ses pas») is not necessary once one enters the regime of silence (I do not know if there are ghosts, but I do know that the floating ascribed to them would be due to the diegetic silence-over). This would explain the impression of somnambulism, why one feels then that one is not walking but is being carried and hence makes no sounds.

While John Cage emphasizes that there is no silence—even were one to enter an anechoic room, one would still hear the body's presence (a high sound, that of the nervous system in operation, and a low sound, that of the blood in circulation)—Jalal Toufic stresses the presence of (a diegetic) silence(-over) despite the sounds. Real *presence* is conveyed by the diegetic silence-over that falls over ambient sound ("presence": «the background sound that conveys the sense of an identifiable space. Without room presence all other sound seems artificial»), and that maintains itself even if sounds are heard, since the latter are superimposed on it (hence a silence different from that produced in an anechoic room).

The silence that forms the fraction of a second pause between exhaling and inhaling, and that is now extended indefinitely, is simultaneous with a continuous breathing, a breathing that has done away with the back and then forth movement of the air (*what* is breathed then is more proximate than the air found in space).

In Bergman's *Persona*, the actress becomes silent for she hears a diegetic silence-over in the theater. How can one be sound in this silence? How not to feel an apprehension that decay, error, fallacy (the opposite of sound reasoning) is on the verge of happening or already happened (whether or not in the form of this silence).

One cannot know when a minute of silence ends since for silence to exist no clock (a second is the duration of «9,192,631,770 periods of the radiation corresponding to the transition between the two hyperfine levels of the ground state of the cesium-133 atom») can be ticking.

From Dreyer's script *Jesus*: «For a moment there is a profound silence. Then Jesus cries: Lazarus, come forth.» It is this silence that should make the people around Jesus feel how impossible it is raise the dead.

Fear:
The inability to scream caused by fear is the beginning of a deafness. This specific deafness is a signal of the approach of eternity (Fini, in Herzog's *Land of Silence and Darkness*, says: «One thinks of deafness, that it is complete stillness. But oh no, that is wrong. It is a never-ending noise in the head, ranging down to the lowest ringing.» Is it these unmotivated sounds that inject time into the world of the deaf(-blind), without which their conception of time would be almost as drastically different from ours as the schizophrenics'?).

Fear makes one unable to speak—even in the form of inner monologue.

Sometimes the absence of sound/voice caused by fear is redeemed through faith, but then one abstains of one's free will from speaking (Alexander in Tarkovsky's *The Sacrifice*). This indicates that fear is subsisting.

A person sees the vampire and is so scared that he cannot utter the scream. In rare cases the bite of the vampire is acupuncture that releases the scream.

There is a doubling between Bergman's script of *Persona* and his film *Persona*. We read in the former: «Sister Alma, in terror, turns off the radio and the steaming female voice...»[96], when in the latter it is Elizabeth who turns off the radio in terror. Fear is taking hold of Bergman, hence the distortions that take place between the script and the film (David Pirie, who is himself set on correcting mistakes— he mentions that a number of early shorts have wrongly been included into filmographies of the vampire: *Vampires of the Coast* (1909), *The Vampire* (1911), *The Vampire's Tower* (1913), *The Vampire's Clutch* (1914), *Vampires of the Night* (1914), *Tracked by a Vampire* (1914), *A Village Vampire* (1916); many of these movies used the word vampire in the sense of femme fatale/vamp—writes on page 46 of *The Vampire Cinema*: «Later he sees a snowy-haired wrinkled old woman and watches her being handed some poison by the village doctor.» It is the other way round: the vampire hands the doctor the poison bottle. On the same page, the caption of a still of Gisèle (played by Rena Mandel) tied in the vampire's lair reads: «Leone, the vampire's victim in Dreyer's *Vampyr*, is played by Sybille Schmitz.» He also mistakes, like so many others, the plaster mill for a flour mill. Jean-Louis Schefer writes, «La roue du moulin, la farine, le vampire rencogné contre un mur et sur lequel ce sablier descend dans le film de Dreyer»[97]: he mistakes the doctor for a vampire and the plaster for flour (it would be interesting if the windmill Harker passes on his way from Transylvania to Wismar in Herzog's *Nosferatu* is a tribute to Dreyer's *Vampyr*, Herzog having mistaken the plaster factory for a flour windmill and made his tribute referring to something that does not exist in Dreyer's film). Roland Barthes writes: «In Dreyer's *Vampyr*, as a friend points out, the camera moves from house to cemetery recording what the dead man sees... the spectator can no longer take up any position, for he cannot identify his eye with the closed eyes of the dead man,» when in fact Gray's eyes are open. Isn't that fear, a fear that makes us flee so quickly, swish pan our look, that we do not see clearly? When I write about Gray as dead/ undead I am not making a fear-induced mistake[98]), the script becoming the double of the film as Alma becomes the double of Elizabeth. I do not think that the change in this specific case could be explained away by the changes that filmmakers make in the script when they shoot and edit the film. What corroborates viewing the script as the double of the film in this case is that in the script Elizabeth has interior monologues, that is, she speaks to herself, therefore is different from the mute Elizabeth of the film, who does not have interior monologues.

Fear makes us *under*achieve: what he remembers from the period of fear is his absence of wittiness and his excessively slow thinking conjoined to the swish pan of fleeing (especially when he saw the immobilizations of people) that left him depending on conjuncture as to what he had perceived. I am looking at her reading; her eyes look closed to me. I have to force myself to delay moving my gaze to other things, so as to make sure as she turns the page, her eyes moving to the top of the new page, that they are open. Her eyes are open. But forcing oneself to continue looking at the details as a way to fight the swish pan induced by fear often fails to achieve its aim either because, as in Robbe-Grillet's descriptions, space and time have become *complementary* (as understood in quantum mechanics) entities: the more precision and certainty there is about the one the more there is uncertainty about the other—the more precisely are objects delineated spatially, up to their shadows, to the dust and light patterns on them, the more the time to which the description refers cannot be determined; or because the hysterical presence of the object fills everything, whether the thing perceived remains self-similar (the indefinitely-approaching face Mark Vonnegut saw during the schizophrenic episode he underwent) or metamorphoses (the tree root in Sartre's *Nausea*). What interests the hysteric, and anyone who feels absolute/excessive presence, in a TV/film/video image is that its becoming more and more present has as a limit the degree of presence we normally ascribe to a flesh-and-blood person, normal presence, this shielding him from the sudden excessive presence that persons and objects can have: each at the limit can totally fill the universe, overspread even to the extent of annulling the fuzziness due to Heisenberg's uncertainty principle: everything is filled, even beyond what is allowed by the uncertainty principle (should one deduce from the data provided by Jalal Toufic's experience and that of schizophrenic and hysterical persons that the uncertainty principle applies only in a limited realm (even if that realm admits of non-separability)?).

Fear and the accompanying swish pan bring about a demise of the close-up since one cannot see the details[99]—hence the connection of the fleeting with the mask. The blurriness produced by the fear-induced swish pan is itself the mask (near the end of *The Shining* Wendy looks in one of the rooms and sees two masked persons; were we to search the Overlook Hotel we are sure not to find these masks), hence the mask cannot be blurred. The mask, in this sense, however much it may be specific, for instance with smaller or bigger eyes, nose, idiosyncratic expression, does not denote an individualization at all, hence the indistinguishability of the adult female Lucybelle from a 3-year old male (*Lucybelle Crater & 20 yr old son's 3 yr old son, also her 3 yr old grandson—Lucybelle Crater*, 1969-70); from a legless female (*Lucybelle Crater & 20 yr old son's legless wife Lucybelle Crater*, 1969-70); from a 15-year old male (*Lucybelle Crater & 15 yr old son Lucybelle Crater*, 1970), etc. The different masks in Meatyard's Lucybelle Crater series are as little differentiable as the identical masks-faces of the eight librarians in Patrick Bokanowski's *L'Ange* (it is not one and the same librarian sitting at the table in a position of authority—any of the eight could be the one sitting at the table and being consulted).[100] In the case of a mask, the blurriness is to be considered a formal element, whether decorative or reflexive (as an index of the photographic process), or else as due to the dead's being an out-of-registration composite. These masked faces are our remoteness—the beauty of the shot in Patrick Bokanowski's *L'Ange* that begins as a very high-angle extreme long shot of the handless seated man and the maid bringing him the vase and depositing it once more on the table, the set, with the exception of the two figures, who occupy less than ten percent of the frame, in total darkness, and ends with a zoom-in movement. For what we perceive at the end of the zoom-in movement are masks, i.e., our remoteness. Was the zoom-in really a zoom-out? Was there a crossing of the imaginary line during the zoom in, so that, imperceptibly to us, it became a zoom-out (a labyrinthine structure)?—and excessive slowness with respect to the fear-induced swish pan/tilt.[101] While the blurred version of the mask is emphasized in Adrian Lyne's *Jacob's Ladder* (the blurriness of the demon-like figures Jacob sees both in the car and in the subway is caused by his fear-induced swish pans) and the frozen version of the mask is emphasized in Bokanowski's *L'Ange*, both are equally prominent in the work of Ralph Eugene Meatyard: a) the out-of-focus version of the mask—will not be included here any of the photographs of the No-Focus series, since it is clear that in that series we are dealing with a no-focus due to the lens being out-of-focus rather than to the blurriness that is produced by a too quick movement or too slow exposure time or both; also will not to be included photographs, such as Untitled [Girl twirling in front of shed], 1965, and Untitled [Group of children with dolls and masks], 1963, where the blurriness can easily and justifiably be construed to be due to the *normal* movement of the one in the photograph (can one convincingly write that one can always detect when one is dealing with a normal movement of the person in the photograph and when one is rather dealing with a swish pan of the character/photographer/viewer or the two superimposed? If there is a site of an occultation of the fear in his photographs in Meatyard's work, it is to be found in the temptation such photographs present both us and Meatyard to consider the blurriness in his photographs in general as due to a normal movement of the characters); will be mentioned only photographs where either the persons are not moving, such as Untitled [*possibly* self-portrait in room wallpapered with newspapers],[102] 1967-68, Untitled [*it could be* interior with two boys], 1961, *To—El Mochuelo* [*maybe* boys with noose], 1962, Untitled [*I have the feeling it is* male nude in bathroom], 1970, Untitled [*perhaps* two boys, one seen through hole in wall], 1962, Untitled [*conceivably* child as a bird], 1960 (the hands of the child are as still as the two wing-like figures of peeling paint above him and which they echo), or else where the blurring can be considered to be due to the fear-induced swish pan of the person in the photograph, for instance Untitled [Georgetown series: woman entering store], 1955-56, or to the fear-induced slowness of thinking and reacting, rendered here at the level of the photographic process through the long exposures; b) the frozen version of the mask: Untitled [*perhaps* sitting boy with mask and masked hands—*Lucybelle Crater*], 1960, *Romance (N.) From Ambrose Bierce #3*, 1962, Untitled [*perhaps* woman and child framing parallelogram window—*Lucybelle Crater and Lucybelle Crater*], 1970-72, Untitled [*perhaps* girl atop woman], 1970-72; c) and the conjunction of the two in the same photograph: Untitled [*plausibly* masked woman with girl on ladder], 1970-72, *Occasion For Diriment* [*apparently* young girl and masked boy beating his breast], 1962—we are dealing with a swish-tilt in the case of the latter two photographs. The fear-induced swish pan/tilt must have made Ralph Eugene Meatyard sensitive to the swish pans/tilts of REM (also the acronym of his name) that are intrinsic to the process of vision itself and that make it possible; he managed to render them, to find a literal equivalent for them in his Light on Water series, for instance *Light #3*, 1959, and *Light Abstraction*, 1967. The fear-induced swish pan/tilt is what makes the many aforementioned photographs, which are, at the level of their production, not only posed but also staged, true snapshots. In *L'Ange*, *Jacob's Ladder* and Meatyard's work, the mask serves to hide not the one behind it, but, through the fear-induced fleeing swish pan of averting to look, the one in front of it. Thus to criticize works where a courageous warrior undauntedly fights masked, demon-like figures, as one-sided, simplistic portrayals of heroes that do not show them having any fear, is to miss the point, i.e. the swish pan, completely. The masks of these demon-like figures are the hero's fear made visible. If we may find the masks of these demon-like figures and in general masquerades somewhat unfair, it is not due to a moralizing attitude that condemns hiding the truth, but because of the added advantage whoever dons the mask has by reason of the association the latter has to the swish-pan and fear (fogginess in the mind, slower thinking and reaction, etc.).

We fear fear because often fear either discloses to us or makes us sense what we know (i.e. we fear fear because we are basically gullible enough to think that what we did not know that we know is the truth)—fear is courage. Courage is not the absence of fear but the absence of the fear of fear, of the swish pan that hides what fear could have revealed. Courage resides in confronting what fear discloses. Madness is the fear of death-as-undeath that *frightens one to death*.

That is certainly not what one wants: to be cornered between boredom and fear, between being stuck in the closed thing that chronological time is and disorientation (time's absence or delirium).

A fear so pervasive it blocks even the dissociated, hypnotized, unaware part from performing automatic writing.

The main character's hair is standing on end throughout David Lynch's *Eraserhead* (1977): a fear that has become constant, ordinary (punk hair out of fear). To write a novel where there is no mention of fear, where fear, as in Patricia Highsmith's novel *Ripley's Game*, is displaced onto such phrases as «*I'm afraid* I can't help you» (p.36[103]), «*I'm afraid* I haven't changed my mind about that» (p.55), «*I'm afraid* it's no go» (p.86), while the character acts detached, indifferent.

Some physical characteristics of what has no image:
With the exception of the downy hair on his palms, the grass which grows every night in time-lapse cinematography over the vampire's grave is the only hair he has.

This vampire is not bald a la Herzog's Nosferatu; his forehead, by expanding into the scalp, rather than making the scalp bald has itself become bald (Frank Auerbach's *Head of E.O.W., 1960*; *Head of E.O.W., 1956*; *Head of E.O.W., 1957*).

Broken Mirrors/glass:
Mirrors do not reflect what is in front of them when it is a vampire/undead: the mirror remains blank. This gets relayed in Maya Deren's *Meshes of the Afternoon* where the front of the head of the mysterious figure is a mirror. This indicates that the blank we see in the mirror before which the vampire is standing is not necessarily a sign of the absence of image of the vampire but could itself be an image of the face of the vampire. The mirror at the front of the head of the mysterious figure is a face. Since it is a face, i.e. since at any one moment the reflections on it are part of it, when parts of the glass/mirror fall to the ground, they maintain what they have "reflected." The glass covers the (absence of) face of the vampire and hence reflects as any mirror does, but when it is broken it turns out that it was itself the face.

A window-glass/mirror on whose broken pieces on the room's floor subsist the reflections of the landscape. In *La Clef des Champs*, this effect is due to a sort of refractory period of the mirror in Magritte's work. In Francis Bacon's work, such a phenomenon would be due to mirrors' pinning/absorbing effect[104] which leads to part of the thickness and life being transferred from the person to the reflection—the limit case being the total absorption of the person in the mirror, as is the case in the right panel of *Triptych Inspired by T.S. Eliot's Poem «Sweeney Agonistes»* (1967), in *Lying Figure in a Mirror* (1971), in *Study of Nude with Figure in a Mirror* (1969), and in *Triptych* (1987). On the way to that total absorption we have *Figure Writing Reflected in a Mirror* (1976) then the right panel of *In Memory of George Dyer* (1971), where the tug is no longer, as in the former painting, between the person and his reflection-presence in the mirror but is instead between the reflection-presence in a mirror and that in the reflecting surface of a table, the part of the body still outside both deploying as much acrobatics to maintain itself outside both as the trapezist in the left panel is deploying not to fall off the tightrope. In *Study for Portrait* (1981) the body has become so adroit at maintaining its balance between the two tugging mediums that it can sit half outside the mirror and half inside it with neither medium exerting an attraction on the part of the body in the other medium, and without even the minimal displacement due to the index of refraction from one medium to the other; as a side-effect of this one starts separating in half outside the mirror (*Study from the Human Body*, 1981) or inside it (*Portrait of George Dyer in a Mirror*, 1968)—one having now to deal with the *false threshold* since the threshold is no longer the obvious dividing surface between the mirror and what is outside it? Bacon painted no broken mirrors with subsisting reflections, probably because they are implicit in the aforementioned paintings.

Haven't taken a shower or looked in a mirror for days. Walking, hearing sometimes the sound of glass as it breaks (where is the sound coming from?), of steel dishes becoming rusty in lapse-time cinematography.

The off-screen and/or the set:
By seeing the shadows of persons in wide shots without seeing the persons themselves, for instance in Dreyer's *Vampyr* seeing the reflection in the water without the presence outside the water of that of which it is the reflection (one subject reporting his hypnagogic experience: «Reflection in a lake of old houses that did not exist!»[105]),

one is seeing the off-screen as such on screen—an off-screen that itself has an off-screen. One cannot see this off-screen in the screen without feeling that one is apprehending telepathically what is on the screen (this off-screen in the frame foreshadows Gray's coming dissociation). The guard is sitting, his chin propped on his hand; his shadow comes in, rests his rifle next to the chair and sits in the same position: it is only then that the image becomes in-sync.

Another version of an off-screen in the screen can be found in Herzog's *Land of Silence and Darkness*. The things the blind-deaf is touching in the frame are synesthetically seen by the spectator. To see objects on the screen that the blind-deaf has not touched or is not touching is to see the off-screen on the screen. The swimming pool's water surrounding the blind-deaf child's body is an all-pervading touch: here we come the closest to a superposition of the two frames, that of the blind-deaf and that of the spectator.

Bazin's prohibition of montage, isolating what is under danger (both Chaplin and the lion in the frame-as-cage), reproduces at the level of the individual the kind of isolation that one encounters in horror and science-fiction films at the level of a community or a city: a sort of an automatic *sous-entendu* quarantine taking place, an event horizon forming to shield the outside world from the singularity, the stricken town or city suddenly isolated from the rest of the world (no off-screen past the boundaries of the town), and this through no plausible mechanism.

In some altered states what lies beyond the perceptual horizon is not a homogeneous extension of what lies within that horizon (in film terms, the off-screen is no longer the homogeneous extension of the on-screen but is either radically heterogeneous with it or has totally disappeared): directly beyond the windows of one's room, where a TV is showing a local-channel program, may be interstellar space or the void; the disappearance of the off-screen in many cases induces a feeling of being imprisoned in the on-screen (on the Chicago El, we are separated from the outside by harsh night rain and the vapor on the windows. The train goes underground. We are in a prison. The people inside the train, ugly, dead, deformed. In the corner a sad man, withdrawn, a filament of liquid in his eyes tinged with red, and his sadness makes the others look human, alive. The liquid in his eyes moving down the vapor of the windows, which become transparent. Once again I am in a mere train going to specific places). In other altered states one is no longer sure that one is in the same on-screen that one thinks one is in: the room one is in may be identical to one's room but one may look out of the window and discover that one is in Chicago rather than New York, or in the desert rather than in a town.

The suspension of chronology, of history, of inscribed progression is often linked with this sudden disappearance of the off-screen, hence with the divestment of the space, which has become closed, from the rest of the world (if there is something to the other side of what one still vaguely remembers to have been the door through which one entered the bar a short time ago, it is at present an extension of the bar—the bar as the world). And it is then that the words of *Breathless'* protagonist: "informers inform, burglars burgle, lovers love," take on a meaning that has to do less with essences than with this closure of the space. People in a bar are people in a bar. This phenomenon made, for the first time, bearable, gave a different perspective on, a different slant to those people who (as in *Cheers*) seem to spend their life in bars.

If a scene starts with a close-up, there is an ambiguity for the duration of the close-up as to what the off-screen is. In films dealing with altered states this ambiguity should not be abolished once we go to the master shot to establish the location and the situation where the action is happening, but is to be renewed within the same scene whenever we return to a close-up. The shot change would then correspond in the diegesis to what it is in the filming: a lapse, an interruption. What is a close-up (then) except a shot of a person trying to remember—the rest of the space that was disclosed by the master shot?

The smooth pans of *Ordet* —some are up ten minutes long— where the characters never block each other,[106] i.e. never create any off-screen within the frame, though continuous at the level of on-screen space are often discontinuous at the level of the off-screen space: we suddenly discover the existence of a person we did not know existed in that location (it sometimes feels that Dreyer's characters, who do not look at each other but look in other directions (*Ordet*,

Gertrud), are following with their eyes such *presence*s). We are dealing with the same process as a René Thom catastrophe: continuous change in the variables resulting in a discontinuous change in the system's behavior. The beginning and next-to-last sections of *Ordet*, sections where the off-screen is continuous, show people looking for someone, while in the other sections, where the off-screen is discontinuous, i.e. where we may and often do suddenly discover the presence of a person we had reason to think is not at that locality (the invisibility of these Dreyer characters is equivalent to the absence of the reflection in the mirror in vampire films), nobody is searching for anyone.

In Straub-Huillet's *Moses and Aaron* (1975), where the main subject of the film is God, the camera pan often becomes the tracing of a creation: what appears while the camera moves laterally is being created as the camera moves. Therefore, the two sides of the frame when the camera movement stops are not symmetrical: to one side there is nothing, an uncreated, while the other side is simply the homogeneous extension of the screen, which we already saw. *Moses and Aaron* should be shown in conjunction with Miklos Jansco's *Red Psalm* (1971). At one point in the latter the villagers are ordered to retreat and they do. But one can say that the whole film ends up becoming a retreat, an exodus: even though the eye is at times no longer in the mood or able to continue to follow not only the path but the rhythm prescribed to it by the continuous long shots of which the film is composed, it does not lag behind but is *carried along* by the movement of the camera. The eye is in retreat. Therefore it is quite appropriate that the film that was on the same bill with *Red Psalm* at Anthology Film Archives, *Jelenlét* (1965), was a portrait of a synagogue, that is, dealt with a people linked to an exodus. The movement of creation, which makes the two sides of the frame asymmetrical, produces as a side-effect an amnesia in regard to the left-behind, already-created off-screen. It is this amnesia, rather than inertia, or rather than inertia alone, that in large part explains how being carried along by the retreat or exodus can take place: there is no place to rest. It is only once the camera stops that amnesia clears and the off-screen to one side exists. Peter Rose's *Analogies* (1977), in which the screen is often subdivided into three frames that cover in sequence the same space being shown by a pan or a tracking shot, allows memory: the amnesia is suspended and the eye can relax a little. Hence one can treat *Moses and Aaron*, *Red Psalm*, and *Analogies* as a triptych. It is said in the Prologue section of Rose's *The Man Who Could Not See Far Enough* (1981) that an object is a sort of visual oasis marking the place where vision (that of *Analogies*?) rests. Section One, which at first shows three frames that consecutively cover the same section of space-time, soon shows three frames, each of which contains fades to varying times of the day, so that while the three frames still consecutively cover the same space, each shows it at a different time of the day: no resting place. The eye in exodus once more.

«There are no wings to the screen. There could not be without destroying its specific illusion, which is to make of a revolver or of a face the very center of the universe»[107]. The centrality of the on-screen that Bazin writes about must be reconsidered in light not only of dissociative experiences (whether in near-death situations; due to chronic migraine...)—where the out-of-the-body component is simultaneously on screen and off-screen (in reference to the body left behind, for instance that of Gray on the bench—which has its own off-screen)—but also of *virtual reality*, which permits telepresence, and, through the use of sensors, telesensing. Is the out-of-the-body off-screen or in the wings?

Reality is as distant in situations of dread/anxiety/deep trance as the film set is from the finished film. And just as reality does nonetheless sometimes appear in these situations, the set on rare occasions protrudes in the film! The set is not included in the film in documentaries, nor through the use of master shots (who tells us that the set itself is not filmic, hence possibly containing jump cuts, abrupt place changes, time idiosyncrasies?). Hitchcock, the director who cautioned the most against respecting the integrity of the set during the filming (François Truffaut: «to inject realism into a given film frame, a director must allow for a certain amount of unreality in the space immediately surrounding that frame. For instance, the close-up of a kiss between two supposedly standing figures might be obtained by having the two actors kneeling on a kitchen table»; Alfred Hitchcock: «That's one way of doing it. And we might even raise that table some nine inches to have it come into the frame. Do you want to show a man standing behind a table? Well, the closer you get to him, the higher you must raise the table if you want to keep it inside the image. Anyhow, many directors overlook these things and they hold their cameras too far away to keep that table inside the image»[108]), enjoining one to be concerned only with the film images that will be extracted from the set, the arrangements they will enter into and the off-screen they will suggest, nonetheless extracted a set from the filmic space in many scenes in his films. The set is, of course, not reinscribed through the accurateness of the settings in his films—«I am very concerned about the authenticity of settings and furnishings. When I can't shoot in the actual settings, I'm for taking research photographs of everything»[109]—but through the presence *in* the film of anomalies along the line of the aforementioned two standing people who are kneeling on a table that is nine-inch taller than its height, for instance, in *North By Northwest*, the miniature razor (which is not only to be inscribed within a contrasting relation to the giant faces of Mount Rushmore, but is also to be considered as an appearance of (an element of) the set in the film) and the clothes that are too short and thus do not fit the person that the hotel maid and the valet boy as well as Vandamm and his three cronies take for Kaplan: that is why, when the protagonist's mother comments that the trousers "are perfect," we are not to take this as only ironic, but also as earnest. The same way the farmer in the deserted area of *North by Northwest* wonders about a crop-dusting plane spraying a section of the field where there are no crops, the spectator may wonder what are these quasi-incarnations of the set doing in a film. Indeed we can think of that plane scene as a shot of the plane that was to be part of the film in abstraction of the context/set where it was filmed but that for some reason the rest was seen in the film, the set appearing in the film. It is in these instances rather than in *Rope* that we have a relation with the set (the scene in Kaplan's hotel room in *North By Northwest*— one of the sites of the resurgence of the set—begins by a long shot that becomes a pan, then continues in mostly medium shots, i.e. does not give us a comprehensive view of the hotel room, nor an exhaustive enumeration of its contents). A drop of red ink falls on the sleeve of the heroine of *Marnie*, this unleashing a traumatic reaction on her part and ushering a behavior pattern that one would associate with someone reacting to wounding himself/herself: her dash toward the restroom, holding, with the other hand, her forearm parallel to the ground. It is clear that the red of the ink blot functions as an association with blood and this is why it unleashes the traumatic episode; but it should also be seen, in an overdetermined way, as an instance of the intrusion of the set into the film—red ink or paint often stands for blood during the filming. Resurgence of the repressed in the film, of the set, in a totally different way than in self-reflexive films that manifest the film production process whether by uttering the meta, self-reflexive "cut," or by showing part of the crew and the production equipment or both.

In Fritz Lang's *Secret Beyond the Door* (1948), the seventh reconstructed room is identical to a film set, both because it is a transcription of a room from another locality (its being in its entirety authentic is no objection since we know that some directors, like Kurosawa, have the set constructed in full, even parts that will at no point appear on the screen) and because, like the set, which is extra-diegetic, it is not to be witnessed (I could not suppress a smile of recognition when I saw the heroine take hold of a flashlight before she headed to the room. Bazin: «The screen is not a frame like that of a picture but a mask which allows only a part of the action to be seen... "The theater," says Baudelaire, "is a crystal chandelier" ... we might say of the cinema that it is the little flashlight of the usher»[110]): the person who reconstructed the room, the husband, is entranced when in the room, i.e. is not himself, is acting a role then: he sees the room without seeing it. When the taboo against witnessing the last room is transgressed, the uncanny effect one has is that of seeing the set in the film.

A set can be extracted from diegetic space-time by means of certain kinds of inventories (Christian Boltanski's Inventories: *The Clothes of François C*, 1972; the different versions of the inventory of objects belonging to a person after his/her death, for instance *Inventaire de la vieille dame de Baden-Baden* (installed at Kunsthalle of Baden-Baden, April 1973)). Death (Boltanski's *Inventory of objects that belonged to a woman of Bois-Colombes*, 1974 (installed at the Centre national d'art contemporain, Paris)), disappearance (Calle's installation *Last Seen* at the Isabella Stewart Gardner Museum in Boston, about thirteen works of art (*The Concert* by Jan Vermeer, etc.) stolen from the museum and still untraced—a sort of *Inventory of objects that belong(ed) to the Isabella Stewart Gardner Museum in Boston*), inexistence, or dissociation are linked to the appearance of the set, hence in Sophie Calle's series of photographs *L'Hôtel*, which show, while the guests are outside their hotel rooms, on outings, the sundry items they brought with them, the listing of entries from the guests' journals and the chronology established by Calle in her commentaries are there to exorcise the aforementioned dangers attendant on the appearance of the set (the opening of both the closed drawers (showing items of underwear, etc.) and closed closets (showing hung shirts, etc.) and the opening of the notebooks and journals indicates that we are dealing with something similar to the transportation of the different items to another location in Boltanski's Inventories, i.e. that we are dealing with a set—the images are extracted from the set, but a set in turn can be extracted from the latter images).

Close-Up:
If we begin a scene with a master long shot, each hand we see in the shot is a superimposition of many hands (everything that is not precise is not individual since it can be confused, not merely subjectively but at the objective level, with others), and it is only one of these that becomes actualized as we come close enough for it to become the close-up of no one, i.e. the hand becomes the most particular when we've lost not only to whom it belongs (indeed when the hand becomes a close-up in hypnosis, for instance in hand-levitation induction—where the subject is asked to concentrate his attention on his hand and any sensations that may be occurring in it—it no longer belongs to the subject both because it is no longer subject to his will but to that of the hypnotist and because as far as the hypnotized subject can tell it undergoes changes that render it different from his hand as he knows it: longer or fatter or more hairy) but also where and/or when it is at that moment: the close-up, achieved in life through meditation or hypnosis (because they usually make the background out-of-focus, enhance attention, etc.), makes possible,

as in cinema, cutting to a completely different time and/or location—the hypnotist repeated, "where are you now?".

A medium or close shot of Siamese twins remains a long shot of one of the Siamese twins. Hence, Siamese twins are, as it were, a prefiguration of what we witness in many postmodern works, for instance in many of Warhol's works (*Campbell's Soup Cans* (1962), *192 One-Dollar Bills* (1962), *Thirty Are Better Than One* (1962), *Statue of Liberty* (1963), etc.) and in Robert Flick's *Along Ocean Park, Looking West, Summer, 1980*: the medium or close shot remains a long shot. Nonetheless, the close-up and the medium shot subsist, but now in the form of the content of the image, i.e. in the form of persons with deformities: in Tod Browning's *Freaks* (1932), in which two of the characters are Siamese twins, the man deprived of legs is a medium shot even when in the background plane of a long shot, and Prince Randian, the black man who has only a head with a small piece of trunk attached to it, is a close-up; in Francis Bacon's work, where the person and his reflection form a Siamese twins, for instance in *Figure Writing Reflected in a Mirror* (1976), we witness a disappearance of some parts of the person—part of the leg or the face or the bust, etc.—this making of the person a close or medium "shot."

Extras:

In some altered states of consciousness, once others exit the frame, they either continue to exist but are transfigured into extras, or become immobilized or else simply disappear. In their case, Bazin's assertion that the frame is a mask is false.

The double for the voice of a person is a stunt woman/man (the character of Gene Kelly in *Singing in the Rain*, who begins his career as a stuntman, falls in love with a woman who becomes a double for the voice of another woman, hence a stunt woman), i.e. his/her doubling of the other person can have utterly dangerous consequences for himself/herself (Robert Aldrich's *The legend Of Lylah Clare*). Strangely, his/her doubling of the other person can have dangerous consequences also for the one who has been doubled for his own safety: in one shot in *The Gold Rush* Chaplin feigns being frozen by the snow, so that when the man who finds him tries to carry him to the cabin, he is in one block, stiff, with the consequence that the man carries him horizontally, by the waist, parallel to the ground, the same way he would have carried the mannequin used in dangerous situations to replace an actor—a preventive measure on Chaplin's part against the possible pernicious effects of the traditional replacement?

The aristocrat Count Dracula is also the coachman that drives the guests to the castle: he is his own diegetic extra.

Since most of the actors were hypnotized during the filming of Herzog's *Heart of Glass*, at least some of them must have watched the edited, final version of the film not remembering having acted in some or all the scenes in which they appear, feeling that some of the shots were played by a stand-in for them.

The poet tells Gertrud that the day before at a party he met a young musician who mentioned his last conquest: her. He weeps since he himself loves her. All this to the accompaniment of the music («It is Heinrich Heine who said that where the words come out short there music begins»[111]) coming from another hall, composed and played by that same young musician, who thus becomes just (becoming meanwhile an extra to the meeting in the other room) to his injustice[112].

Time-lapse cinematography permits one to see violence that would in most instances otherwise pass unperceived: for instance red starfish feeding slowly on white ones. But maybe the violence of time itself feeding on these predators even as they prey on others is then hidden by their violence and can be better felt in normal motion when nothing *seems* to happen (the first part of Akerman's *Je, tu, il, elle*, 1974). Two dangers: that one try to occult the violence of time by drowning it in one's violence, or that one become an extra to the passage of time (*Jeanne Diehlman*, 1975)—in *Toute Une Nuit* (1982), there are no longer any extras, nobody is treated as an extra (the only extra that subsists is a diegetic one: a person who loves a woman who is already in love with another).

Out-of-sync:
According to Bresson, one should not present both the sound and the image of a door closing, but only one of the two. This eschewal of redundancy is made possible by the ability of each, the sound and

the image, to stand for both, i.e., it is due to an implied redundancy. In the case of both the distracted and those in some altered states this implied redundancy subsists no more: the sound "of" a closing door has separated from—one was on the point of writing "the closing door"—the image of the closing door, which is now conjoined to a sound that does not (always) accompany it in real life, for instance the sound of waves—in a film, the filmmaker must establish that this is not because there are waves nearby or because someone close-by or a neighbor is listening to a playback of the sound of waves or because in the coming scene waves will be heard or seen. In such cases one has to try not to fall into either the absolute solitude that consists in the sound track and the image track separating completely (and for this, prior to reaching the critical disjunction, one must have established words as not referring to an image, even when they seem to be describing it with precision, but as secreting their own referent: in Toufic's *Ashoura* we see on a first monitor two subway trains passing each other in opposite directions then a person fainting, while on a second monitor we see the following words: "Two trains passing each other in opposite directions—person fainting during Ashoura. The previous words do not refer to an image but have to create their own image-like sensation"), or into the paranoid one, since both distraction and many an altered state, by unlocking the *a priori* conjunctions (for instance the conjunction of the image and the sound of the sea) that in a way ensured that no excessive correlations would occur (two bodies for one voice in Syberberg's *Parsifal* (1982), one body for two voices in the case of possession (*Exorcist*)), make the fight against paranoia—once the distracted discovers the latter state of excessive condensation during an altered state—much more difficult.

When the sound is divested of the image, whether completely or by becoming out-of-sync, etc., repetition will often occur, whether in the same film, as in both Werner Schroeter's *Alternative Currents*, where certain images and sounds recur, and Syberberg's *Parsifal*, where two on-screen bodies utter the same played-back voice; or in a later film, as in Duras' *Son Nom de Venise,* where the entire sound track repeats that of *India Song*, with the consequence that *India Song* haunts *Son Nom de Venise*, which becomes a ***double*** *feature* (the Vice-consul says to Anne Marie Stretter: "We are the same"—so are *India Song* and *Son Nom de Venise*) even when one sees it on its own.

We witness in hypnosis both sync: the *pacing* of the subject by the hypnotist; and out-of-sync: the separation of the image and the sound track: «while he was still unable to speak, his hand, out of awareness, was able to write automatically the names of a number of the items that he had been able to picture but not speak about»[113].

Voice-over/Sound-over/Image-over:
Don't you hear something? Both Gisele in Dreyer's *Vampyr* and Dr. Sarah Roberts in *The Hunger* hear what others have not heard (the latter twice asks her lover, who did not hear the phone ring, to pick up the phone; later in the film she picks up the phone only to hear her co-worker remark that the phone did not ring. While signing copies of her book at a bookstore, she looks at the female vampire, whom we did not hear say anything, and says: "I am sorry, what did you say?" "Nothing, but I would like to talk to you"). It is surprising no vampire film has shown an interaction of the vampire or the telepathic person(s) in the diegesis with the voice-over and music-over which should be *over*heard by these characters. Often the ability to hear the voice-over (do schizophrenics hallucinate voices or do they rather hear the voice(s)-over superimposed on life?) and/or sound-over (the music in *Sauve qui peut (la Vie)* —with the exception of the one instance of its incarnation: in the last scene we are shown an orchestra playing it) is achieved at the expense of or achieved through not hearing sounds and voices that are very close by, sometimes voices that are addressed to one (similarly, overlooking is required for over-looking). Examples of voice-over: the voice of the master/guide trying to help the dead (as in the *Bardo Thödol*); or that of the hypnotist: «although deep asleep you can hear me clearly... You will always hear me distinctly no matter how deeply asleep you feel.» The master has to achieve with the dead disciple what the hypnotist can achieve with the hypnotized person. The voice-over of the master is there to fight the *sous-entendus* of the dead/undead in the Bardo state.

The discovery in altered states that a double can think in one's head facilitates one's later detachment from the stream of consciousness that goes on in one's head in traditional states: it becomes a voice-over. The master always treats the stream of thoughts passing through his mind as voice-over.

While *still* speaking to and looking at Wendy in the hotel's kitchen near the beginning of Kubrick's *The Shining*, the cook turns, looks at the child and talks to him. This look and speech is an image-over and voice-over, a diegetic *aparté*.

Aparté in the form of verbal reporting ("I am speaking to Kathy") occurs in the hypnotically-induced age-regression that does not reach full revivification.

In *Psycho*, both the overhead shot of the son-as-the-mother stabbing the detective on the staircase and the overhead shot of him transporting the mummy of his mother play the role of an out-of-the-body pov— a diegetic image-over. The voyeurism in *Psycho* is to be located not only in Norman's looking in the peephole at the woman, but also in his looking at himself-as-his-mother from an out-of-body position (someone reporting his out-of-the-body state: «Mostly, I was just observing... It didn't feel as though it was happening to me at all»).

The mourner and the dead/undead:
Among the Guaycurus in Paraguay, when a death took place, the chief would change the name of every member of the tribe: «from that moment everybody remembered his new name just as if he had borne it all his life.»[114] When someone died everyone else died with him/her, or took the risk of becoming his/her double to connect with the dead/undead, the one who has been replaced by his/her double (the Masai in East Africa change the dead man's name immediately after his death). If the name of the dead happens to be the same as the name of a tree or animal, the name of the latter is changed. «In the seven years which the missionary Dobrizhoffer spent among Abipones of Paraguay, the native word for jaguar was changed thrice, and the words for crocodile, thorn, and the slaughter of cattle underwent similar though less varied vicissitudes.»[115] Hence, due to the changing of the name after the death of a member of the tribe, no history. Mourning should create, and often did create, not forgetfulness (loss of connection with the dead), but amnesia (connection with the amnesia of the dead), producing a zone of

indiscernibility where it is no longer known who is who (in the Mekeo district of British New Guinea a widower becomes a social outcast: he is prohibited from showing himself in public and has to hide if he senses anybody's approach—as if the mourner is being mistaken for the dead, who is invisible), for amnesia dissolves personality. One accompanies the amnesiac not by remembering him, but by becoming amnesiac oneself. It is related in Katherine Hurbis-Cherrier's video *All That's Left* (1992) that when asked by a priest at the funeral mass to share anecdotes about Hurbis-Cherrier's dead aunt a long time passed without any of those attending saying anything, until the priest, no longer expecting somebody to speak, ended the service with a few edifying words. This is the real minute of silence. And if that silence can, in an overdetermined way, be attributed to psychological factors, a supposed shyness of the people, who would therefore have anecdotes to tell about the dead woman but are somewhat embarrassed to speak about them in front of so many others—this is Hurbis-Cherrier's reading—structurally we are dealing with the truest minute of silence, a minute of silence that denotes, also structurally and outside any psychology, the amnesia that strikes us about the dead, and which is a form of accompaniment.

Between *Distracted* and *(Vampires)*, between the suicidal and the undead, between distraction and the absolute concentration—yoga attempts to penetrate the Bardo state lucidly—needed to evade/neutralize the underworld of undeath, between forgetfulness and amnesia, between the perforation of walls and tunneling, there was (the) amnesia (of LSD) and the encounter with the double (-in-the-mind). All along (see the Author's Note and the last page in *Distracted*) the apprehension that one's reception from the threatened amnesiac version of one in a bifurcation branch would result in a book that is the double of *Distracted*, signaling the latter's ruining and demise. It is only now, having encountered the double in my mind and undergone amnesia, that I not so much really felt and realized that my father is dead (he died five years ago, in 1986; the narrator in Proust's *Remembrance of Things Past* really felt his grandmother had died only a year after her death took place), but entered a relation with him as dead—or is he by now totally dissolved (into clouds and towels) or reincarnated?

Wilhelm Wundt writes, to explain the taboo upon the dead, that a loved one changes at the moment of death into a demon from whom the survivors can expect nothing but hostility. Whether one calls the changed-into entity the double or a demon, this change is objective (as objective as the slowing down of time and the shrinking in size in the direction of movement depending on the frame of reference) and not to be reduced to and explained away with Freud's *projection*. Hence the taboo upon the dead and their treatment as enemies is not to be explained by an ambivalence of the others toward them during their life (Freud), but is the result of their possession or replacement by the double. One is confronted with the uncertainty over whether the dead person has been totally replaced by a demon—the constant refrain in *Dracula* to justify the mutilation (impaling/beheading) of the undead, for instance of undead Lucy: s/he only has the figure, likeness of the living human being, s/he is not one of us; or whether s/he is possessed (even if the only remnant of him/her is the hidden observer), in which case s/he ought to be helped («if you prick us, do we not bleed? If you tickle us, do we not laugh? If you poison us, do we not die?» No we cannot die), for instance through writing.

Persons with obsessive neurosis have obsessive guilt feelings in relation to the dead person. «It is not that the mourner was really responsible for the death or was really guilty of neglect, as the self-reproaches declare to be the case. None the less there was something in her—a wish that was unconscious to herself—which would not have been dissatisfied by the occurrence of death and which might actually have brought it about if it had had the power. And after death *has* occurred, it is against this unconscious wish that the reproaches are a reaction.»[116] Was Freud's placing the "has" in italics a lapsus? That is, did Freud want to put everything else rather than this "has" in italics? For why is it only after the death of the other person that the obsessive neurotic begins to feel guilt if the unconscious wish was all the time operant? If it is only after death *has* occurred that the obsessive neurotic's self-reproaches appear, it is for two reasons: it is only after the death of the other (and in the case of the schizophrenic, after death in life), that is after his becoming an unconscious-come-to-the-surface (s/he can affect only what is not guarded by consciousness: the schizophrenic and the dead), that he can be affected radically by the consciousness, subconscious and unconscious of others (one should try to shield not the living from the dead (vampires), but the dead and those who died-before-dying (the mad, etc.) from the living: Harker enters Dracula's castle without invitation in Browning's *Dracula* (the door opens on its own): the living can always and so easily enter without permission or obstacle the minds/souls of the dead). The second reason for feeling guilty would be that by not helping the undead, one has not only left him/her to his/her double, but—because the unconscious is a danger to the largely autonomous self of the one still living—one's self is subconsciously fighting what is trying to invade it or to make it invade it. During a psychedelic trip a doubling may have occurred: while one is back on the other side (as happens 8-10 hours after taking LSD), one has left the amnesiac version of oneself behind; the person who has gone back to normal knows that sooner or later, he, like everybody else (these are not in concert in their attack that produces a surrealist *exquisite corpse*, although the one attacked most often feels that they are), may be subconsciously attacking the schizophrenic or the person on a psychedelic, or the amnesiac version of himself, who is fighting what is imposed on him by the double. If the dead is attacked, it is by all, by those who knew the person and by those who didn't, by those who speak his/her/its language and by those who speak a foreign language unknown to him/her/it/they (of the thirty-two schizophrenics who hallucinated in English in one hospital, sixteen could not speak in this language[117]). Hence the provincialism of the attacks of the folklore peasant vampire, first against his family and relatives and then against the inhabitants of his village, sheds less light on the mechanism operating here than do the modern versions,[118] which make the vampire attack through the plague, that is through contagion, hence indiscriminately. Guilt may be a signal from the plane of undeath or from a reality that one left in the past and that is still unfolding (bifurcation) that something can and should be altered in that reality to alleviate what in its scale of harm and suffering is totally out of proportion to the stimuli (the master can help through the voice-over/telepathy that guides the undead in the Bardo state; one can help through amnesia or writing, etc.). Though this guilt can turn into the traditional guilt if after a period the undead has either dissolved into everything else or reincarnated (*life goes on* even for the dead) and the person still continues to feel guilty.

Composites:

The first thing one notices in many nineteenth century photographs is the blurriness of the living. Indeed, photography at first preserved the dead (and not the living) since the early daguerreotypes and calotypes required long, multi-minute exposures. But even at present, one can see clearly (if the fear of fear did not force one to swish pan) that when the non-moving living and the frozen/immobilized undead are side by side, the frozen brings out the blurriness of the non-moving. Everything that is not frozen is blurred—the shutter cannot be fast enough. This blurriness of the living is different from the blurriness of the dead, which we see in some of Gerhard Richter's blurred paintings[119] and in Dreyer's *Vampyr*. The former is due to the living's movement even as they stand still, the latter is due to the fact that the dead, who has lost the body (and in the case of the one who *died before dying*, who feels disembodied)—in Gerhard Richter's paintings, the image has lost any existential trace with the referent since Richter paints the photographs—the *circle of confusion* of the different composites of which the person is composed, is in the process of decomposition ("I am Prado, I am also Prado's father. I venture to say that I am also Lesseps... I am also Chambige... *every name in history is I*"[120])—a blurriness we witness in Francis Galton's and Nancy Burson's composites. Richter: «In the Photo Paintings for example, I tried to grasp this beautiful lack of meaning from the point of view of the *sujet* (choicelessness of the choice...)»[121]; more precisely, this choicelessness of the choice reveals itself not only by the fact that the *sujet* is arbitrary («the door, windows, shadows, all of which I dislike») but also by the fact that the *sujet* is a composite of itself and everything else: each photopainting in Richter's series *Eight Student Nurses* (1971) is a composite of itself with the others in any of the different possible ratios[122]. The living person is a composite that, in death-as-undeath or during some altered states, dissociates first into the separate elements that are themselves composites,[123] most of them uglier than the original composite (Francis Galton, who did some composites in the nineteenth century, already noticed that the composites looked more beautiful than the individuals (the same is the case in Nancy Burson's composites[124])—this embalming of the living), then into non-composites, becoming alien. Each of us is common, not alien, both because each of us is a composite of all the others, even of those who lived yonder and who are long dead, and because each of us is part of the composite that constitutes the others. That is why we do not find others or for that matter ourselves alien, and that is why they in turn do not find us alien. In certain altered states, though, we see the dead, people who have become not merely uglier, but alien, and that is because they are no longer composites (the withdrawal of the cathexis of the world).

Reception and its absence:
The blind-deaf of Herzog's *Land of Silence and Darkness* are an element of us (or are we an element of them?). Fini: «I watched their faces very closely, I wish you could see that too, once.» Long shots of skiers, without cuts to their faces. The blind saw more than us. But also we can't see any of her past except that shot. Her past is our blindness. Hearing the blind-deaf Fini utter that phrase, we are rendered blind), the blind-deaf child is our other childhood (it is his/her inability to identify with us that makes our becoming him/her or knowing that s/he is us divergent from an identification). We can neither identify with the blind and deaf with their reduced spectra, nor with the dead with their excessively extended spectra. We feel that the deaf-blind are an element of us, that the blind-deaf child is our other childhood, but the undead, despite their excessively extended spectra, do not view us as an element of them, as their life.

There are many forms of the inability to receive:

— That of a limited spectrum: all that exceeds the spectrum is not received (exception: Freud's unconscious affect, which is related to the *après-coup*).

— In the *amnesiac syndrome* there is a dissociation between the capacity to learn and the patient's knowledge that he learned anything. An inability to receive receiving.

— An extreme closing, a turning off, a catatonia. The schizophrenic fighting death-as-undeath, the absence of death, with catatonia/thanatosis.

— A total opening in death, where everything penetrates us (do not the concept and validity of receiving lose their meaning in death, since everything is received, even that which is being withheld?), but also where that which penetrates us is itself transgressing/wounding its boundaries and vomiting itself in us (this emergency one feels when everything around one is emergent from itself): this induces an intense feeling of utter suffocation, of an absence of space—greatly more intense than the one that can be induced by such works by M. C. Escher as *Regular division of the plane III*, with horsemen for figure and background, or *Symmetry Work 22*, with birds for ground and fish for background, where everything is full, with no emptiness, no gaps at all. It is precisely when we experience the plenitude, the suffocation of existence that the blind-deaf child in the pool in Herzog's *Land of Silence and Darkness*—the child who fears going into the plenitude of the water touching him all over—is no longer our other childhood.

It may be that what one writes about the experience of being a vampire will be enacted later when one is no longer able to express it, speak about it (*strange* is not so much a word, as the words' withdrawal), think about it, no longer able to write (from Virginia Woolf's suicide letter: «you see I can't write this [the suicide letter] even, which shows I am right [to commit suicide]»), being then in an altered state or because the double-in-the-mind has taken over: writing is one's chance to utter what one will later be unable to (or what the amnesiac version of one, in a bifurcation branch, cannot), to receive what will later be imposed. There is a radical difference between the reception, as presents, both of thoughts (after the perforation of a wall) during the writing process and of sensations, and the imposition of even arbitrary ideas on one (when the two different meanings of *certain, inevitable/irrefutable* and *particular*, become one—*dead certain*), as in schizophrenia, hypnagogia and death (montage is important in films about hypnosis, doubles, and/or undeath because it imposes an interpretation on the spectator, doing away with the democracy of interpretation Bazin found to occur with certain usages of depth of field. The interpretation it imposes can then enter in contradiction with another interpretation it also imposes, as in Robbe-Grillet's cinema), whether

— through ideas associating/linking on their own: the movement of objects before the vampire should not be interpreted as caused by psychokinesis, but as induced by a state of fascination, when ideas and words but also things function on their own (Mark Vonnegut feeling the approach of schizophrenia wanted to be hypnotized by a friend, i.e. to lose control to a friend rather than to autonomous thoughts/affects/things). Since hypnagogic images/ideas are active by themselves, autonomous[125] (the use of negative footage renders the sensation that near-death persons, hypnagogic subjects and people on LSD have that objects are illuminated by their own light. In Hithcock's *Suspicion*, not only do the wife's thoughts begin to link on their own, the glass of milk is illuminated by its own light (Hitchcock hid a light in the glass); in the last section of Patrick Bokanowski's *L'Ange* there are so many projected lights that it is as if the images on the screen are projecting themselves, the screen illuminating itself), the attempt to alter them has to resort to what can change the active into passive: hypnotic suggestion.[126] What will be the psychic consequences of the proliferation of smart houses—should one head at night toward another part of the house, «lights will come on one at a time to show the way» and the doors will open and close on their own; once the alarm clock rings in the morning, the curtains open, the shower starts, the coffee brews...»[127]—smart bombs, smart cars, etc., of objects becoming automobile? Will we wander in a hypnagogic world?

— or through a doubling in the mind, hence by the double in the mind; an imposition which is conjoined to the ambiguity/uncertainty in the fantastic (Todorov[128]) and in undeath (the Bardo state is the *uncertain state*) concerning whether things are real or imaginary/an illusion (this uncertainty paralleling Heisenberg's uncertainty principle in quantum physics), and/or to the ambivalence (Freud) of the living toward the dead revealed in the taboo on the dead. The uncertainty is between two necessities, two kinds of submissions: one to natural laws, and one to the necessity in doubling. The received, though being necessary, is within creation, for it becomes necessary only if *also* accepted-affirmed (hence a modicum of detachment/freedom is necessary for one to receive). If the dead don't think it is because it is now language or their double that does *all* the associating.

Eisenstein: «The material of the sound-film is not dialogue. *The true material of the sound-film is, of course, the monologue...* How fascinating it is to listen to one's own train of thought... How you talk "to yourself"»[129]. Let us sidetrack this «train of thought» and the «of course» off course. The material of the sound-film is the monologue from which oneself is ever in danger of being excluded (Eisenstein maintains his *inner monologue* outside any possession, multiple personalities with no amnesiac barrier between them or the double-inside-the-mind thematic).

Can what has stolen any reception from one itself receive (also one's style)? In most cases, this is tantamount to asking: can a black hole receive a particular thing when it reduces everything to just mass, electric charge and angular momentum?

Asceticism and proliferation, or is the iris a halo or a matte?

Murnau: «Un de mes rêves est de réaliser un film de six bobines avec pour tout décor une pièce et pour tout mobilier une chaise et une table. Le mur du fond serait blanc et rien ne viendrait distraire du drame...»[130]; Dreyer: «The director can give his rooms a soul through simplification, by removing all that is superfluous...»[131]. This laconism and simplification at the level of the set often secretes a proliferation at the level of subject matter: in *Vampyr*, the doubling and then tripling of Gray during his dissociation, and the doubling of the guard; an overinclusion at the level of form: the overdetermined editing in *Nosferatu* that creates floating, telepathic connections between Mina in Bremen and Nosferatu in Transylvania.

Asceticism as negative proliferation, not in the sense that it is what is opposed to proliferation, but in that it is a proliferation preceded by a negative sign (as in *negative energy*). One must be careful when trying to simplify, since if one removes too much, one will end up with a matte and hence proliferation (the reverse is less frequent: the beautiful way the mimes in Antonioni's *Blow Up* fill to the brim the small truck transporting them to the park only to play there a tennis match with no ball). The iris can function as a halo, creating a certain autonomy, a further separation from the off-screen, but also as a matte. We encounter the same reversal in yoga (yoga is to allow one to get detached from the world/nature). The yogi moves from physical withdrawal to the withdrawal from psychomental life. Of paramount importance is: the reduction of all possible positions of the body to one (the yogic posture, *asana*: maintaining the body with no movements in the same position to attain «a complete suspension of attention to the presence of one's own body»[132]), the reduction of all the possible rhythms of breathing to one, the reduction of all distractions so that the attention can be concentrated on one object. But these reductions have to counter a side-effect that they themselves create; asceticism, while making it possible to suppress the senses at will, establishes a new power over them—the possibility of passing beyond their limits: telepathy (which we would have expected as soon as we saw the blankness that was created in and outside the yogi), but also clairvoyance, clairaudience, mind reading, etc. Inversely, only what is telepathic and subject to overinclusion is surrounded by a halo (before 1959, the blue screen traveling matte technique produced a blue halo around moving objects and frequently around non-moving objects). Walter Benjamin writes that the sorcerer, unlike both the surgeon and the cameraman, does not penetrate the patient, maintaining a distance between himself and the ill person, hence maintaining the latter's aura. But that is made possible only because the future sorcerer/shaman/medicine-man has to undergo initiatory states and ordeals one of which consists in seeing in visions his body being dismembered by demons who clean his bones, throw away his bodily fluids, «cut off his head (which they set to one side, for the novice must watch his own dismemberment...) and hack his body to bits, which are later distributed among the spirits of various sicknesses. It is only on this condition that the future Shaman will obtain the power of healing... His bones are then covered with new flesh, and in some cases he is also given new blood».[133] It is the reconstituted body of the shaman, his new body that has an aura.

Darkness scares us, more because it makes us feel a *presence* than because it is already a matte making possible a telepathy that undoes locality. The black of the iris is a matte that could not later be replaced by a visible element, hence the iris in Murnau's *Nosferatu* points to the presence of an invisible (that cannot be reached even by telepathy or the uncanny ability of the dead/undead to materialize whatsoever in the Bardo state)—or better to a *presence*—and hence belongs to a phenomenon whose other manifestation is the absence of the vampire in the mirror.

Presence:

In Robert Altman's *Vincent and Theo*, Van Gogh is shown twice trying to paint the field with crows. The first time the *presence* of the crows is signaled by the fact that although no crows can be seen in the field both we, the spectators, and he hear the sound-over of the crows, this making him paint them over the field. Later in the film, he stands once more in front of the field, but is unable to paint it. Holding a gun in his hand, he walks straight ahead and fires, to force the crows to manifest themselves, to become visible, to no longer remain a *presence*.

The need to materialize the *presence* is in many cases conjoined to the need to etherealize the hysterical, obscene-obstinate substantiality of the object the person sees or hears.

One feels different after taking both a depressant and an antidepressant: the alteration is a side effect of nothing, hence haunts as any *presence* does.

The Vietnam war and *presence*: these thick forests and bushes where the Vietnamese could not be seen induced a feeling of *presence*. The American revenge: the Stealth fighter—more a response/reaction to the Vietnam war than to the arm race with the USSR.

Many of *Despair*'s shots begin with an in-focus plane inhabited by nobody to then rack to the till then out-of-focus plane where the character, who will soon become dissociated/have a double, is positioned.

Haunting:

In rare cases, deserted ruined houses give one the feeling that the inhabitants' departure was in relation to *our* coming (this foreknowledge is the haunting).

Carpenter's *Halloween*: due to the identification of the camera with the character in the first scene, the rest of the shots in the film, even those that follow his death, are haunted by him.

The distracted's never being on time (*Distracted*) makes it impossible for him to exist only when perception happens (Berkeley) and not to appear before perception starts or subsist after perception ceases, i.e. makes it impossible for him not to haunt; late against late: haunting *presence* against refractory period.

Telepathy:

We aristocrats, who value distance and hence prefer chance connections, know that there is no pure chance: telepathy is a fluctuation of chance. Telepathy is *false chance* (as in *false vacuum*).

Eisenstein stresses the need to undo all transitions between phenomena shown in two different shots, and he finds a justification/example in Kabuki: «the purely cinematographic method of *acting without transitions*... the black shrouded Kurogo obligingly conceals him from the spectators. And lo!—he is *resurrected* in a new makeup... now characterizing another stage (degree) of his emotional state.»[134] This laconism that Eisenstein insists on, condemning the European's emotional transitions, is part of his emphasis on montage. In *Potemkin*, when Eisenstein shows us the close-up of the woman with pince-nez followed «immediately—without transition—» with a close-up of her with pince-nez smashed and eye bleeding, the importance of this kind of editing is not that, as Eisenstein writes, it is an example of «an artificially produced image of motion» (the animation of the statue of the lion is another one of the examples he gives), giving the spectator «the impression of a shot hitting the eye» (the actual impacting of the bullet against the face cannot be seen except if the collision is shot with a stroboscopic camera that works at a speed of less than a millionth of a second). What is really being subtracted is the lag (about 0.05 second) between the time when the bullet actually hits the body and the time when, impulses from the injured pain nerve cells having reached the brain, awareness takes place that the body has been hit. If we subtract a frame (1/24 of a second (0.0417 second), or to be more precise, since we are dealing with a silent film, 1/18 of a second (0.0556 second)) between the time the bullet hits the body and the time we see the face of the injured woman mouth open in a scream, hence cognizant of the pain, the delay is eliminated both for the wounded woman in the diegesis and for the spectator. This is the shock (the film shot (and the photograph) by Harold Edgerton that catches the bullet hitting the apple is not, in this sense, a shock, since there is a 0.05 second interval between the light from it hitting the eye of the spectator and its reaching his/her brain); a strange form of telepathy that consists in removing the exceedingly brief delay that exists between the periphery of the body and the awareness in the brain. Thus a telepathy that may go unperceived. The jump cut is precisely an attempt to do away with this delay; the jump cut is a form of telepathy.[135] This form of telepathy with the past is often conjoined to the telepathy with the future that we encounter in Arnulf Rainer's work; with Rainer's scratchings the present and the future are simultaneous but this simultaneity needs *postponement* to occur (which does not mean that it occurs in the future).

In the case of the telepath, a shot showing him/her looking may be followed by a shot which, although showing what s/he is seeing, is no longer a *point of view shot*, since it has nothing to do with the actual angle of view, position or distance of the person from the object; the term *pov* should be replaced by another, more general term that can apply to situations such as near-death, in which some patients have been able to see what is going on at a section of the hospital room not directly accessible to their vision[136] (the monitor behind their heads—). For the duration of the telepathic episode, often there is a superimposition after the shot of the telepathic person's face of both his pov and the shot that represents what he is entering in contact with (but it is not only the image he is seeing that is a superimposition, over every image of the vampire is superimposed one or more images, giving one the sensation that what is shown in the image that is underneath and/or the image that is underneath is buried (Brakhage's *Dog Star Man*; in many of Bruce Baillie's films, even when one sees a normal image one feels that it is superimposed on an absence of an image or that an absence of an image is superimposed on it), and, over the long run, inducing in the spectator an inability to breath similar to the effect of strangulation that the closing of the iris creates in Murnau's *Nosferatu* (victims of vampires constantly report that the vampire smothered them before proceeding to suck their blood). There is no telepathy without the burying of superimposition). It is why he feels then that there is too much light: he suffers from the brilliance, the excess of light in the two normally lit superimposed shots. And indeed one has often heard vampires speak, while in a normally lit room, of the «too much light» there, of «the madness of the day». This then has a lot—if not everything (the fact that they live most of the time in darkness, their eyes adapted to low light, contributes a little to it)—to do with the fact they are telepathic, i.e. with the fact that the image they are seeing or in which they are is superimposed onto the one in the future or that is far distant, so that a *double exposure* is produced that makes both images overexposed (and often renders the illumination sourceless and non-directional (in cases where the main light sources in the two images are directed differently), as it is in hypnagogic, near-death, and psychedelic experiences) if each image is rightly exposed, and does not create overexposure only if the two images are *under*exposed. Hence all images have to be underexposed in their case. Vampire walking in dark places so that the cumulative light would be right for each of the two images (one ends up feeling that an underexposed shot is that way only because the other shot that is to be superimposed on it is not there yet). When that second shot is in the future, one can say literally that the future illuminates the past and the past illuminates the future. Superimposed on this first reason for the excessive brightness is the circumstance that telepathy requires the neutralization of the body, which normally plays the role of filter, one was almost going to say, an ND filter. It is always too bright for the undead. But conjoined to this light and image overinclusion is a kind of catatonia of light: Herzog's Nosferatu appears in Lucy's mirror as a silhouette and not as a reflection, however much artificial light there is in the room.

Why did Mathias, king of Hungary, imprison the historical Dracula? «Apparently the Germans of Sibiu... had forged three letters in his [Dracula's] name which revealed him as meekly submitting to the Turks, and then had allowed them to be intercepted by servants of the Hungarian king...»[137] We read in the 19 May entry in Harker's diary in Stoker's *Dracula*: «Last night the Count asked me in the suavest tones to write three letters, one saying that my work here is nearly done, and that I should start for home within a few days, another that I was starting on the next morning from the time of the letter, and the third that I had left the castle and arrived at Bistritz.»[138] A non-local correlation between two sets of three forged letters.

Telepathy creates an off-frame of pieces that have been withheld due to *resistance*, as in the case of Freud not including the third case study, that of Foresyth, in his paper "Telepathy and Dreams." If not all the material that deals with telepathy (since two of the three cases are mentioned by Freud in his article), then at least part of it must be elsewhere, outside the horizon-frame of the other work and only *affect it from afar*. These papers on telepathy are not just theoretical works about telepathy, but are already an instance of it.

The doubling of Alma and Elizabeth in *Persona* has to be preceded by a transference of memories. One of the two people keeps totally silent, acting as a suction for the words of the other person. But that is only the first movement, for the indirect transfer of thought which takes place via spoken words from Alma to Elisabeth is complemented by a direct one in the reverse direction, a *thought-transference*, something many psychoanalysts (who sit silently listening while the indirect transference through words is taking place from their patients to them) have had the presentiment is occurring in the seance. Both Freud and Ferenczi[139] accepted the possibility of thought transference and experienced it.

If the difference in temperature ΔT between the upper and lower layers of a fluid is small, we observe thermal conduction, a heat movement through collision of molecules from the lower, hotter layers to the upper, colder ones, which is then lost to the environment. But at a critical value ΔT_c, there is an onset of thermal convection. Prior to ΔT_c the fluid was sensitive only to temperature gradients, but at ΔT_c it suddenly becomes sensitive also to gravity («Un système physico-chimique peut donc devenir *sensible*, loin de l'équilibre, à des facteurs négligeables près de l'équilibre.»[140]) The same could be happening in altered states of consciousness (attained through non-sleep, fasting, drugs—), these far from equilibrium states of the mind. This could help explain telepathy, the sudden ability to sense a stimulus that was in normal states either not sensed or remained at at the level of transient perturbation, whereas now, due to the very large *correlation length*, it has long term effects on the system's behavior.

Ways to evade the permeability of the present with the future and the past:

— By creating the new, one replaces the future which would have been felt simultaneously with the present with what is not felt simultaneously with the present (but this is not always the function of the new: one can create the new precisely because the future, or part of the future, is already felt in the present).

— By changing fast enough, one may exceed or equal the *escape velocity* (one's personality attracts one as gravity attracts one's body), evading the pain and affects from the future felt telepathically (even the ones due to Arnulf Rainer's scratches are short-circuited), evading this permeability of the different times to each other: by the time the affect from the future reaches one, one has changed, so that the *escape velocity* (a critical rate of change) defines an event horizon for telepathy with the future. The untimeliness of people who change radically leads at times to a serenity due to, at times to grievances against a frequent absence of sensation/feeling/thought due to their having evaded that part of the future which was telepathically permeable to them.

When one has gone too fast through radical changes a total breach occurs between the past and the present, whereby one escapes the future (hence the disjunction between the two dates, 1964 and 1969, in Borges' *The Other*[141]) but then the double may appear (in *The Other*, the doubling is not between the young Borges, living in 1918, and the very old one, living in 1969, who meet on a park bench— both are the same person merely at different stages in his development, or rather, since they have different tastes and ideas, both are the same person only because the younger one exists in the memory of the other—but resides in the disjunction between the old Borges living in 1964 with whom the young Borges is conversing and the old Borges living in 1969 who is having the same conversation at the exact same time with that same young Borges).

— Through the over*painting* (*Overpainted Crucifixion*) as anaesthesia against the simultaneity of the present with the future (and the past).

Ellen is telepathic; she tries from Bremen to warn Harker in Transylvania. Before leaving Bremen to Translyvania, Harker had told his friends: "Take care of her." How can those limited to the local take care of the telepathic or of the unconscious, of that which is branched on the outside, on the far? Harker might as well have said to them: "Take care of me."

The air current caused by the passage of a train in one shot undulates the grass in another shot on which the first is superimposed (Bruce Baillie's *Castro Street*), this creating a shallow depth where the two superimposed shots function as the different planes of one shot, with what happens in one shot affecting what is going on in the other shot though it has *little to do* with it (nothing affects one in altered states as much as what has *little to do* with one), without there being *inter*action, nothing which would have acted as a carrier between the two shots. But as a condition for this deployment of telepathy between unrelated shots, whether superimposed (*Castro Street*) or not (Murnau's *Nosferatu*), the planes within each shot must gain a detachment from each other (even the reflections in Bruce Baillie's films seem to be, might be superimpositions), and within each plane the characters should, as in Dreyer's *Ordet* and *Gertrud*, no longer look at each other. While in Zemeckis' *Who Framed Roger Rabbit* (1988) the human characters acted as if the animated characters were with them rather than matted later[142], during the filming of Jalal Toufic's *Night for Day*, in many of the shots where both characters appeared one actor performed alone, with the other actor matted in latter, although both actors were present at the set (what applies to the actors applies also to the objects and furniture, this often resulting in an impression of floating, one sitting on a chair that is added later through matting or that, as in Eric Fishl's layered works on glassine, belongs to another glassine layer, a shallow nonrepresentational depth the width of the glassine sheet separating the person from the chair on which s/he is sitting or the table on which s/he is resting his/her hand). And maybe then certain parts of the body of each actor will be unaware of the marshalling of forces taking place, becoming sites of the obtuse sense that Barthes follows in the film still—in *Potemkin* the chignon of a woman points downward contradicting her raised fist, yet without this having «the slightest symbolic (intellectual) value». One notices the obtuse sense much more in altered states, states where immobilization occurs.

Vampire films that deal with telepathy and the unconscious (Dreyer's *Vampyr* and Murnau's *Nosferatu*), that is with phenomena where the correlations extend far, favor a flat, two-dimensional space (superimpositions (and mist/fog), which proliferate in many vampire films, create an absence of perspective, a flat space). Similarly, in condensed matter physics, if the *correlation length* is greater than the thickness of a thin film, the film—which otherwise would have behaved like the bulk three dimensional material—will behave two dimensionally.[143]

One can consider links such as the one created by the juxtaposition of the shot of Nosferatu in Transylvania walking from screen left to right with the shot of Ellen in Bremen hands outstretched toward the right in Murnau's *Nosferatu* either in terms of telepathy or in terms of filmic editing; is one, in the latter case, not to infer from them any desire on the part of those in the diegesis, consider them extra-diegetic elements? Or is one to consider them a cinematic instance of the unconscious, hence diegetic, whether or not, as is the case in some altered states, the cinematic unconscious comes to the surface, reality becoming filmic? Detachment does not occur at this stage, on the contrary; later, not only telepathy but also the normal emotions/desires may be considered/lived as due to extra-diegetic montage. If the yogi still looks like he has some desires it is only an effect created by the editing (Kuleshov effect), hence no further karma is created.

The future can be apprehended directly only with primary processes—which do not acknowledge time—processes considered primitive, part of the past. There will always be a struggle to entangle the objective from the false in these processes; the same is true in the case of telepathy: telepathy's unveiling of the absence of distance (between two people) unveils in turn the presence of a distance in the same person, the double between the two between which there is telepathy.

New York, 6/24/90. I enter Waverly Cafe for the first time and look for a banana honey muffin. There is none left (there are twelve other kinds of muffin). I ask for a bran muffin. The person who works there asks: "Banana Honey muffin?" Telepathy?

Coincidences(?):
— The day before leaving Milwaukee for New York, I took my car for inspection. I was told that the brakes are 95% worn. I informed Amy about this. We decided to take the trip without replacing the brakes since I intended to dump the car once we reached New York.
— After we finished loading the car and the trailer, I discovered that the tire, concealed in part behind the yesterday-snow, was flat. We decided to drive to the closest garage, but the car was immobilized by ice around the tires. We waited until some people helped us push it onto the street.
— On the point of leaving Milwaukee, I hit the rear of a TV van. The driver took my name just in case the expensive sensitive TV equipment inside the van was damaged.
— It was dark by the time we left Milwaukee. After a while we noticed one then a second truck driver trying to indicate something to us. We pulled to the side and discovered that the lights of our U-Haul trailer were not working. I turned on the flashing lights of the car. One hour later we were stopped by a police car and given a warning. We took an exit and tried to find a place to fix the trailer's lights. None. We drove again on the highway. Another police car stopped us a little later and gave us another warning.
— It was five in the morning when we stopped at my friend's apartment in Toledo. Later in the day he mentioned in passing that he still had the earlier copy of the manuscript I was continuing to expand. I had sent him a copy of the earlier version the previous year so that in case I suddenly died he would have a copy to send to publishers. The manuscript was then ninety-eight pages long. It had become two-hundred pages long. Suicide, murder or any unnatural termination of life was not accepted by ancient people and continues to be so by many traditional cultures: in Maramures in the northern part of Transylvania, Romania, if an unmarried person of marriageable age dies, a *wedding of the dead*[144] is performed in which the dead person is dressed in wedding clothes and symbolically married. So the fact that my friend had the older, shorter version of the manuscript,

rather than the new version, seemed almost a defense against my sudden death. Except that, since I postpone, leave things unfinished *as far* as the deadline is concerned, my dying in an accident would actualize that trait at the level of the book, and hence cannot be inscribed within the taboo on unfinished business. The distracted, those who postpone, are more open to and more at risk of accidents.

— My friend's wife mentioned that his parents were recently seriously injured when a car that had no brakes or cylinders veered off the road and crashed into their car. She also mentioned that before leaving on a trip to Florida a few months prior to our visit, her husband took his car for brake inspection: the brakes were so worn, especially the cylinders, that when he said that he won't be replacing them before his trip, he was asked to sign a form stating that he had been informed about the defective state of the brakes, relieving the garage of any responsibility in case an accident happened to him.

— Back on the road, we wondered why the gas stations in this area are called Sohio. A little later the subject of how one usually disregards omens and signals though they are staring one in the eye was brought up. Shortly after that Amy pronounced Sohio as S-Ohio. How could we have missed the connection of Sohio with Ohio?! Was this an indication that we are disregarding clear signals against continuing this trip?

— We stopped at Pittsburgh to see a close friend of mine, videomaker Prajna Parasher. Prajna and I had a discussion concerning Hopper's *Conference at Night*. After several hours on the road, Amy said: "at long last we're driving during the day," just as we passed the sign *conference section*.

Either we have a car accident, and the mode of thinking allowing me to notice these omens is valid and objective, or we don't, and then I should forget about this mode of thinking. The car "accident" would show that there is no accident, but the cooperation of heterogeneous elements. These independent elements resist being joined together (maybe resisting the stranger applies not only to most people, but also to the elements, animals, plants, timings), this giving signals time to reach one in the form of omens (clairvoyance). We reached New York without a car accident, let alone a fatal one.

Two days later, Amy phoned her parents: in the same time period that these omens were being registered by me, her brother had a very serious accident and was still at the hospital, while a friend who was with him in the car was killed. Were the omens right but underwent displacement (as in dreams) onto another person (me)? It is as probable that the omens we encountered were totally unrelated to his accident. The doubt/uncertainty, the ambiguity subsisted, therefore so did the alternatives and hence the possibility of faith and choice.

In Antonioni's *The Passenger*, 1) the jeep Locke drives in a desert in Africa gets stuck in the sand and he has to leave it; the car he rents after exchanging identities with Robertson breaks down in a landscape of parched hills in Spain and he abandons it. 2) Locke follows a desert man leading him to the rebels' camp, but as they reach the top of a rocky hill, the guide sees a patrol of soldiers in the distance below. Both step back (the camera panning with them) and kneel down while looking at the soldiers (the camera pans from them to the soldiers). In Spain, after his exchange of identities with the dead Robertson and while walking on a rocky hill, Locke sees two policemen in the distance below. The exact same camera pan accompanies his stepping back movement then moves back from Locke, who is looking while kneeling, to the two policemen. These duplications between events to either side of the exchange of identities perhaps indicate that Locke is stuck in himself, and hence that no metamorphosis occurred (the other title of the film is *Profession: Reporter*, implying that Locke remains an observer); or they may indicate, since they are not recognized by Locke, that he is an altogether different person by the time the recurrence occurs. The latter interpretation conflicts with the fact that coincidences he recognizes as such begin to occur to him once he exchanges his identity with Robertson: he sees the same woman first on a park bench in London then on a bench in a Gaudi building in Barcelona. In both instances he is standing in the same position relative to the woman who is sitting reading (the first time he saw her, in London, he was still Locke, even though he had already exchanged his identity with Robertson; by the time he saw her in Barcelona he was already Locke-become-Robertson)[145]. The latter coincidence indicates that he has become another while maintaining his memory; had he not exchanged his identity with Robertson, there would have been no coincidence: a young woman would have been seen once in London by Locke and soon forgotten, and once in Barcelona by Robertson and soon forgotten. We will always hear about coincidence from people who are dissociated, who have out-of-the-body episodes, or who have doubles. It is around this time that Locke's wife suddenly begins to feel, "perhaps I was wrong about him." Since Locke is not really dead and hence has not reverted to superimpositions or been changed into/by his encounter with the double, this thought that occurs to her indicates that the exchange of identities that took place between Locke and Robertson truly ushered in a becoming. Did the becoming fail, so that by the end of the film Locke was Robertson? If so, he died, like Robertson, of a heart attack in a hotel room that looks onto dusty places (having exchanged personalities with someone who died of a heart attack, Locke should have checked the condition of his heart).

One looked at the clock just before being anesthetized for the operation. The minute hand did not move. One asked those around and they confirmed this. A few moments later one went under and when one came back to awareness time had stopped. It is the coincidence between the stopping of the clock this side of the lapse and the stopping of time in the altered state to the other side of the lapse—the coincidence a bridge over the discontinuity of the lapse—that makes it very difficult to dismiss off-hand the coincidences that occur in the altered states as delusions or hallucinations.

Faith:
Fright Night's vampire tells the person aiming a cross at him that the latter has to have faith for the cross to have the power to deter him. If it is through faith that one has a chance of winning against the vampire, it is also through faith that, initially, one gave the vampire a chance of winning against one, that one gave objectivity to the vampire, since faith replaces uncertainty (is the vampire real or imaginary/an illusion?), which is part of what constitutes the fantastic (Todorov), with the virtual, which produces real, measurable effects (virtual photons alter the electron magnetic moment by 0.1159652%). Nonetheless, *everything* is not lost, i.e. one may still be

able to lose everything, since the faith deployed in one's fight against the vampire may allow one to commit suicide in spite of the anticipation of what it will most probably result in, one's becoming an undead, for one might then as well have faith in the paradoxical (that's how it seems to one at that stage) state of a death-as-extinction.

Science is moving toward religion (primitive or Hindu or Buddhist variety),[146] so that soon enough it will take faith to be a secular person. It is not modern science that makes one not believe in religion, but the presence of atheist schizophrenics, for the latter shows that other worlds different from this one can be undergone without the necessity of interpreting them in religious terms.

— I lied to you.— I too lied since I be*lie*ved what you said.

Coexistence of tenses:

Dracula passes without shredding it through the spider's web that extends laterally from one side of the staircase to the other. That may have happened through tunneling or because Harker is speaking to the past, to what existed before the spider built its web. Similarly, the absence of the image of the vampire in the mirror may be due to a temporal disjunction: the film spectator is in the presence of two times.

In previous historical eras, the person who moved from a large distance (i.e. beyond the possibility of direct instantaneous communication) toward a second person belonged to the past of the latter, the reference, until they met. They were separated by as much time as it would have taken a message to get from one to the other by the fastest means available then (nonetheless, in relation to events like an eclipse of the sun, they were contemporary). With the advent of telecommunication, if one person goes to visit another, he would be in the past of the other, but were he, while on his way there, to decide to phone the other, both would become contemporaries. Then once he resumed his journey toward the other, he would be once more in the past of the latter. A fluctuation between being in another's past, present or future.

Backward Movement:

It is more interesting when the backward movement affects a movement, like that of the waves, that is itself a forth-and-back movement (*At Land*).

Raoul Ruiz's *Un couple (tout à l'envers)* is a palindrome that does not have the same meaning forward and backward: in one direction, a woman wakes up her husband and prepares a meal, in the other she kills him. We (almost) always resurrect another than the one who died. This is different from the use of reverse motion to resurrect the dead flower (putting the petals back on the receptacle) in Cocteau's *The Testament of Orpheus* (1960) and Godard's *King Lear* (one can sense the pain and annoyance Mina feels in Murnau's *Nosferatu* when Harker gives her flowers he cut for her if one relates these flowers to the aforementioned two films: he cut the resurrected flowers for her (though he has many flowers in his hands, we actually see him cut only two)).

The finality with which the envelope was deposited on the table so that it lay there in total stillness and immobility, exactly as if it was not deposited in a forward time movement but by a reverse motion that brought it back to its initial position. *Dead stop*.

Some films that have a script should be shot in inverse order to the order of appearance of the shots in the finished film: the last shot of the film would be filmed first, the next-to-last second, etc. So what would be during the screening of the film and according to the diegesis a temporal progression from less old to older in the age of the character would be in the case of the actor or actress a regression to a younger age. With regard to the actor, Cocteau's «le cinéma filme la mort au travail» is valid only in films and videos that do not use editing (Warhol's one-shot films, etc.) or in films where the order of filming coincides exactly with the order in which the characters appear in the diegesis. In traditional films Cocteau's words only partially apply since there is frequent shuffling of the order of the shooting in relation to the order in which the shots appear in the finished film. «Le cinéma filme la mort au travail» applies within each shot.

The vampire woke up and looked at the sunset. Around half an hour later, he was already uncertain whether he still had about eight hours till sunrise or half an hour in the reverse direction of time till just before sunset. It turned out to be the latter: he could see a wave going backward, then he felt his head turned to the side, as when a barber adjusts the position of one's head, and soon was, as in *Meshes of the Afternoon*, going backward down the stairs.

Time idiosyncrasies:
Henrik Galeen writes in his script for Murnau's *Nosferatu* that the man who goes down to the ship's sleeping quarters comes up, having seen Nosferatu, with his hair suddenly turned white. Is this a fear-induced fast-forward that can be explained by biological science (accelerated reactions—) or is it a time-lapse signaling that the person is already in the realm of undeath? This time-lapse, made possible by the immobilization—not sleep or rigor mortis (these as well as suspended animation are not true immobilizations but can be fully subsumed within the domain of the biological and life)—of the vampire in the coffin, recurs in vampire films (myriad flies moving in a lamp (*Fitzcarraldo*), turning it into something similar to a sand clock: a fly clock. Time flies): the time-lapse decomposition of the vampire in *The Horror of Dracula*; the time-lapse progression of the clouds (added to an otherwise anemic sky) in the last shot of Herzog's *Nosferatu*.

In Boorman's *Exorcist 2*, people and animals flee in all directions during the passage of the devil above them, but one should have also seen the landscapes themselves fleeing the devil's passage in time-lapse cinematography.

Above all, he wanted to know at what rhythm the decomposition after death will occur (Peter Handke's just, beautiful lines, «like the fear of dying in summer / when you decompose more quickly,»[147] remain at the level of the relative changes that affect one specific duration, here the human; they do not reach the unjustice residing in the different durations that used to inhabit the world inhabiting the undead), whether as far as it would be felt by the body, the decomposition would be at the rate of decomposition of a mountain or at that of the reactions that happen in the body, a sort of time-lapse decomposition. We don't protect ourselves only from things, but also mainly from their rhythms: the too quick or the too slow.

Memory, amnesia and flashback:
The traditional flashback, memory, can happen at present only because a *flashback* (as in a post psychedelic trip or in post-traumatic stress) has made possible its actualization. The only memory he had now coexisted with amnesia, since memory at present implied that he had a *flashback* to the state of being alive, to the state when he could remember.

The return, in the last aphorism of *Distracted*, to three countries that have been devastated and to which Toufic is biographically related—Lebanon, Iraq, and Palestine—has less (or at least as much) to do with memory, nostalgia and the biographical than, as in the last shot of Joseph Losey's *Mr Klein*, with accepting to be mistaken for another.

The huge amount of papers she had written from school until her graduation from the university, there, in an obese drawer; sometimes, on someone mentioning a subject, she would show him/her the paper(s) she had written on that subject. "You, so laconic, selecting, discarding, are nonetheless no more selective than me, for all the past is still somewhere, and can be resuscitated (despite your falsifying voluntary memory) by hypnosis [hypnosis can, through a preliminary suggestion, falsify what is relived] or by near-death experiences." One should be able to pass in quick review (like the fastforward of one's life in a near-death experience) the past, selecting what one needs (only the telepath/clairvoyant should do this), becoming amnesiac in relation to the rest. Not merely an aphoristic memory, but an aphoristic past (real amnesias and not just the diluted ones which are due to the repression by an agency of the psychic apparatus of the person). It is perhaps in this empty time, in this portion of temporality empty of duration that the vampire can reside.

Following an initiatic experience, he tries to restore a bridge to the past, going to meet his old friends in the various cities where they live (the many long-distance phone calls having led him to believe that everything was the same): in each instance the old relation is very quickly broken (has he, have they been replaced by the double? Is he in a different branch of a bifurcating universe?). During that period he called the publishing companies to which he had sent his manuscript a year earlier. One publisher told him that he was highly impressed by his manuscript and felt as if he already knew him. Because the publisher said that even if it turned out that he could not publish the manuscript, he would try to help publish it elsewhere; that he will introduce him to writers and video makers; that he had felt somewhat guilty for not responding and contacting him after the first version of the manuscript reached him years earlier, and hence was relieved by the opportunity the phone call afforded him to try to compensate for that; and because he suggested they meet soon, he himself also felt during that first phone conversation that he already knew the publisher. For how long? Up to age twenty-five, that is up to three years prior to the phone conversation, this was the way he expected at least some publishers to conduct themselves, hence he felt he knew the publisher from the period that preceded the disillusionment, i.e. for at least three years. But seven months after the conversation neither the meeting nor any of the other promises had materialized. Is it that he had to lose all his friends, including the publisher, in this period? The Lyapounov time is the duration of friendship.

Amnesia: he has changed from a person with a large portion of his memories of an episodic type (autobiographical, with the memories dated) to one having all his memories of the semantic type (recalling a word in the vocabulary does not require recollecting when it was learned).

Forgetfulness is still not amnesia, and if the silence between the sounds has to be extended until the structure (of the music piece) is forgotten (John Cage), there is still an underlying continuity, silence itself is still continuous. But amnesia cuts the silence. Amnesia produces a discontinuous forgetfulness. Amnesia is a lapse in both memory and forgetfulness.

There is no advent of retrograde amnesia: it is already there when it occurs having erased the point at which it began.

There is an element, a presentiment of amnesia whenever any surprise happens.

The past now exists almost exclusively in the mode of retrospective corrections to illusions: «Still further on, a very young girl... is attached to the trunk of a tree, her hands pulled behind her, her mouth parted in terror and her eyes dilated by what she sees appearing before her: a huge tiger only a few yards away, staring at her for a moment before devouring her. This is a group of life-size statuary carved out of wood...»[148] Yet the same way memory sometimes falsifies, these retroactive corrections are sometimes an attempt to counteract a knowledge one had, turning what is exoteric into a secret. Mobile film sets make it possible to fool the spectator into believing an illusion, later showing him the truth of the matter; but in rare cases the later modification is introduced to make us call what we saw before an illusion: having seen someone tunnel through a wall in a long shot, imperceptibly to us the film set changes during a zoom-in shot to reveal that there was an opening in the wall when we were sure that there was none. But here our criterion for whether there was a tunneling should be the form of the movement itself, for the body moves or remains still or both (in somnambulism) in a specific way in the case of tunneling: in Deren's *Ritual in Transfigured Time*, which begins with a cross-section of two rooms that seem to be separated by a thick wall through which Maya Deren tunnels, even when later in the scene we see that indeed there was an opening between the two rooms, we can still be quite sure that Maya tunneled, if not through a wall, then through the *space* separating the two rooms.

"This morning I went to a cafe. A woman is sitting with a man. She keeps looking at me. The only way to respond to that is to take out a notebook and write (as the pointed tip of the pencil sinks slightly in the paper, I feel I am on the beach) while looking at her. There are two other men each sitting alone at a table. I stayed for a short time at the cafe, after which I wandered through the streets, and then, feeling tired, went to the nearest subway station. While waiting for the train I saw a young man standing on the platform playing music. A train stopped; people, most of them with earphones, came out of it; the train moved, its noise drowning the music; two of the people with earphones threw each a dollar in the guitar case. At night I saw a film and went back to my hotel. I read for a while. Thought how sterile the day was, for the young woman who was sitting by herself in the cafe in the morning and whom I went to speak to..." We read these lines in a short story by Jalal Toufic. It is a structure that recurs in his writing, films and videos. An episode will be narrated, if we are dealing with a short story, or shown, in the case of a film or a video, with a minimum number of cuts/ellipses, and then later the character, either while remembering or while mentioning the episode to another person will mention an event that was not narrated/shown. Is it a delusion/confabulation, or did it really happen?

The diary as letters from the amnesiac to himself.

There is a strong connection of memory to miniatures: in one shot in Tarkovsky's *The Sacrifice*, in the foreground we see the child's birthday present to his father, a miniature of the family house, and in the background the real house; in *Nostalgia* the camera pans over a small hill of sand in a house and then zooms in through the window, the outside, background scenery seeming to be a continuation of the miniature sand hill. But were we to see a miniature of the child's gift in the same shot with the house and its miniature, we would then have entered into proliferation (fractal self-similarity) and amnesia.

Was my walking to you, a stranger, yesterday and giving you a book already a memory? Did it make me so happy that I wanted to repeat it today? But there is often the fascination of the *always* once one does something twice: "and I have always walked up to you and given you this Gogol book that has a short story titled 'The Nose'". The unexpected repetition of an action, not necessarily the first such repetition but perhaps the second or third, instead of making of the action a second occurrence, a #2 episode, may suddenly unleash the regime of the n+1, a realm that either imprisons one in eternal recurrence by keeping the n indefinite, or, if n = 0, cancels the first time the action happened, turning the repetition into a first time. That is probably what happens in *Last Year at Marienbad*: the second repetition of their meeting attains the n+1; but for her n = 0, so that it is the first time she meets him, while for him the n remains indeterminate, so that he is imprisoned in an eternal recurrence of the events. A conjunction of amnesia and eternal recurrence. The good or bad memory either of them has or is suffering from in no way characterizes the respective person prior to the establishment of the n+1; they belong to the n+1: he has good memory because the n in $n+1$ remained indefinite, she has a bad memory because n took the numerical value of zero. The repetition that triggered the n+1 does not have to be the same in every respect with regard to the first action. Repetition has hence to do not with an exact duplication of the actions but with the attainment of the n+1. Parts of what is being repeated can be missing, different and there will still be adequacy and hence repetition (in *Last Year at Marienbad*, there is a frequent discrepancy between the description he gives of what she was doing or wearing and what the images show); memory reduplicates this facet of repetition. Memory is falsifying, not because it omits and even alters certain facets of what happened, but because this is done by memory as an external imitation of this aforementioned facet of real repetition. Memory does not give us back the event, nor falsify it, except indirectly, for its direct relation is not with the event but with repetition: it *imitates* not the event but its real repetition. When I suddenly decide to do a repetition of my giving you the book on the previous day (acting as if this were our first meeting), and find that I came dressed in a different shirt, and can't find the Penguin edition of the Gogol book at the bookstore, so I give you instead the Norton edition, which also contains "The Nose," between the two meetings there already elapsed the time it would have taken me and you to forget what I was wearing, what I exactly said, and what edition I gave you on the first day—a year? To flee the regime of eternal recurrence one has to repeat what is repeating itself without one, against one's effort—to stop it from repeating itself; one must repeat the second time so that maybe one will reach n=3, short circuiting the n+1.

Dissolves:
In traditional cinematic flashbacks the shot of the person beginning to remember and the first shot of the episode s/he is remembering, in which s/he appears, superimpose momentarily before the first is replaced by the second: a mirror image. Someone who has no mirror image either has no memory or can remember the past of others (i.e. can have flashbacks in which s/he at no point appears). The latter memory may turn out to be a hallucination, a memory that can be confirmed by the one whose past has been remembered or a memory of a bifurcation version of the other person. The fleeting superimposition

of the two Gertruds during a flashback in *Gertrud* (1964), with neither looking at the other, may in large part explain why the characters in that film do not look at each other: the way the characters look when they are speaking to each other has as its paradigm that of their positions and the directions of their looks during remembering. It is this that makes *Gertrud* a film about memory («Have I lived? No, but I have known love»). Memory rendered visible otherwise than by a flashback (the film contains two flashbacks of Gertrud; in both we have a memory within a memory (as in *a dream within a dream*): in the second, Gertrud's whole relationship with the poet abruptly becomes a memory upon her discovery that his relationship to her comes second with respect to his creative work; in the first, we have the aforementioned spatial positioning *within* the flashback). An answer to Duras' *Hiroshima Mon Amour* (1959), where we are still dealing with an external memory, its occasional resurrection, and the fateful knowledge that it will fade?[149] Gertrud's dream that is visible to all in the form of a painting finds an equivalent in this memory visible to all (a memory other than the one rendered by the traditional flashback), including the film spectator. A film about memory that, unlike *Sunset Boulevard* and *Fedora*, can begin "at the beginning".

The dissolve from shot 213 (Nosferatu almost in miniature) to shot 214 (Nosferatu in normal height/dimension) within a pov of Harker in Murnau's *Nosferatu* should be replaced by an overlay of one shot on the other, for what should be made clear is that the reduction in the dimensions of Nosferatu in shot 213 is perhaps not due to perspective rendering (perspective having been undone) but is a literal reduction (often in hypnagogic states the subject sees three-dimensional miniature apparitions (micropsia) of people: «although small, the images are not felt to be seen at a great distance; in fact, they are never located farther than a few feet from the eyes»[150]).

The dissolve in film should mainly be used to denote the maintenance of a state beyond the threshold of a phase transition.

Acting:

It is not enough to create the lapses and jump-cuts in the image and sound as in Robbe-Grillet's films if one does not also, as he did so well, neutralize the feelings and acting in his actors, for otherwise in order to achieve the emotions they think the role asks for, they would have created in their imaginations a series of objectives that would have restored a continuous off-screen (Stanislavsky stresses the need for continuity for the actor to achieve a *true to life* performance: «going back to the imaginary scene when I made my morning call on Famusov, I recall an infinite number of physical objectives which I had to execute in my imagination. I had to go along a corridor, knock at a door, take hold of and turn the doorknob, open the door, enter, greet the master of the house and anyone else present, and so forth. In order to preserve the truthfulness of the occasion I could not simply fly into his room in one movement,»[151] and: «You cannot step from the first floor in a house to the tenth [but that is precisely what we find in Maya Deren's films (*Meshes of the Afternoon, Choreography for a Camera, At Land*)]... You must go through and carry out a whole series of consecutive and logical physical and simple psychological objectives.»[152] This continuity has to be undone even in the form of the authentic set: Kurosawa has «the sets made exactly like the real thing,»[153] even those parts that will not appear on the screen—he mentions this matter of the authentic sets in relation to actors, and how they make the latter's performance natural; the same applies in the case of Tarkovsky, who insisted for instance for *The Mirror* (1974) on having the garden planted and the house reconstructed, resurrected exactly as it was forty years earlier when his family, which the film portrays, lived there, so that the actors would feel at home), if not to the film—this is impossible in the case of Robbe-Grillet—then at least at the level of the scene or even at the level of a few shots.

In *Le Camion* Depardieu reads his lines for the first time during the actual filming of the shots (Duras: «Aucune répétition du texte n'aurait été envisagée»). Thus in no way can the actor be the character invoked in the text, if only because he has the text in his hand. The book found in the hand of Depardieu (and the photograph of Ann-Marie Stretter next to Delphine Seyrig in *India Song*) parallels the knife in the hand of Thornhill in *North By Northwest* (1959). Duras and Hitchcock are two directors who neutralize the actor, the latter in the name of the storyboard, the former in the name of the written text, the book. In the former case, it is so that the actor will be mistaken for the character, who himself is mistaken for someone else (the *wrong man*); in the latter case, it is so that the character will remain the same, untouched by the actor, the latter's performance shedding no light on the character, just as the ruins of the palaces where many of Duras' films were shot remained untouched by the filming (except for the occasional use of a flashlight, no film lighting was used both in *Son Nom de Venise* and in *Le Cimetière Anglais*, the interview with Dominique Noguez on *Son Nom de Venise*).

The actor plays different characters in various films: a sort of reincarnation—exception: Bresson's *models* (Humbert Balsan, who was Gauvin in *Lancelot du Lac*: «c'est justement en terminant la... post-synchronisation, et en disant au revoir à Bresson, qu'il m'a dit: surtout ne refaites plus jamais de cinéma»). The risk of playing the role of vampire, of what does not decompose, is that reincarnations will cease from then on: «Lugosi often protested that he was trapped by the role» of vampire[154] (like the victims of the vampire).

In the *you* mode:
The *you* mode applies
— during disorientation: you suddenly don't know what your name is, where you are, what hour it is. Disoriented. Then things begin to clear up, you know now who you are, but you don't know where that faint light illuminating the room is coming from and why you have this open book in front of you, your palm feeling the texture of its paper. You close it and walk like a somnambulist to the door, turn the light on, and look at the room.
— in somnambulism.
— in some precognitive remote perception experiments. Waiting for the train, you look around the station: the same kind of people, the same floor, the same kind of lamps, the same clocks as in other stations. All of these similarities (including the similarity of the boredom you feel here as in other stations) make you feel that the actual stations are abstract and minimalist, and that what fills them

is traveling with you. You think that you might soon have a déjà vu experience, but nothing of the sort happens. It dawns on you that the statistics monitoring the remote perception experiment (in which a percipient has to describe an unknown geographical location where an agent either was, is or will be) of which you are one of the elements, the agent, should be altered, since all the percipient has to do is to describe any station from memory and the station in question would fit. You close your eyes and try to evoke a station and describe it, sure that you would then end up simultaneously having described the one in which you are standing. Still closing your eyes, you take out a notebook and a pen from your pocket and... nothing! You seem to have lost all memory of any station. A little later, you suddenly look to your left and see a woman who is not the kind that attracts you. Yet you keep looking at her. You don't feel any curiosity about her, yet you have an urge to look at her socks to see what color they are. You see that they are yellow and folded at the edge. «On a few occasions, agents have reported informally that while at the target their attention had been inexplicably drawn to rather minor or peripheral details of the scene, and later learned that those details were prominent in the percipient's description.»[155] The clear desire forced on the agent to see a specific but rather neutral phenomenon or object (a clarity that contrasts with the vague terms used by the percipients in the remote perception reports in the experiments conducted by Jahn and Dunne[156] even when their description was precise: *what seems like, it could be, or, have the impression, maybe something like, possibly, I have a feeling of*) is not necessarily, indeed is often not at all that of the percipient, whose state remains in most cases one of apathy and detachment. Between the percipient and the agent there is that «third who walks always beside you» (T. S. Eliot),[157] and it is this third, the double of the percipient, who wants to see these specific things. This *you* will become very prominent when virtual reality becomes operational; in the case of commands and actions performed in/through virtual reality, between one and the machine one can control at a remote locality, there will be the «third... always beside you». The noise which is being abolished in digital as against analog modes of communication (where it can be only minimized) would be transferred to the person's own mind (a phenomenon equivalent to what happens in the case of *squeezed light*).

— in hypnosis: you hear the hypnotist saying, «staring at the target so long has made your eyes very tired. Your eyes hurt and your eyelids feel very heavy. Soon you will no longer be able to keep your eyes open. You will have stood the discomfort long enough... Your eyes are moist from the strain. You are becoming more drowsy and sleepy.... It would be a relief just to let your eyes close and to relax completely, to relax completely».[158]

Gutless:
Blood gives health to the vampire, but does not alleviate his hunger. Hence the appropriate title of a vampire film, *The Hunger*. Hunger subsists after drinking blood, for the vampire, like many a schizophrenic (Daniel Schreber «lived for a long time without a stomach, without intestines, almost without lungs... without a bladder»), has no guts: no stomach, no intestines, no lungs, no liver; if hunger does nonetheless stop at times, it is due to a *flashback*. Hunger can be assuaged only in a *flashback*. Not *food for thought*, but thirst for thought; not the thirst of the person drinking, but the thirst of blood: blood removed from the body clots in about six minutes. Drinking the thirsty, drinking the thirst.

He never needed blood to give him vitality; on the contrary, it was when he could no longer bear what he was experiencing, the madness of reality, reality transformed into an indefinite bad psychedelic trip, it was then that he felt the urgent need to drink blood, for the blood that passed through his perforated teeth seeped from him since he was without guts. If seeing a lot of blood made some of his victims faint, drinking blood made him faint, exactly as if it was his blood that was seeping from him.

Unlike in Anne Rice's *Interviews With the Vampire*, he did not, when drinking the blood of someone, hear two hearts pumping. Each vampire either has two hearts («Wilhelm Hertz makes mention of a belief that a revenant is born with two hearts») or has none, hence, when sucking the blood of someone living, he would hear either three hearts or only one.

He vomited through the only gut he still had, the only thing close to intestines and alimentary canals: his throat. This made him all the more conscious of all the tunnels inside (and outside) the walls (Bacon's *Figure standing at a washbasin*, 1976; *Three figures in a room*, 1964; *Triptych*, May-June 1973. Terry Gilliam's *Brazil*). Then he vomited his throat; all the tunnels in the walls disappeared and he looked for a long time at the smoothness of the walls, like a trap that has snapped shut (like the door closing behind the victim of the vampire).

The vampire swelled into a great mass (*Carmilla*[159]) during the meal (a sort of bingeing), similar in this to the vampire bat, who must consume 50-100% of its body weight in blood every night[160], but shortly afterward he had to vomit (like an anorexic using purgatives) what he drank or ate, since it did not dissolve in him (the ability of things, this coffee for instance, to dissolve in others, to become part of them always amazed him). Anorectics often take over the family cooking: lean Nosferatu (who, while not appearing in mirrors, has the thinness of Andre Kertesz's *Distortion No. 113*) prepares Jonathan Harker's meals—but not for long, since those who, like Harker, live for some time on very high altitudes (Nosferatu's and Dracula's castles are situated on very high altitudes) soon begin to suffer from a loss of appetite and their taste becomes dull.

Masters:

Hegel stressed that mastery and philosophy come from facing death and the negative. What comes from facing undeath (can undeath, the realm of over-turns, be faced?)? What comes from facing death not as annihilation—as pure nothing—nor as a determined negation (once one inscribes one's death in a larger cause: the revolution, etc.), but as a realm of total non mastery. The two most typical kinds of masters: the one who risks his life, the one who has guts, the Hegelian type; the one who has already died before he dies, the gutless, the guru/sheik. By risking his life, the Hegelian master shows his freedom from given life, but the other master, the guru, has to get free from both life and death (a matter of *life **and** death* precisely in that it is not just a matter of life and *its* absence), acceding to a nonconditioned mode of being, and for that he has to become detached from the world/nature (whenever this is needed the guidance of a guru, a master (who himself had at one point a master) is necessary). The same non change in the Hegelian master, whose basic action is risking his life (Kojève), and in the yogi/guru who has reached nirvana.

Vampire Sexuality:
The bite of teeth into flesh, the love bite, never interested him, only the kiss of teeth, teeth kissing teeth. To be precise, one other kind of kiss attracted him: in a video by Su-Chen Hung, *East/West*, the screen is vertically cut in two, each containing one half of the mouth of a talking person. The moving lips of one mouth sensuously touch the moving lips of the other mouth, each two lips closing and opening non-synchronously in relation to the other two lips (what the person is saying becomes voice-over). One of the two frames contains just a little more than half of one mouth, which creates a virtual overlapping from one part to the other, a touching without touching.

Clothing the body of the victim in what is inside it: blood; the paradoxical nudity of the victim then: the interior is clothing the exterior. Then the vampire clothed this nude body with its shit, i.e. with the exterior-inside-the-body.

The tenderness of her skin. He knew that the *stratum corneum*, the surface skin cells, hard-filled with Keratin, were dead; since cells cannot survive exposure to the air, even the skin showing up at the surface to replace the summer skin that is being shed is already dead. The tenderness of her skin. He wanted to touch all her skin, even that under the nails.

The vampire's victim may have the feeling that the vampire's erect penis going inside her is full of her blood, which instead of being distributed to all the vampire's body, went straight to his penis (erection is produced by an afflux of blood to the genital areas).

We encounter a strange kind of necrophilia in vampire films, since it is the corpse that is acting like the alive person, while the alive person through the hypnosis to which the vampire has subjected him/her or through the immobilization due to fear is acting like a corpse.

There is zoophilia in vampire films. The bat into which the vampire turns during his flight is still present in the vampire that is making love to his victim. There is hence multiple-partner sex in this contact with the vampire, the vampire being a bat, a wolf, a man, a mist and a breath (the vampire does not breathe but he can metamorphose into a breath); sometimes the other animal and human forms-constituents get the woman or the man to the edge of a climax leaving it to an inanimate element (for instance a breath) to effectuate the orgasm.

Blood cells have no nucleus and hence cannot reduplicate. The vampire, who renders men impotent and women sterile, is also in love with this facet of blood. The sucking by the vampire of the blood of the female plays for her the role of a different *period*, therefore she cannot have a child for that time interval (it does not matter that in this case the blood she is losing is not that carrying the residue of the egg—*conversion*). «Here there are no children nor dogs» (*Vampyr*): neither filiation/reproduction nor what defends the territory. Contagion, genetic splicing, video/TV inlay/overlay and film matting, which create recombinant images, replace filiation.

Absence of breathing:
«Meanwhile driven by the fatal breath of the vampire the vessel moved rapidly towards the Baltic» (Murnau's *Nosferatu*). The vampire, similar in this to the yogin, whose breathing is suspended for very long periods (indefinite suspension of respiration is a goal in yoga), and contrary to what Murnau would like us to believe, does not breathe (not only did he not breathe, he did not feel the breathing of others when they breathed near him; he had the sensation of breathing only when he heard Sufi flute sound (whether played on a *nay* or a synthesizer)). That line can best be understood as hinting at what is strangely absent from *Nosferatu*: the use of miniatures. Other people cannot see their image in the mirror in winter since their breath, visible then, hides the surface of the mirror (one of the first tests to check if someone is alive is to see if mist forms on a mirror held next to his mouth). But, as vampire he did not breathe—inexistent mirror-image hidden by inexistent breath; even in winter

one did not see any visible breath coming out of his mouth; only, somewhere nearby was mist or fog.

Absence of sitting (exception: sleeping in a sitting position):
The vampire, like anorexics, almost never sits (Browning's *Dracula*), but either lies horizontally or stands. Indeed, the height of the dining room chairs in Nosferatu's castle in Murnau's film is that of a standing man. One looks with incomprehension at Magritte's painting *Perspective II: Le Balcon de Manet* showing a sitting coffin; but then one realizes that were one to open the coffin, one would discover that the person inside it is not sitting but standing. Similarly in *Perspective: Mme. Récamier* were one to open the coffin one would discover that Mme. Récamier is either lying horizontally for the length of the horizontal section and the height of the vertical section of the coffin, or standing for the height of the vertical section and the length of the horizontal section (cafe late at night. On and on he looked at the section «Sleeping» in *Weegee's New York, 335 photographien, 1935-1960*: the only sitting acceptable to him is that of people sleeping in sitting positions in bars, in cafes, behind the wheel of parked cars late at night (chauffeurs), between nightclub performances (performers), on park benches or in crowded night shelters for the homeless[161] (some of those sleeping, though having enough space to fully stretch, have one leg held straight up: *On a parkbench in Greenwich Village* and *Cellule de la maison d'arrêt*)). In Topor's novel *Le locataire imaginaire*, Tralkovsky's neighbors' garbage is extremely, conspicuously clean. They are mummies, hence do not shit in the restroom (when a female neighbor who is shunned by them wants to take her revenge on them, she smears excrement in front of their doors), only stand still there: they do not have to sit even for that minimal time during which even writers who wrote while standing (Virginia Woolf) or walking (Nietzsche) had to sit. She said, "you're short." But I walk or lie in bed and rarely sit. I am taller than most people, for the latter sit so often (how short is a sitting body).

Different Spectra:
Sometimes he, an undead, would see, in a *flashback*, things and people as they are seen by human spectra; but in general, he felt

disoriented by too many spectra. These were, in comparison to the normal spectrum, sometimes too extended, in other cases too constricted. At times he would see things as they appear in a microscope, and the magnification would differ on specific occasions: he saw some parts of the person, animal or thing with 1,000,000x magnification; other parts he saw with 1,000x magnification. Hence he could see the microbes and amoeba in her face. Also the pores in the skin. He had the urge to suck the blood, that (lukewarm) lava. He felt that his teeth could penetrate her neck without wounding it. Yet though he was seeing her neck with a magnification that showed it full of holes, he had to make sure that his teeth were not themselves distorted and magnified, as if by a wide lens, becoming bigger than the holes in her neck, in which case as he closed in on her neck he would suddenly feel that he was wounding what he had just seen perforated with large enough pores. Sometimes the neck, except for a small part magnified enough so that penetration could happen without wounding, was seen with little or no magnification; it is to that small part he directed his teeth if he didn't want to pierce the neck, but to the other parts, if he wanted to bite and wound. Sometimes his field of vision was subdivided, like the dragonfly's (her hair, simultaneously flowing under his sliding hand, braided under his dragonfly look), or as in Peter Rose's *Analogies*, into a large number of compartments. Each of these quadrants he saw with a different spectrum or lens: in one quadrant he saw with dragonfly vision (her lips have the multiplicity of teeth); in another, part of the person behind him seen with the field of vision of a horse (a 360° field); in another yet the same or another part with that of a fish eye (180° field of vision), so that the image was distorted whenever he moved, looking fatter than in the other quadrants. In one quadrant, part of the person in a normal lens, in another in a telephoto lens; the person appeared to be moving toward him much faster in the wide-lens quadrant than in the telephoto lens quadrant, where he appeared to be barely moving; and the same things appeared at a distance from each other in the wide-angle lens quadrant, but crammed together in the telephoto quadrant. What *scared* and disoriented him the most was temporal mixing: in one section of his field of vision seeing the person's face at a particular age, in another section seeing the same person's face but much older, and in a third section seeing the face putrefying.

Hibernation:
In our encounter with most things, living or not, and events, our reduced sensory spectrum plays the same role as low temperature (or dryness) does in the case of hibernating (or estivating) animals: the same way a certain range of temperature induces hibernation in certain warm-blooded animals (which are very vulnerable to any animal who finds them then) and its dipping below the lower limit or rising above the upper limit of that range awakens these animals, by limiting our spectra, we have been forcing everything that exists, including ourselves, to hibernate (undeath (with its extreme extension of the spectra) is the return of the repressed). The extension of the spectrum is a provocation, since it raises things and events from hibernation (was it the extension of the spectrum of a person or an organism that woke the vampire from his hibernation?). Humans have a very strong interest in limiting their sense spectra (they can be extended by prolonged fasting or sensory deprivation or the intake of a psychedelic, etc.) and then extending them by slow increments (the atomic bomb showed that we've transgressed a certain critical limit, but many further critical points exist). The bat who had just awakened from hibernation awakened again from yet another hibernation for the person perceiving it (telepathically?) had extended his spectrum.

The extension of the spectrum is very dangerous because it may put one in relation with another organism whose power resides in that part of the spectrum, so that while we were stronger than it in our normal spectrum, it may be much stronger than us in the new section of the spectrum.

The Edward Hopper people inside a room but not looking at the objects or people inside it or at the room itself, nor at the visible outside, are present not in order to see the location where they are but to make it and maintain it as what it is: a room.

The doubling between the vampire and the mad:
Both Dracula and the mad men/women in the mental hospitals found so often in vampire films are in death: the latter are submerged by it, the former in control of it.

The vampire penetrates the skin, sucking his victim's blood, while in the mental hospitals schizophrenics experience the infinity of holes in their skin or shoes and the *bleeding* of sounds into each other. The vampire's corpse remains non-pierced: however much one zooms in on the unwrinkled face of Kinski no pores are visible in it (just the veins under the excessively white skin). Or did the vampire actually bite his victim? Behind the vampire's closed lips there are no teeth, no opening; the victim hears voices-over in his head and blood oozes out of his neck through stigmata.

Schizophrenics often use a cryptic language («Recreat. Recreat xangoran temr e xangoran an. Naza e fango xangoranan. Inai dum. Ageai dum»[162]). The letter that Nosferatu, the one who lies in the crypt, sends to Renfield is written in a cryptic, foreign writing. Stoker's Dracula asks Harker to help him speak English without an accent, for otherwise on arriving in England he would be «a stranger in a strange land,» hence scrutinized. The undead being intrinsically a stranger in a strange land, foreign actors are often used in vampire films: the accents of Kinski, Gans, Adjani, and the other non Anglo-Saxon actors in the English version of Herzog's *Nosferatu* (there are two versions of the film, one in English, one in German); not only are there three versions, each in a different language, of Dreyer's *Vampyr* (Dreyer insisted that his cast should not be dubbed, but that the actors should speak their lines in three languages whether they knew these languages or not), but also the vampire, who does not speak throughout the film, has an accent to her silence; Catherine Deneuve's accent in *The Hunger*; the accent of Lugosi in Browning's *Dracula*; the many versions-copies of Murnau's *Nosferatu* (French, German, Spanish—); and since in Wenders' *The American Friend* the still-living painter Derwart is thought by everybody to be already dead, the film is tri-lingual: German, English and French.

In vampire films, we encounter not only vampires, those aristocrats[163] who do not dissolve in the earth (how does the earth "feel" about its inability to digest the non-biodegradable, plastic and vampires?), but also the mad, those who undergo the dissolution even as they live: «in acute schizophrenia... the patient feels that he is part of the plants, animals, clouds, or of the whole world, and that they are part of him.»[164] As a hinge between the two, Kinski in the role of Nosferatu, the one who does not disintegrate in the grave into particles that will become parts of all that exists: «everything that exists—the animals, the trees, the clouds—is in me because I'm part of everything. I feel it *physically*... It makes no sense to do what I did when I was young and say, "I want to do this part or that part." I don't care anymore; they are in me anyway, all of them. And if I bring out this one or that one, there are a hundred million still left... People call this acting because they don't know any better»[165].

During the early Renaissance, a large portion of the madmen were put on the *Narrenschiff*, boats that carried the insane from town to town. Parallel to these ships of the mad is the ship of the dead, for instance the one around which revolves Raul Ruiz's *Les Trois Couronnes Du Matelot*; the ones that transport Dracula to London, Nosferatu to Bremen/Wismar. An intertitle in Murnau's *Nosferatu* reads: «The men little suspected what terrible cargo they were carrying down the valley.»[166] The same can be said of the men who accepted to take Jonah, that other undead, on their ship [during the storm which threatens to sink the ship, Jonah suggests to the sailors that they throw him into the sea to appease the God that has unleashed the storm. He thinks that death is total extinction. God sends the Whale to swallow him. Jonah in the dark of the Whale's belly (like Nosferatu in the coffin) experiences death as undeath]. This though does not seem to have been the case with the men asked to transport Murnau's coffin on their ship on their trip from the U.S. to Germany: «When the coffin had been put on the boat the sailors at first refused to sail with it on board. It was twice taken off the ship before they would agree.»[167] Was Murnau an undead?

It is not only the dead that have been forced into confinement (Baudrillard's *L'Echange Symbolique et la Mort*)—it is not by living in a cemetery, as the three quarters of a million Egyptians who live in the City of the Dead in Cairo do, that one will reach the dead's space, the labyrinth where one is homeless, ending the dead's confinement— but also the mad (Foucault's *Madness and Civilization*; at least until the 1960's—after which deinstitutionalization started). The confinement of the dead and the insane is encountered even in cosmology, where it applies to black holes, i.e. to *dead* stars that contain a *singularity*.[168]

Sensitivity to initial/final conditions:
Immortality for ancient Egyptians depended on the continued non-decomposition of the corpse. Faults in the preparation of the mummy or damage inflicted on it by thieves trying to plunder the contents of the tomb caused the loss of immortality. Ancient Egyptians' manner of insuring their immortality is interesting precisely because of its precariousness. This precariousness, though itself perhaps accidental, is revealing, because it points to the most noteworthy characteristic of the state following death: the extreme sensitivity (and suggestibility) to initial conditions (here they would be the final conditions of life, the initial conditions of death). Whenever we are dealing with the unconscious we find, as in any far from equilibrium (dynamical) system, an extreme sensitivity to initial conditions.[169] Anyone, even the least subtle person, can then throw us into a bad trip (night—I sat looking at him slightly distorting his face, repeating certain phrases with the air of having said them only once, speaking in a modified voice, and certainly there was a part of me that saw clearly through the brutal thing this shallow person was committing, but there was another part that, oblivious of what the other part knew (Brechtian *distantiation* fails in situations as these), began to feel an intense anxiety, the presentiment that paranoia and an altered sense of time was looming close), into the endless (not that it is infinite but that during it time stops or bifurcates) paranoid trip that death and madness can be. It is therefore not surprising that disciplines that are concerned with doing away with or at least having mastery over the Bardo state, for instance yoga, mention, among the «powers» that can be obtained through Samyama, the power of knowing the moment one is to die. Such knowledge would permit one to try to be in the best condition to face death (in meditation, hence unaffected by set (having complete control over one's stream of consciousness and/or absolute detachment from it) and setting, detached/withdrawn from them), for that state, just prior to death, is critical since it is ultra sensitive. The same emphasis on this last moment is found in

fifteenth century Christianity: whereas in the twelfth and thirteenth centuries «the balance sheet is closed not at the moment of death but on the *dies illa*, the last day of the world... [the great gathering] in the fifteenth century had moved to the sickroom... The dying man will see his entire life as it is contained in the book, and he will be tempted either by despair over his sins, by the "vainglory" of his good deeds, or by the passionate love for the things and the persons. His attitude during this fleeting moment will erase at once all the sins of his life if he wards off temptation or, on the contrary, will cancel out all his good deeds if he gives way. The final test has replaced the Last Judgement...»[170]

Beyond supersaturation (contributing factors: off-film—), *precipitate***ly**:
Dreyer: «A Danish critic said to me one day, "I have the impression that there are at least six of your films that are stylistically different, one from the other." This moved me, for that is something I really tried to do: to find a style that has value for only a single film, for this milieu, this action, this character, this subject.» This clarifies why *Vampyr*, unlike Herzog's *Nosferatu*, joins all the traits of a particular conception of the vampire. Since the credits inform the spectator that the film is based on Le Fanu's *Through a Glass Darkly*, the fact that the plots of "Carmilla" and the other stories of the book are very different from the film's plot indicates that spectators should supplement what goes on in the film with what goes on in the stories of *Through a Glass Darkly* (the spectators, like the manservant and Gray, and like the victims in Dracula stories and films, have to read a book on vampires). *Through a Glass Darkly*, in particular "Carmilla," is an off-film of *Vampyr* (hence it is like those characters in *Ordet* whom we did not know were in the room and that we suddenly see after many minutes of a continuous shot). Similarly, in *Lightning Over Water* an off-film is created by the inclusion in the film of a rehearsal, directed by Nicholas Ray, of a section from Kafka's *Report to the Academy*. It is far less Nick's direct attacks against Wenders («What could make it funny would be if I'd puke all over you. Come on, my leader... leader with my tail up... you're making me sick to my stomach») that show his view of the filming of *Lightning Over*

Water these attacks could be merely the venting of anger over the frustrations encountered in the process of making a film, especially a joint one (is Wim (with his crew in Ray's apartment proliferating like the rats in Herzog's *Nosferatu*) the vampire? Or is it the camera over the empty junk (like (Herzog's and Murnau's) Nosferatu or (Browning's and Badham's) Dracula on the empty ship transporting them from Transylvania to Bremen, Wismar or London; same circular movement around the empty ship in Herzog's *Nosferatu* and in *Lightning Over Water*), with both Nick and Wim its victims?)—than the inclusion of his rehearsal of Kafka's *A Report to an Academy* in the film. There is a statistically significant deviation from chance in the concordance between the first version of the film (edited by Peter Przygodda) and Kafka's short story («They were good creatures, in spite of everything. I find it still pleasant to remember the sound of their heavy footfalls which used to echo through my half-dreaming head... When they were off-duty some of them often used to sit down in a semicircle around me; they hardly spoke but only grunted to each other. If I were to be invited today to take a cruise on that ship I should certainly refuse the invitation... there was one of them who came again and again, alone or with friends, by day, by night, at all kinds of hours; he would post himself before me with the bottle and give me instructions. He could not understand me, he wanted to solve the enigma of my being... there was no attraction for me in imitating human beings; I imitated them because I needed a way out.»[171] Wim: «Are you ready? I didn't come to talk about dying, Nick.» Nick: «I didn't come to talk about dying, Nick.» Wim: «But we might have to». Nick: «But we might have to.») This concordance is for the most part lost in the second version (where the film crew and the shooting of the film in Ray's apartment are far less manifest), the one which Wenders edited. Did Nick Ray begin working on his production of Kafka's story before the filming began, or did he decide to work on it and include it in the film in response to what was taking place in the film so that surreptitiously an off-film would be created (the part of Kafka's short story included in *Lightning Over Water* is not the relevant one)? Nick's *A Report to an Academy* is, unlike *Hammett*, not an interruption of Lightning Over Water.[172] Were more of the rehearsals shot (the more relevant paragraphs) but edited out by Wenders? Or, a much more interesting hypothesis, were these more relevant paragraphs intentionally left out by Ray, as a new kind of (inaudible) voice-over? Nick will have also edited the film because he introduced the off-film, making *Lightning Over Water* also *Nick's Movie*. This off-film, whether in *Vampyr* or *Nick's Movie*, is a form of supersaturation of the film. Yet, *Vampyr* still became too saturated, most probably because it is also part of *Ordet* (1954): *Vampyr* (1932) happens between Inger's death and resurrection in *Ordet* (from a 1954 interview with Dreyer: «— When did you first come to think of filming Ordet?— It happened one evening *twenty two years ago* when I attended its first performance at the Betty Nansen Theater...»[173]). Inger's bite-like kiss in *Ordet* just after her resurrection can be considered to be a lingering reflex from her stay in the undead world of *Vampyr*; figures grouped around a death bed as painting in *Vampyr* and reality in *Ordet*. *Ordet*, which is about a pregnant woman who gives birth to (the faith in) her husband who is older than her, can have its first part (up to the death of Inger) be earlier than *Vampyr* which was shot before it.

Unlike Dreyer, in an interview Herzog says that he would like to have the rights of distribution of his films because he may one day want to join them into one film.[174] *Nosferatu* had to be made in order to make it impossible for all of Herzog's films to join together: all of them have elements of the Vampire Film: crossing the *imaginary line* in *Fitzcarraldo* (1982): the two tributaries of the Amazon, the Pachitea, which flows into the Amazon upstream from the city of Iquitos, and the Ucayali, which flows downstream, run parallel to each other; the Pongo das Mortes rapids blow the flow along the Ucayali. «Fitzgeraldo... who disappeared upstream, is coming back from downstream! It can't be, someone who's gone upstream *has to come back from upstream*»[175]; in *Land of Silence and Darkness* a blind-deaf says: "When you let go of my hand it is as if we were separated by a thousand miles," which echoes the ability of the vampire to tunnel through long distances; madness in *Signs of Life*; repetition and déjà vu in *Last Words*; sleepwalking in the diegesis and hypnosis in the filming of *Heart of Glass* (Sepp Bierbichler, who played the part of Hias, is the only actor who was not hypnotized); hallucinations in *Aguirre, the Wrath of God*; ruins and the absence of reflections and shadows («in paradise you cross the sand without seeing your shadow... There you cross the sand without seeing your face») in *Fata Morgana*. Or rather, the presence of *Nosferatu* makes it possible to join the other films together without them forming a unity. A wise move by Herzog: dissociating the elements, rather than putting them in the same vampire film, may have saved him from having a nervous breakdown, something that happened to Dreyer just after finishing *Vampyr*, necessitating interning him for a while.

Accidents:

I could see him, a very old person, walking very slowly toward the car, his worn eyes almost totally closed. He was one of those unfortunate enough to have no susceptibility to hypnosis (no age regression was possible in his case). He was so old he felt almost nothing, his senses, but also his memory, were so dull. Half-way to the car, he paused for a moment. He was puzzled: he had forgotten why he was there. He was put in a car with no brakes. They knew he could go through the accident without undergoing a near-death state. But the past, which had become a rare commodity, had to be recorded. What the experimenters suspected the first few times, they know at present: in some cases, they are observed from some out-of-the-body position by the person whose dying body they are observing. He could see himself lying on the ground near the crushed car. Under him, on the ground, were the doctors and historians observing the bruised body from which they will extract, like a black box, the camera they inserted earlier in his brain, which recorded not only the accident but the flash review of his life (they put a very slow film in his brain so that it would not be overexposed).

The car accident is the ultimate way to get the Photograph, hence it is no *accident* that in Ballard's *Crash* the main character, who is obsessed with car crashes, is equally obsessed with photography (especially photographs depicting the effects of the crash on the car and the victims), and that the main character in Hitchcock's *Rear Window* (1954), a photographer, has his legs cast because, while he was taking photographs of a car race, a car veered off track and smashed into him (when near the end of the film the murderer tries to kill him, the photographer, who cannot move since his leg is still cast, can stop him only by directing an intense flashlight at him, i.e.

taking a photograph of him without using a camera. The murderer is immobilized/cast for the duration of the developing time for the photograph (we are as it were witnessing the first polaroid)). Likewise, we could not have obtained the photographs that we have of the subatomic world without crashes between elementary particles in particle accelerators.

One day in 1906 a filmstrip jammed in Méliès' camera. He managed to get the camera to function again and continued filming. At the projection of the reel a horse-drawn tram suddenly became a hearse. An accident between a hearse and a horse-drawn tram both moving at rather slow speeds, hence having enough time, even had their drivers found themselves on a collision course, to avert crashing into each other (in Franju's *Le Sang des bêtes* a horse led by a man moves about nonchalantly (the horse even lowers his head to smell the ground, as if nothing could happen to him), then is suddenly killed (first a Behr-gun stuns him by percussion): an accident (hence the symptomatic presence of the butcher who lost a leg in a work accident and now walks on a wooden leg). So strong is this unawareness of the horse—unlike the horse, the sheep readied to be killed sense what is going to happen to them—that it imposes a specific kind of montage: the cut from the long shot of the horse nonchalantly smelling the ground to a close-up of him being shot. We most probably have a law of montage here: every time two persons, or a person and a domesticated animal, are within a frame and one of them is totally unaware of the danger she/he/it is in, there will occur a cut, whether the director wants it or not, between that shot and the shot in which she/he/it is killed or injured. But even in the absence of a cut, we would still feel that the killed or injured animal or person has been replaced within the continuous shot by a double (we infer that we went through a lapse at some point), that it is his double that is killed or injured or else that it is himself/herself that has been injured or killed by a double of the person or animal in whose presence s/he is, because his/her surprise is that of being eaten by a mimicry animal (small fish eaten by angler fish))—an accident produced in the camera. A crash between their images. It is not accidental that that mixing of two things that had nothing to do with each other which ushered editing was related to death: the hearse that appeared.

Animals:
Rats and mice have been subjected to myriad memory experiments: in some of these (for instance those conducted by Karl Lashely), lesions were inflicted on different parts of their brains to see if memory resides in a specific area; in many other experiments, they had to find their way through mazes. With the plague the situation is reversed (rats can become carriers of the plague) and humans are now the subjects of the experiment: many of those struck by the plague become amnesiac and are lost in the plagued city become a maze.

The man-animal figures, or to be more precise, god-animal figures that populate ancient mythologies (Minotaur, etc.) and religions (ancient Egyptian falcon-headed god, etc.) may be coming back to actuality with the advent of recombinant DNA. They were already present in a virtual way through the use of psychedelics: «the Amahuaca training for hunters included group ingestion of ayahuasca. Under the influence of the psychedelic brew, participants invoked visions of animals hunted by the tribe. They were able to tune into them and identify with them so fully that they got to know intimately their instincts and habits»[176] (if the hunt often ends in a possession of the animal by humans, it is preceded by a *possession* of the humans by the animal). Yet in many instances the hallucinated animal was a mutated one (in the majority of cases these metamorphoses are not autosymbolic representations). Could it be that the hallucinations of people on psychedelics were laboratories that pointed to species that certain mutations are good while others are very dangerous and sterile?

The suffering humans inflict on veals (through constraining their movement—) and on many lab animals (rabbits don't shed tears, so the noxious products being tested on their eyes, to determine how bad they may be to humans, damage the eye without any defense...) is possible perhaps only because almost all humans suffer much more during the Bardo state.

Pain:
This tremendous sudden pity which at times takes hold of a person who lived in solitude for a long time and is living at present with someone, becoming an almost unbearable pain. Pity is an infinite phenomenon. Only the sudden memory (a memory that surfaces to save one) that they think of sooner or later having children gives one respite from the pain of pity, the pity of pain (is pain sometimes the pity one has for the body?). To see/hear someone else suffering or to think s/he is suffering is in most cases harsher than to undergo his/her suffering, for during life there is a limit to the duration and/or intensity of the pain and suffering that can be undergone, beyond which one faints, one goes into a coma, one dies, one has an out-of-the-body experience. But suffering because someone else is suffering (due to pain or pity) can increase indefinitely and not in proportion to the suffering of the other person or animal (that's why we may ask to suffer in his/her/its place (is this then a sacrifice, or is it rather done to evade a bigger pain?), something which may benefit both persons, for the person one is sparing the pain may not be prone to pity, may be someone who does not suffer too much because someone else is suffering), that is why, since it has no negative feedback mechanism, it may not be part of life but already part of death (unless even death has suffering thresholds beyond which there occurs a reversal back into life; one reason for accepting the possibility of reincarnation (which in the schizophrenic's case is undergone while s/he lives: «I am Napoleon...») would be that any organism has built-in mechanisms to arrest its operations once it cannot deal even inefficiently with its surroundings (it is itself one of its surroundings), whether through fainting, hibernation, catatonia, thanatosis, dissociation or even death: when the stimuli become radically unbearable for the undead, the only way out would be Life), since death may be the realm of the absence of reversal points, of escape velocities (there is no escape from death, not in the sense that we will all die, for that remains an external characteristic not so much of death itself as of its relation to life, but in the sense that death itself has no reversal thresholds or escape velocities from it).

It is humorous that it is hypnotic analgesia, through the distinction in it between overt and covert pain reduction, that permits one to give utterance to the almost abstract pain one often feels, a pain that is not necessarily confined to the body's boundaries: the subliminal pain in one's exhaled breath indicated by the scratches close to Arnulf Rainer's face in his *Untitled*, 1971 (one can see in yogic diagrams of the energetic conduits the same extension beyond the boundaries of the body). Rainer's photographs with their scratches and overpainting (the series *Self-portraits*, etc.) can be viewed as rendering the *hidden observer*.

The vampire is moving closer to her. He cannot reduce pain through his reflection in her pupil, for he has no reflections (her pupils his blindness), while in Bill Viola's *I Do Not Know What it is I Am Like*, whose next to last section documents a ceremony in the Mahadevi temple in Fiji in which the participants stick needles in their bodies and then perform fire-walking, Viola appears in the pupils of birds, in drops of water, on faucets' surfaces. The streak of light in her dark pupil (light kills vampires) is his reflection, his reflection that will kill him (another story of the double)—but to an undead being killed is not a possible way out of pain (in Herzog's *Nosferatu* the vampiric Harker does not replace Nosferatu, but is Nosferatu). Yet sometimes he could feel the pain vanishing: was it that in reality-as-film he was within an iris, hence already an image— an iris being a frame inside the frame—which feels no pain? At other times, during the early stages of metamorphosis, depersonalization/ dissociation occurred and the vampire watched what was going on without feeling pain, and with detachment, as if the pain was happening to a stunt. Are there few or no mirrors or equivalents of mirrors in Herzog's films, since he stresses that one should not get rid of pain[177]?

What of trying to evade pain through disappearing: the half faces in Francis Bacon's *Triptych, three studies for a self portrait* (1980); the half head in the left panel of *Triptych* (1983); the half-leg and half-bust in *Triptych* (August 1972)? The circles around the face in *Studies from the Human Body* (1975), the circle over the foot of the right panel in *Triptych* (1974-77), the eyeglasses in *Triptych* (1986-87)—in the case of the eyeglasses we should concentrate on the role they play in the painting, rather than on their referential function—are magnifying glass enlarging to normal size what is decreasing in size toward disappearance, so that the parts of the body often maintain their normal size. The effect of the frame-in-the-form-of-a-circle, namely less pain, is countered by the magnifying glass aspect of the circle.

A shot of a person looking in a specific direction is followed by a shot that begins as a static pov then continues in a pan to the side; the third shot is not a return to the person who was looking, with the consequence that the film spectator is no longer sure whether the second shot was in its entirety the pov of the person who was looking, who must in that case have at one point moved his head to the side, or whether either the shot had become objective or the person had just gone through a minimal dissociation (the sketch with charcoal displaced over the painted face with pale, luminous cheeks in Frank Auerbach's *Head of Catherine Lampert VI*). The two possibilities produce a decrease in pain since the uncertainty is objective.

It [the altered state] happened and is over with, and it is still unfolding in a bifurcation branch. And it [resurrection] did not happen:
The modesty which insinuates itself following the period of fear and the presence of the double is both an extreme danger (and indulgence) and a warning that one is forgetting that this subsequent period—a credit—is simultaneous with the period of the encounter with the double and fear (what occurred in an altered state at a previous time, or what will occur later, is still unfolding even as one is back in a normal state) with which it has to get in contact by writing, hence still part of the state of emergency. One should not have the modesty of thinking that one should not write on extreme and strange experiences one is not undergoing at the time, for one underwent these experiences and needs this period to try to replace, at least in part, imposition by reception.

The maintenance of both: it [the altered state] happened and is over with, and it is still unfolding in a bifurcation branch; and it [resurrection] did not happen: the dead J. is resurrected in *L'Arrêt de Mort* and both she and the one who witnessed the resurrection act normal, as if the interruption of death did not occur: «judging it [the illness] as though it had followed its natural course—I found her much better than I would have imagined after everything that had been written to me» (Harker tries to *under*play/*under*state what happened to him in the letter he sends to Mina; he shouldn't have done that but should have acted as if nothing had happened («don Juan had insisted that I had to proceed as if nothing had happened»[178])). In Tarkovsky's *Solaris*, Chris Kelvin begins to doubt his sanity when he meets a copy of his dead wife, a copy who herself dies and is resurrected: resurrection of the one who was alone in the world of death has to occur in front of many as in *Ordet*, otherwise the one who resurrects another or witnesses such a resurrection is at a high risk of being projected in time either past death into undeath/madness[179] or, still this side of death, into senility. Dreyer succumbed to neither of these two eventualities and yet at the opening in Paris of *Gertrud* many critics wrote that he should have died ten years earlier, after finishing *Ordet*, *Gertrud* being according to them the product of a senile director[180] (their attack on *Gertrud* is also an attack on *Ordet*, a film that resurrects the dead, permitting what ended to continue. *Gertrud* itself had to be resurrected from the oblivion in which its bad reception buried it). Only the resurrected can resurrect someone else: only Johannes, the one who *died before he died*, the mad for a time, hence the dead/undead for a time, can resurrect the dead Inger, and only resurrected Inger can resurrect her husband into faith. In *L'Arrêt de Mort*, the narrator can resurrect J. only because he himself is already dead, since the doctor had, seven years earlier, given him only six months to live (J. does not include him in her will, not because she is angry at him for advising her to commit suicide, but because he is already dead, and only the living can carry out/be included in a will), and though he otherwise belittles the doctor (*Death Sentence*, Station Hill Press, p.5), he writes: «One last [but not least] thing about this doctor... he was, it seems to me, a great deal more reliable in his diagnosis than most» (p.9). If doctors are to be conjoined to vampires and the undead, and they often are in books and films on the undead, this should not be in the manner shown in Dreyer's *Vampyr*, where the doctor is merely one of the aids of the vampire, but in the manner in which it is shown in Blanchot's *L'Arrêt de Mort*, where the doctor puts a certain limit to the span of time a person would live, so that by surviving that *deadline* one becomes either an undead as in Blanchot's novel, or the double of who he was as in Patricia Highsmith's *Ripley's Game*, a novel where the doctor projects that Jonathan would die from his myelocytic leukemia after 6-12 or even 6-8 years—Jonathan was entering his sixth year at the beginning of the novel. In the latter cases the doctor's prognosis becomes a performative; the doctor is reliable not so much because he proffers the right diagnoses and prognoses, but rather because his prognosis is a performative.

Only the resurrected, or one who forms a pair with the resurrected or the undead, can kill the dead/undead: in *Vampyr*, were it not for Gray's undeath, the manservant would not have been able to kill the vampire.

Bifurcation:

Bifurcation. Hence, the expression "I can talk/write about it because I've been there" is somewhat misleading since one is still there.

One may sense that a certain (altered) state that one found oneself in in the past following a lapse and/or found that one has left after a lapse is still unfolding (the vampire film works within closure since it attacks anyone who dies before his time, with unfinished business. Both this closure and the more specific one consisting in the obliteration of the vampire and the end of the plague at the end of films that deal with the latter theme are subverted by bifurcation). The period which "follows" the one of altered consciousness is both later than and simultaneous with the latter: a credit in the form of a kind of parallel montage. This period plays the role of the guardian in cases where one has no guardian (the one without guardian (in the form of a *hidden observer*, or of a writer connecting, unbeknownst to one or both of them, to what is occurring to the person in the altered state, or of this credit period) represents a danger to *invariance*). Hence there is something anticlimactic about the passage from the altered state to the normal state. How can I help him (my mother calls me in New York from Lebanon because she had a presentiment that something bad happened to me or might happen to me if I am not very cautious. I tell her nothing bad happened to me. But perhaps the premonition is about the version of me in another bifurcation branch, about the amnesiac Jalal. The amnesiac Jalal has no mother, but my mother may have a premonition about him since what happens to him affects me)? It is not oneself that can be the master/guide/ guardian of oneself-as-amnesiac fighting the double (in the mind) in one of the bifurcation branches, but one's writing. One has to help with writing, with what is received (received also from the amnesiac version of one, who feels that he is receiving nothing, creating nothing, but only resisting ideas and sensations imposed upon him by the double): interference between one's version in a bifurcation branch and oneself as writer, oneself-as-person the go-between (a dangerous position (Joseph Losey's *The Go-Between*)). Some use their characters and/or their amnesiac version(s) as the experimental sample, while they themselves-as-writers become the control sample; other writers use themselves-as-amnesiac-version(s) as the experimental sample, and their characters as the control sample (not in the sense that their characters are normal people, but that their characters become the amnesiac-version's guides/masters/hidden-observer)[181].

It all begins very innocently in George Landow's *The Film that Rises to the Surface of Clarified Butter* (1968): someone is drawing the outline of a figure on a white paper. The light grows a little dimmer and we see, as in a child's drawing book, the faint preexisting outline the person is merely re-tracing. Then we see a shot of a woman who looks at us. The same shot recurs a little later, and we feel that we too, who thought that we were seeing the film for the first time, were already here before. To know that something that is occurring to us for the first time has already occurred to us before in an *absolutely* identical manner can be withstood. But knowing that it is has never stopped happening and is still occurring even as the mental blocking induced by fear happens is to be no longer able to directly report on it to another since this experience means by the same token that I myself, who am watching a film where a certain shot repeats itself, have never and could never leave the auditorium, that I have always been here, that this recurrence of the shot has retroactively and objectively erased my having entered the room, that if I go out it would be as another person and that my knowing that another has remained here is not a continuous knowledge that passed with me through the threshold but something that I have received indirectly from him. Even when it seems to me that I have absolutely experienced eternal recurrence as the deepest, most intensely felt experience of my life or death, it is still only something that has been indirectly received by me from someone who is imprisoned by his experience and who has *one* experience: the horrified realization that he has always been here and that he cannot leave from the unlocked place where he happens to be (the present of the eternal recurrence is the aforementioned realization, which is itself, this realization, what recurs each time in relation to either the same or a different scene/moment). What is to live the present but no longer to trace this preexisting line? What is sloppiness but the attempt to approximate what preexists (the Zen master lets the line trace itself, hence the absence of sloppiness, of imprecision)? The present without trace, freedom, cannot be achieved except by confronting and accepting the eternal recurrence of events.

The indefinite number of moments of realization of the eternal recurrence, "Oh! I've always been here!," hence of moments that are not and cannot be transitive to form linear time must both exist (as refractory periods) and be occulted—i.e. one has to be amnesiac about them; at each a bifurcation occurs—in order for linear time to be constituted.

One should continue receiving from the bifurcating branches as long as one considers that what is being received is not issuing from or is itself something completely lacking (not only in any consciousness but also) any negative feedback mechanism. Not to automatically take the sudden cessation of a segment for a negative feedback: this sudden cessation is a characteristic facet of a bifurcating time. Parallel time does not necessarily imply that the other branches are continuing in a linear fashion; it is often the case that, whether indefinitely-scanned or not, the parallel segments are interrupted. One criterion by which to judge whether a branch that is out of one's awareness—for one is then in another branch—is still continuing to unfold may be that one continues receiving from the version of oneself in it. Two pitfalls: thinking that an altered state is over just because one is back to the normal state (an ignoring of bifurcation): it is often the case that while over the altered state is continuing as (voice/image)-over (one's dread that one has, by taking a psychedelic, made an disproportional blunder is a translation of the fact that one intuitively senses that a bifurcation has happened and hence that the sudden disappearance of the altered state a few hours after the intake is misleading since another version of one is still there); and thinking that the interruption in one version, one now in another branch, necessarily implies in all cases unfinished business and therefore that that version is continuing.

Must one promptly commit suicide, since only that will by the same movement end the terrible plight of the other versions of oneself, some of them in frightening psychotic worlds? Except, it is possible, even very probable, that the temptation to try to end it all (i.e. get rid of all the bifurcation branches) by committing suicide is a ruse of the other sections to get rid of the linear and more normal section, the other sections continuing, one having lost one's refuge from them. Hence *I should think* one should not feel guilt for not committing suicide (one ought not to try to exterminate the vestige of guilt that haunts the *should*).

One must not immediately equate the indeterminacy produced by the fact that the bifurcation branch that will be taken cannot be predicted with choice, since if, due to a change in the non-equilibrium, a dissipative structure is forced to retreat in its evolution, *as long as there are no strong perturbations*, it takes the same path in the reverse direction (traditional memory). Choice is a matter of either a two-way indeterminacy, and hence applies only in the case of dissipative non-linear structures that undergo strong perturbations and hysteresis, losing their memory of the path that led to where they are (this amnesia is part of choice); or, in the case of a crossing of a threshold of no return, of the creation of a bifurcation. We the amnesiacs leave for traces only another version of us (bifurcation). Choice consists in *having created* a bifurcation point rather than in selecting one of many alternatives. If, as is often the case, the threshold of no return is not itself a real choice, one has to turn up back at a bifurcation threshold prior to it. Choice is signaled by the existence of a bifurcation, and is hence unknowable (except through faith; though it is then no longer clear whether the bifurcation was already there or whether faith, which produces real effects through the agency of the virtual, created the bifurcation), since it is taken by another version of me. Choice also entails a certain link, for instance by writing, between the two versions.

Over-turns, or the discrete way in which an angle can widen toward the obtuse:
One or more of the following hands/lines/bifurcation branches is superimposed on the handless, faceless clock we see in the dream in Bergman's *Wild Strawberries* (1957): we move from jump cuts due to a narrower than 30° angle between two consecutive medium shots or close shots or long shots (signaling a lapse); *to* the awry looks in *Ordet* (in vampire films, it is not only the eyes that do not meet; the mouths do not meet in the kiss: mouth over neck); *to* the 90° translation that affects Munch's mouth in *The Scream*: it is not so much that the mouth opens to utter the scream but is unable to do so because of panic; rather, the mouth is a normal mouth that has been translated through a 90° turn. And it is this normal mouth, which is not screaming at all, except for its vertical translation movement, that shows that from an external point of view nothing warrants the attack of anxiety or panic—the two friends who were accompanying him continued their normal walk; *to* the cathexis of the matte line itself in Nabokov's *Despair*: «a film actor in a double part can hardly deceive anyone, for even if he does appear in both impersonations at once, the eye cannot help tracing a line down the middle where the halves of the picture have been joined.»[182] Similarly, the eye cannot help tracing the same kind of line, the matte line, in Bergman's *Persona*, one side of the face from half of Liv Ulman's face, the other from half of Bibi Anderson's face; *to* the partial crossing of the imaginary line in *At Land*: the two chess players who are at first sitting at opposite sides of the chess board are suddenly sitting on the same side in the following shot and still continuing their game; the crossing of the nun behind the camera in Dreyer's *Vampyr*; *to* the crossing of the *imaginary line*, a matte line between the shots: Nosferatu's ship moving from right to left in a first shot, then from left to right in the next shot (of the ship); the back and forth of the coach during the journey to the vampire's castle in Bram Stoker's *Dracula*: «we were simply going over and over the same ground again»; in *The American Friend*, a stranger proposes to Jonathan to kill someone for a certain amount of money. His reply is: "You must take me for somebody else." Later, a frontal tracking shot of Jonathan going to meet the same man in the airport is followed by a tracking shot, at the same pace,

toward Jonathan sleeping on a couch in the airport. The latter shot could be Jonathan's pov; in which case we are dealing with a dissociation. We can consider the dissociation revealed by this two-shot sequence as the decision to commit the crime;[183] the crossing of the 90° *imaginary line* in Munch's *The Scream* is conjoined to a crossing of the 180° *imaginary line*—the withdrawal of the world: now he is looking in the opposite direction to the two friends and the fjord. This position induced by the 180° over-turn is in no way to be mistaken with that of the jealous person looking at us, the spectators, in Munch's *Jealousy*, away from woman and the man *behind his back*. Jealousy may lead to anxiety; the two may display many similarities—after all jealousy and anxiety are the two paradigmatic interminglings—they are, nonetheless, not the same. Munch's *Jealousy* and *The Scream* deploy the same spatial arrangement of the three figures, except that unlike in the case of *Jealousy*, we cannot say that in *The Scream* the foreground figure is looking at the spectator, for two related reasons: although the spectator of the painting can see the face of the figure in the foreground, the latter cannot see the spectator, for he has undergone a 180° turn (a labyrinthine circle: although a straight line can be traced from the two men walking away in the background to the figure in the foreground to the spectator, the two 180° turns undergone by the foreground figure, one away from the spectator he was facing and one away from the two persons in the background, do not add up to 360° or deduct to 0°, do not return him to his starting position); and the turn to the frontal position in relation to the viewer of the painting, is, unlike in *Jealousy*, discrete rather than gradual; in Philip K. Dick's *Eye in the Sky*, «shuddering, Hamilton grasped the railing and began to climb back upstairs.

«He had gone only two steps when his legs, of their own volition, refused to carry him farther. His body comprehended what his mind refused to accept. He was going back down...» The immobilization of Hamilton has nothing to do with the freezing that fear creates but, on the contrary, it counteracts the swish pan that fear induces and which can hide the crossing of the imaginary line. «"Is—there anything I can do? Won't you turn toward me? Must you have your back to me?"

«Hamilton laughed wildly. "Sure I'll turn toward you." Gripping the railing, he made a cautious about-face—and found himself still facing the gloomy cave..."»[184] Even if Orpheus wanted to look back while ascending the passage from Hades, he would have been still looking in the wrong, that is the just direction, away from Eurydice (life and death are separated by, among other things, an *imaginary line*). Orpheus wanted to look at her, began looking at her way back in Hades; it is only when he reached the sunlight and life again that he could turn. These increasingly pronounced turnings most often induce an attempt to turn away from them, though past a certain stage this turning away is no longer possible; *to* a more enigmatic crossing of the *imaginary line*, the turned back of the reflection of the person facing the mirror in Magritte's *Reproduction Prohibited* (1937) and of Nosferatu in the dissolve-as-mirror in Murnau's *Nosferatu*, 1922 (within one of Harker's povs there is a momentary superimposition of a shot of Nosferatu standing at the end of the corridor and a closer shot of him, both shots with the vampire facing in the same direction). Interpellation fails in both *Reproduction Prohibited* and the dissolve-as-mirror in Murnau's *Nosferatu*; the "hey, you there" is not answered by the 180° turn that constitutes a subject («Because he has recognized that... it was really him who was hailed (and not someone else)»)[185] since it constitutes a mirror-image (the hailing is a kind of mirror, and the mirror a kind of hailing that succeeds in eliciting a response (the Magritte and the dissolve in Murnau's *Nosferatu* are exceptions), one having made a 180° turn in the mirror to answer one's virtual hailing of oneself in front of it. Munch's use of graphic arts is partly motivated by the fact that they allowed him, who suffered from over-turns (*The Scream*), to have the 180° turn of the left-right inversion, achieving mirror reflections of the painted versions (this inversion is also present in the two photographs titled *Self-portrait in a rented room*, 1906)). The 180° over-turn neutralizes the subjectivization of the interpellation since it overturns the turn to answer the hailing, this *turning one's head* and often producing an about-face, with the new beliefs and opinions either filling one's mind completely or entering into conflict with one's previously-held beliefs, displacing them to the background. Whereas a photograph or a painting in which a person is giving us his back invites identification—both the

Bantam Classics edition of *Frankenstein* and the Penguin Classics edition of *Ecce Homo* have on their covers Caspar David Friedrich's *From the Summit; Traveler Looking Over the Sea of Fog*—the back turned on us in *Reproduction Prohibited*—not in the accidental sense that the one looking in the mirror is looking away from us, but categorically, since both the person and his reflection in the mirror are giving us their back—makes it impossible for us, unless we had at one point died before dying, to identify with the figure in the painting (Bonitzer writes in relation to Robert Montgomery's film *Lady in the Lake*: «the argument against the film is that the *"parti-pris"* of the subjective camera prevented the famous and necessary identification between the spectator and the hero... We cannot identify with someone whose face is always hidden from us.» Who is this *we*? What if we are undead, hence have no face, either because we have no image in the mirror or because the image we see when we look in the mirror is always giving us its back? Even in that case we cannot identify with one «whose face is always hidden from us» but only because we *are* him and he cannot identify with himself. What Bonitzer writes applies to the normal spectator, who cannot for instance identify with Jekyll with whom the camera is identified in the beginning scene of Rouben Mamoulian's *Dr. Jekyll and Mr. Hyde,* and this is fortunate, for otherwise he would have been trapped and hence forced later to undergo the dissociation Jekyll undergoes). Not to *run out on* or *walk out on* the one who is suffering from immobilizations, and not to *turn one's back on* the one who is suffering from the automatic crossing of the imaginary line, the one who is, against his will, turning his back on the world and himself (it may be that only a dancer can endure and counteract, and hence affirm, the latter state: in Deren's *Choreography for a Camera* the dancer's quick revolving movement in front of a two-headed statue of Siva—the ultimate crossing of the imaginary line—produces, and not only stroboscopically, a two-faced being). Those who undergo anxiety, experiencing everything—including themselves (depersonalization)—as strange,[186] must be helped; one helps only strangers (it is through an *aparté* that after the over-turn (caused by the crossing of the imaginary line) s/he can still speak or look at or be in the company of those s/he was speaking to before the turn. Will we be able to over-hear and over-look him/her or will we overlook him/her?).

One should emphasize that these turnings, which range from an angle of less than 30° to a 180° turn, happen in a non-gradual way, do not cover the intermediate arc. One should emphasize this because of the ever-present temptation to occult the discreteness of the turn. This temptation can be discerned in Munch's work. First comes *Study for Despair*, 1891-2,[187] with a man in profile propped against a railing; then *Despair (Deranged Mood at Sunset)*, 1892, where we see two other figures walking in the distance away from the foreground character leaning in profile against the railing—the painting here presents a spatial arrangement that closely follows the one experienced by Munch during an anxiety attack: «I stopped, leaned against the railing, dead tired [my friends looked at me and walked on]»; then, in 1892, come two small pen-and-ink sketches intended to serve as illustrations for the book of poems Emanuel Goldstein dedicated to Munch and for which Munch created the frontispiece, both with the title *Despair*: the first presents the same spatial positioning as the aforementioned painting, but in the second the person in the foreground is looking straight in the direction of the spectator of the painting; then comes *Study for The Scream*, 1893,[188] where one of the two friends is turned and looking either at the landscape or at the figure in the foreground, counterbalancing the latter's full turn that resulted in his facing in the direction of the spectator; last but not least comes *The Scream*, 1983,[189] where the character has undergone a 180° turn while the other two men continue their walk in the background, their back to him. We see Munch moving from the profile position, the 90° turn, which shadows his experience, to the 180° turn, which renders it more exactly (rather than disappearing, the 90° turn is now that of the mouth). Past attaining the latter arrangement the regression to earlier spatial arrangements serves to give the erroneous impression that the 180° turn is gradual: in *Despair*, 1894 (reworked, c. 1915),[190] the person in the foreground has undergone a 135° turn, is introspective, his eyes as if closed, his face directed toward the ground. *The Scream*, 1895,[191] can be viewed as a restatement of the appropriate arrangement but also as placing the 180° turn after the 135° turn, this implying that a gradual turning had taken place.

Hegel's *the road to truth is part of the truth* applies only till Munch reaches the arrangement in *The Scream* (1893). The danger of the serial (for instance Munch's The Frieze of Life) is that it may infiltrate in a moment of lesser sobriety the movement portrayed in a single painting,[192] this resulting in the case of *The Scream/Despair* in the jump cut being occulted through the series as a gradual turning (when Munch exhibited the "Love" series in 1894 in Stockholm both *Despair*, 1892, and *The Scream*, 1893, were part of it). This secondary elaboration also manifests itself in the fact that many of the stages Munch as an artist had to go through in reaching the sudden turn that is rendered in *The Scream* are produced again, past 1893, in different media: lithograph, intaglio, woodcut, pen-and-ink sketches (it is in a letter written on November 14, 1894, i.e. around a year after the definite version of *The Scream*, that Munch mentions that he has begun working in the graphic arts. «Art comes with a person's urge to communicate to another—all means are equally good»; certainly prints would make for a wider circulation and exposure of Munch's work than the paintings, occasionally exhibited in a few museums, could. Unfortunately, the enhanced communication with and accessibility to the public that resulted was due not only to the fact that more people could see the prints than could see the paintings, but also to the counterfeit possibility of communication of the different planes and positions of the discrete turns, most spectators then dealing with gradual turnings) and prose poems. If at all, the gradual turning applies to the theme of jealousy. And it is because there is no fear in this case that Munch does not feel the compulsion to show what can be taken as a gradual turning: *Jealousy*, 1895,[193] *Jealousy* 1986,[194] *Jealousy*, 1907,[195] *Jealousy*, 1933-35,[196] all show the character in the foreground looking in the direction of the viewer of the painting.

In Ted Julian Arnold's *Second Child I* (1993), the seated figure has undergone a "turning into stone," i.e. "in the same movement" an immobilization and a receding into the wall behind it in the painting (were the spectator to come closer to the painting s/he would see that wallpaper patterns in the form of flowers cover the yellow wall, realizing that the receding is into something flat, devoid of depth; it is in this sense that the receding in question is in-place) that imbues it with a flatness (one can take the words "second child" as suggesting that the woman in the painting is pregnant: in which case her belly that does not protrude confirms the receding into the (flat) wall) even when it is in a 45° profile pose in relation to the spectator (the "turning into stone" is what gives this flat figure its impressive sense of solidity); this is what makes such a figure one that is facing us despite the fact it is for all practical purposes a profile figure. The logic then to the series of three paintings *Second Child I, II,* and *III*: to present/juxtapose a frontal figure, a profile figure, and a profile figure that is at the same time a frontal figure; it is not the figure in *Second Child II* that best manifests frontality, but the one in *Second Child I* (the frontality of the profile figure has nothing to do with a cubist simultaneity of the different planes). A difficult and strange achievement: to manage in the above conditions and despite them a profile figure (the figure in *Second Child III* would be a control sample in relation to such a figure). In the painting *21* (1988) the face is painted on the back of a folded piece of canvas, so that actually it is a face that has turned 180° in relation to the open palm that gives the sense of frontality. *21* allows us to better understand the provenance of the shadow on the face in both *Second Child I* and *Second Child II*: it is the shadow of both the flat wall on the figure receding into it and of the 180°-turned face on itself (symptomatically, at the lower part of *Second Child I* there is an illusionistic fold). We no longer are dealing with masked faces but with faces that because they are implicitly turned 180° even when they stare at us have these otherwise unmotivated shadows on them. The lingering sense of frontality despite this implicit 180°-turn is a result of the aforementioned effect of a frontality of the figure in whatever position it is produced by its "turning into stone."

Counterfeiting
An image has to be revivified or decomposed, the former option resulting on the long run in the latter: Rainer's scratches over the death mask of Wagner; the setting of the opera *Parsifal* both inside and on Wagner's death mask in Syberberg's *Parsifal*. The *incorporated* dead is both an extreme permeability in the Bardo state and totally embalmed/shielded in a safe inside the one who incorporated[197] him/her (save: *guard; excepted...* from the birth-death cycle)(when

melancholy ends one can hear the incorporated person fall from the now living person like a prosthesis). The incorporated dead inside the melancholic is the only image that the dead has. But either because the undead has been radically altered or replaced by the double (in Hitchcock's *Rebecca*, the psychological motivation of the maid who wants to hurt the new wife for replacing her dead, former mistress—she tells the new wife that the hung portrait represents her husband's grandmother, when in fact it is Rebecca's—is merely the occasion for us to know that Rebecca has been replaced at least in part by the husband's grandmother), or because s/he has no image (either because s/he sees himself/herself with his/her back to himself/herself in the (dissolve-as-)mirror or because s/he does not appear in the mirror), this image is an imposition of an image on the undead (Tim Burton's *Batman* shows one version of the confrontation between the unliving through *incorporation* (Batman)— maintaining outside of death the person who died and that one finds impossible to mourn maintains one outside of life—and the undead who caused the death of the one(s) the former is incorporating (the Joker); some vampire films show a more just version of the confrontation between the unliving and the undead, this time between the unliving and the undead they incorporated, the latter trying to get rid of the unliving to liberate themselves from the image being enforced on them by the unliving). This imposition of a fake image on the undead leads both to an imposition of an image on the living by (means of) the dead[198] (who have no image[199]), and to the discovery that the dead do not have a (mirror) image or that they are a superimposition of potentialities with the one actualized being determined or at least largely inflected by the particularity of the person looking for their truth or trying to imitate them, which is the same thing. In *Rebecca* the new wife finds herself trying to imitate the dead Rebecca, her husband's first wife; this ensues in the former's discovery that the image-conception she had of Rebecca is wrong compared to who the late Rebecca turns out to be. In Hitchcock we have both the *wrong man*, the male wrongly accused of being the murderer, and the wrong woman (*Rebecca*, 1940; *Vertigo*, 1958), the dead/undead woman who is divergent from her image. Dealing with a melancholic, the detective of *Vertigo* should have throughly investigated Carlotta Valdes' life, for in the case of a coincidence of Carlotta with herself, he would be almost sure that the wife is not a melancholic who has incorporated the dead Carlotta. But there is no coincidence: Carlotta Valdes is insane (hence has no image), and before that there were two different Carlotta's, *Happy Carlotta* and *Sad Carlotta* (the author of *(Vampires)* would also have been fooled were he in charge of investigating the case).

Are we, in *Vertigo*, dealing with history or with forgery, i.e. are we dealing with a relation with the dead as they were when alive, hence with the past, or are we dealing with the dead as undead? If we are dealing with forgery, then in the second part of the film we would still be dealing with Madeleine, i.e. Judy does not exist as an actual body but only as one version of Madeleine. If we are dealing with history, then we are and were dealing with a woman called Judy who helped Madeleine's husband fool the retired detective Scottie[200]. This distinction, forgery or history, is far more important than Hitchcock's alternative between suspense (the audience knows about a certain key fact, while the character doesn't) and surprise (both the character and the audience don't know about something), i.e. between, in the case of *Vertigo*, disclosing Judy's identity to the audience near the end (surprise), as in the book, or doing that, as in the film, near the beginning of the second part (suspense)—it is manifest from his book of interviews with Truffaut that in both cases Hitchcock remains within the perspective of history,[201] i.e. that for him Judy, somebody different from Madeleine, exists in both alternatives. The two, suspense or surprise, would work equally well for history and for the forgery due to the search into the realm of the dead, since in the case of the dead/undead, i.e. the intrinsically *late*, forgery does not require that one begin with what happened earlier, i.e. does not require the surprise alternative rather than suspense, which gives us everything in the beginning. But with forgery in the case of the living (Lubitch's *To Be or Not To Be*), the surprise mode is mandatory. The alternative suspense/surprise overlaps with the alternative history/forgery only in cases of the forgery with the living.

In Bertolucci's *The Spider's Stratagem*, Draifa says emphatically of Athos-father: "He was afraid of nothing." Hence Athos does not betray out of cowardice (Draifa says to him "Athos you're a coward," but this with regard to his inability to leave his wife for her). "Why did he betray?" Because another, Athos-son/undead Athos, was to search for Athos-father's true story after his death, inflecting the story precisely because he did not stick to history. This non-teleological influence of what happened later on what preceded it in the case of the dead—one of the synonyms for *dead* is *late*—is given an explicit, visible form in one scene where Athos-father and Athos-son/undead Athos coexist, with Draifa as hinge between them: in her flashback, facing the camera away from Athos father who is looking out of the window giving her his back, she addresses Athos-son/undead Athos standing in Tara thirty six years later.

Athos (whether son or resurrected father) comes looking for the truth about the martyred Athos Magnani. This leads him to the theater. The goodbye from the sailor—who was the only other passenger to leave the train on which Athos arrived at Tara in the beginning shot of the film and who is at present running away from Tara as Athos heads to the theater—marks the threshold beyond which there is no return: Athos should have left Tara then. It is from then on that he is imprisoned. It may be that he intuited this but chose to risk precisely repeating an incident with the hope of diverting its fatal outcome. The problem with doing this is that even in the rare cases when the attempt succeeds, the person who is thus resurrected or rather who would not have died becomes the double of the person who did the repetition (the person may be his exact replica as in Bertolucci's *The Spider's Stratagem*, but he doesn't have to be, since the double has no image), this presaging the latter's death. But in the majority of cases the exact repetition once set in motion cannot be stopped, hence, in a variant to what takes place in Bertolucci's film, everything is repeated in the theater exactly as it was on the night when Athos-father was murdered there. That is we witness, past a certain threshold, the scanning of the same events in the space-time continuum (i.e., Athos is killed once more. The only index that a double scanning has occurred is that both we and Athos think for a moment that we are seeing his double in the theater[202]— a subjective error that reveals an otherwise undetectable objective duplication). If the resemblance between the two occurrences is not exact and events take place as in Bertolucci's film, then having discovered the truth, Athos son or resurrected father has to arrange for his own murder, so that it would seem that the presumably-fascist killers of Athos Magnani were trying to stop him from divulging their identity, this assuring the perpetuation of a falsehood (namely that Athos Magnani was murdered by fascists) which may have been the truth were it not for undead Athos' or Athos-son's search for the truth. Athos-son II comes, having been invited by Tara's mayor, to inaugurate by a speech the memorial to his father (this therefore happens before the coming of undead Athos or Athos-son, for by the time the latter arrives, the memorial has already been inaugurated and is part of Tara), and while giving the official story about Athos Magnani, the only version he knows, he hears voices in his head, one of which, a voice identical to his, whispers: "Who is Athos Magnani?... A traitor or a hero?... What was the real story of Athos Magnani?" Athos-son II is not trying to know the truth, yet the haunting voice(s)-over and the shots from the flashbacks of Athos-son or Athos resurrected, which have not yet occurred by the time of the inauguration speech and which we see interspersed in that speech, try to make him believe the truth as it transpired in relation to the search for Athos' truth by Athos-son or undead Athos. But in the bifurcation branch where Athos son II is it is much more probable that Athos-father did not betray but indeed was a hero killed by fascists (the legend about the specific circumstances of his death may belong only to the version of events encountered by undead Athos or Athos-son).

Is it out of infidelity that some (especially those for whom substitutions are anathema, for instance *Vertigo's* Scottie, who is very angered when he sees Carlotta's face in the painting replaced by his female friend's face) try to make someone resemble the loved dead person? Are they trying to replace the latter? Instead, this attempt at making someone reproduce the deceased is one of the ways—dying before dying is another—to sense, acknowledge the metamorphosis of the dead (by forcing more change on the dead, I discover the forced change upon the dead by both the dead and the living (and the dead component of the living)(but not by those who transcended rebirth-redeath)), his/her forced alteration/replacement: the double as clone to give us an inkling of the double as division in the mind. This infidelity is thus a fidelity that lingers with the dead beyond the threshold where s/he is replaced (*Life goes on*: the dead is replaced from the standpoint of the living. "Death goes on": the dead is replaced from her/his own standpoint). A fidelity to the dead's forced infidelity to himself/herself (if there is a resistance here on the part of the one being asked to imitate the dead, it would be because the infidelity of the bereaved asking him/her to imitate is a fidelity to the forced infidelity of the dead).

The criterion here to differentiate between those who search for the truth—whether they do so directly or by interposing someone to replicate the dead (someone who has therefore to get to the latter's truth)—to sense the metamorphosing dead, and those, dogmatics, who search for the truth of the dead, is that the latter project this sensing of a real change in the dead person back to the past: "I may have been mistaken about him" (as Robertson's wife says in Antonioni's *The Passenger*).

Since the dead's *reconnaissance* in the fluctuating, labyrinthine, illusory realm of undeath fails because s/he no longer has an image, the living who *create* a portrait of him/her may reach him/her (not a portrait of the dead as s/he was while still alive, nor a portrait of him/her as one guesses s/he has metamorphosed in undeath, nor an ideal portrait), s/he recognizing our portrait of him/her, feeling grateful to us (*reconnaissance* is, besides reconnoitering, both recognition and gratitude).

Unfinished Business:
There was and continues to be a prohibition against someone dying with unfinished business—*the wedding of the dead*, which is still performed into the present era in Maramures in Transylvania, sublates the premature death of an unmarried person of marriageable age; revenants are inscribed within a system of just retribution, of action that always necessitates a reaction—be *living* that unfinished business («the Scots held that the corpse of a suicide would not crumble until the time that he or she would have died had nature taken her course»). The vampire cannot be killed before s/he finishes what s/he set out to do, or before s/he possesses someone else, for instance Harker in Herzog's *Nosferatu*, who has to accomplish the

outstanding. In *The Testament of Dr Mabuse*, the late Dr. Mabuse can, by means of Baum, whom he had previously hypnotized, continue performing the crimes he had planned before his death (in the absence of a posthypnotic suggestion, sequelae to the hypnotic session, for instance age-regression or shrinking in size, may happen if the subjects did not adequately comply with the suggestion during the hypnosis session, that is if they thought of it as unfinished business[203]).

Unfinished business is the biggest obstacle to becoming (the unfinished business of Robertson in *Profession: Reporter*). Indeed, what is personality/consistency if not unfinished business? Of that which has no unfinished business (for instance, the Buddha), one has already always become it: it is our original face, our Buddha nature—without this implying that it is always there, for permanence implies that it belongs to a linear time, that it is extended indefinitely: it is in a structural sense, rather than a temporal one, that it is our original face.

Unfinished business, indebtedness—even in the form of Lyotard's indebtedness of the artist to the blank, of which he can present only a limited number of the indefinite possibilities (hence his/her mourning/melancholy (Lyotard, although against closure and return, is, through melancholia and unfinished business, affirming closure))—has to be dropped. Redeath-rebirth will never catch up with the infinite potentialities of the blank—one infinity is larger than the other. Indebtedness presupposes an interval where one can make comparisons, seeing that what occurred could have been otherwise; but the link itself has to be an occurrence. So that one never feels that other than what occurred could have occurred. No corrections. This is not determinism because even determinism presupposes the conceptual possibility of other alternatives that do not actualize. There is no determinism if one maintains oneself at the level of Lyotard's occurrence/Dzogchen's self-liberation of what happens.

Maybe to die before one's time means to have died before the *die before you die* could have been, not accomplished—since it creates a bifurcation—but attempted.

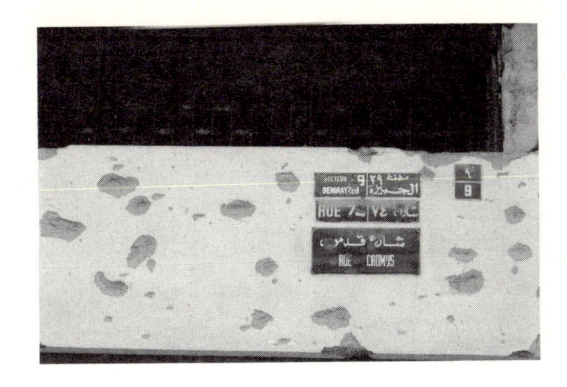

(See pp. 34-35)

Fear of Flying (1991), S. Morrissey

Have a Ball, Sw'theart (1987), S. Morrissey

Tablelady / Office (1991), S. Morrissey

(See pp. 59-60)

Turn-a-bout (1988), S. Morrissey

The Dismay of Mr. Boulager (1992),
Ted Julian Arnold
(See p. 61)

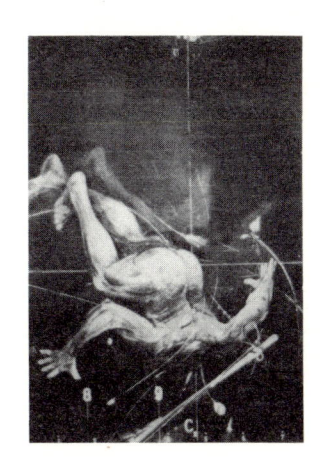

Velickovic and Patrice Trigano,
April 1986. (Courtesy *Cimaise*
#182)
(See p. 76)

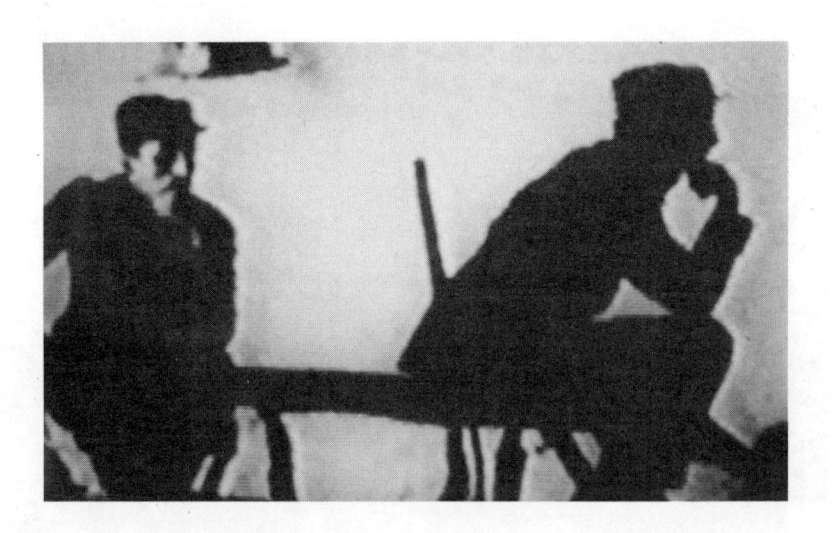

(See p. 87)

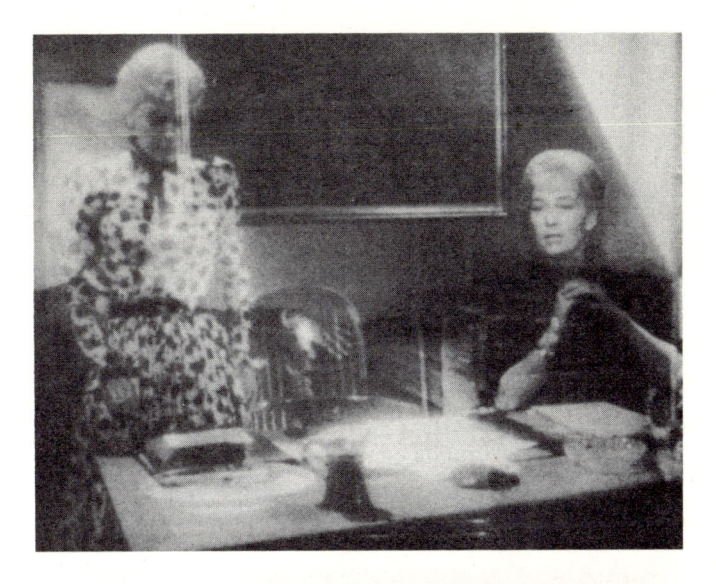

(See p. 128)

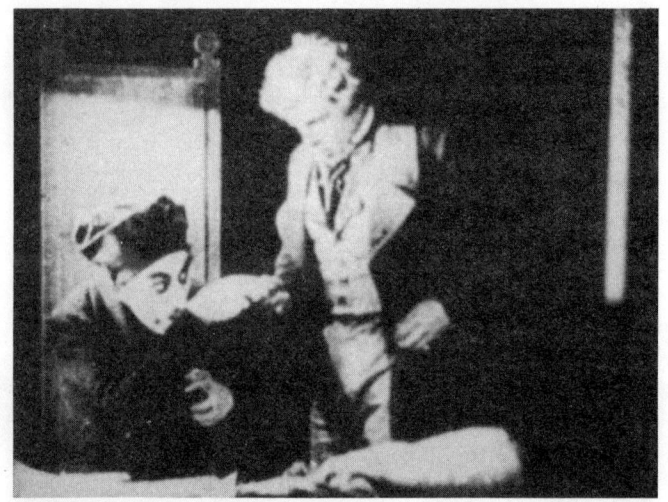

(See p. 136)

(See p. 158)

21 (1988), Ted Julian Arnold
(See p. 162)

(See pp. 161-162)

Second Child #1 (1993),
Ted Julian Arnold

Second Child #2 (1993),
Ted Julian Arnold

Second Child #3 (1993),
Ted Julian Arnold

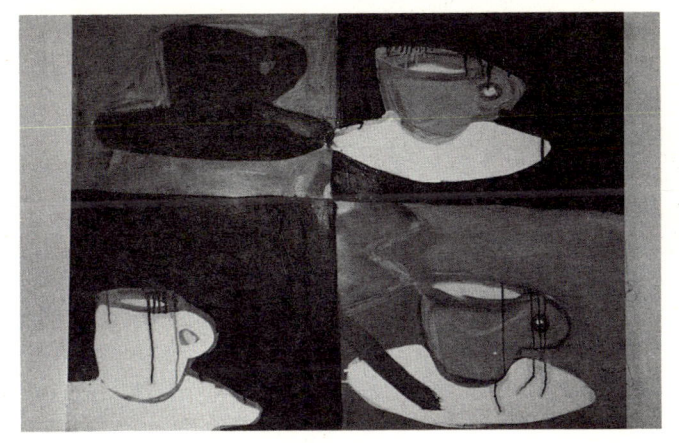

Basic (1989), Casey O'Conner
(See pp. 182-183)

(See p. 212)

(See p. 178)

(See p. 207)

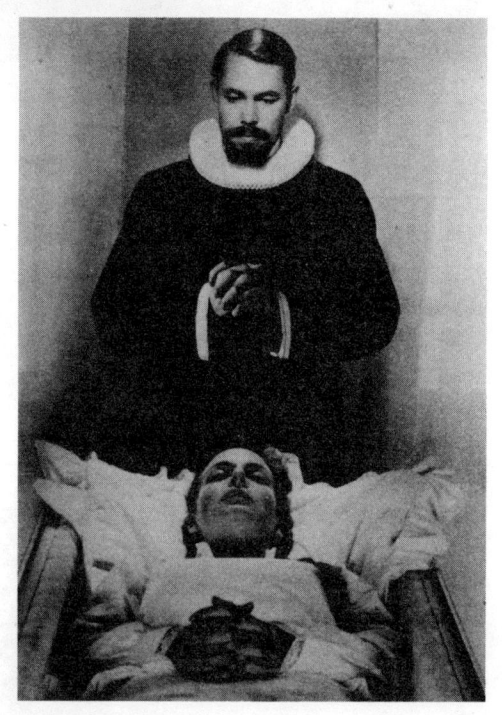

Who of the two is praying for the other? Or is it rather both? No, she is praying for him.

Death:
One can attempt to evade the realm of undeath by reaching either indefinite total immobilization, the freezing of everything, or, beyond *free association* (not only is there nothing free about *free association*, often the one who tries to resist the latter is struck with thought-blocking), universal interaction. The "omnipresent" act of observation that Vertov's kino-eye is can coexist with universal interaction precisely because it is not omnipresent after all[204] but contains refractory periods (in Vertov's cinema they would be the closing of the shutter of both the camera and the projector), for the absence of any refractory period leads to the Zeno's paradox in quantum theory (a radioactive atom would not decay if continuously observed)—the freeze-frames in *Man with a Movie-camera* indicate that *Kino-eye* did manage at times to become a total observation.

Does every aristocrat who affirms life have to die before he dies in order to affirm that cruel carnavalesque period? Is it the case that there is no affirmation of life without the affirmation of death, not as pure inexistence, but as undeath, the life of death, the Bardo state? But how can one affirm the realm that admits of no negation? Certainly logically one can. But really, concretely how can one affirm what admits of no negation or affirmation but only posits (even the uncertainty is posited)? How can one be part of what cannot affirm (itself) and still affirm it (is one to get to the point where death is affirmed or is one to get to the point where one is detached?)? Affirm the realm of undeath up to the point of bringing forth children even though they in turn may have to undergo it?

LSD produces a dissolution of ego boundaries, an interpenetration of outside/inside—during the LSD session he could not smoke because he had lost all feeling of the existence of boundaries between the inside and the outside (exhalation/inhalation thrives on that distinction)—a sudden disappearance of the selective membrane with things. Hence it is immoral to explain a paranoid trip solely by the psychology of the person who took the psychedelic, as, for instance, due to his fear of and resistance to ego loss (those not highly hypnotizable almost never have a *hidden observer*, while in 20% of the most hypnotizable subjects, a *hidden observer* exists) and/or by a bad setting. At that level, Freud's personal unconscious has been supplanted not only with his phylogenetic unconscious and with Jung's collective unconscious of archetypes but also with the transpersonal unconscious experienced by schizophrenics (in a modified version of the double-slit experiment, R. L. Pfleegor and L. Mandel used two independent single-mode lasers. The apparatus was such that there was never more than one photon flying inside it. They still got interference, and here too the interference precluded their knowing from which of the two lasers the photon was ejected.[205] It is the same in altered states in which interference occurs: who ejected a thought?). To be dead is to be haunted by others: the living, the undead, the fleeting (inexistence, like emptiness, is full of fluctuations: fluctuations in the form of thoughts, affects, complete and incomplete phrases, etc.), and the nonexistent (*presence*).

When one is traversed by everything (death being the great intermingling), isn't it natural for one's desire to be transfixed on that part of the human body that has the most to do with what preserves selectivity, that has the most to do with the immune system—blood?

The living win the struggle against the undead by accomplishing death-as-extinction (if there is such a thing) rather than by surviving the struggle, since by becoming survivors they would have turned into the unliving.

Let us opt for the possibility that death can only be experienced in life (through LSD, schizophrenia (the incredible number of people and animals and sometimes plants one becomes, the dissolution of the mind into so many alien modes of thinking/associating), etc.[206] (carnival remains merely a parody of death)), and that once one dies biologically there is a total extinction (a compulsion was taking hold of him, to look at films where someone is cut into pieces or at autopsies, hoping to suddenly be struck by the realization that nothing remains after death). For otherwise we are forced to believe in the world of death/undeath, a world of illusion, as the truth. Psychiatrists who use hypnosis in their practice often use ideomotor signaling as a probe into the unconscious. The unconscious of the hypnotized subject is addressed directly and is asked to raise one of the subject's fingers in case the answer to the question of the hypnotist-psychiatrist is a "yes" and to raise another finger if the answer is a "no." Through a posthypnotic suggestion the ideomotor response registering unconscious reactions and responses can continue even after the person opens his eyes and becomes aware of what is happening around him. The hypnotist can then say: "See, your unconscious is giving a different response than the one you are giving consciously, and it, rather than you, is telling the truth." On being confronted with a finger in his hand answering in the negative in response to a question addressed to the unconscious on whether it accepts to be rid of the pain the person is suffering from—this supposedly indicating *secondary gain*—the subject can always answer that s/he may have been given a posthypnotic suggestion to react in such a way. Is that to be automatically decried as a form of psychoanalytical *resistance*? In rare cases, while acknowledging the unconscious desire, one resists taking it as the truth. For one must not believe death and the unconscious as truth (one must above all not take things in a *deadly serious* manner (death is this absolute seriousness, the absolute literality of everything. An outsider—and who is more of an outsider than the dead?—most often takes things literally (the opposite of the common sense attitude, which is most often metaphorical/symbolical), catches the literal meaning of words and expressions (one should try as much as possible not to use figurative language, with its exaggerations ("I haven't seen her in ages", "I haven't seen her in centuries", etc.), in the presence of psychotics, for many figurative expressions are the transcription in the common language of literal happenings in the altered states), that which was hidden behind the metaphor (Nietzsche's «one is not courageous enough to accept what one already knows» often applies to the literal meaning hidden behind the metaphorical/symbolical (the initiate undergoes death, and not in a metaphorical/symbolical sense)). But that which is *staring one in the eye* in altered states, the literal, is often doing so to hypnotize one), in a *grave* manner, when dealing with the *grave* and death. One must move to other matters (before the stage of fascination and paralysis sets in), since taking things too seriously almost always means one will behave in a cowardly way towards them). Cocteau missed the point completely in his film *Orpheus* (1950), where it is said, "there is no lying in the land of death"—except if this be the lie the dead tell the living. In Kurosawa's *Rashomon* (1950) the testimony of the dead through the mouth of the medium is no more authentic, truthful, than that of the living.

Some have extrapolated from vampires' extreme sensitivity to light and various other symptoms that vampirism is a form of porphyria; this remains merely an analogy since porphyria patients are alive whereas vampires are undead. Schrodinger's cat, which is dead-alive before measurement, in a superimposition of the two states of death and life, is nonetheless not vampiric, for the vampire, except in the less interesting vampire films, in which s/he is a superimposition of being dead and being alive, is undead, that is neither alive—within the known laws of life—nor dead hence extinct.

Sartre writes in *Nausea* that things assume the aspect of adventure only when we relive what occurred from the end side, after it has finished. Death being the end (that never ends), everything that happens after/in it is an adventure. Guide books (*The Egyptian Book of the Dead*, *The Tibetan Book of the Dead*) are of no value there (but a guide, a master is necessary).

It is interesting to compare how two German filmmakers, Wenders and Herzog, dealt with the dying of another person who belongs to cinema history: to those who think of death as pure and simple nonexistence, Wenders would have seemed very well equipped to make a film about/with the dying Nicholas Ray, since prior to the filming of *Lightning Over Water* (1979-80) he had already made several films that dealt in one way or another with the death of film directors: in *Kings of the Road* (1976), the actor Hanns Zischler reads in a newspaper about Fritz Lang's death; in *The American Friend* (1977) Nicholas Ray plays the role of a painter mistakenly thought by everybody to be already dead, and other film directors acting in the diegesis as Mafia men (Sam Fuller, Daniel Schmid (in the role of Ingraham), Peter Lilienthal (in the role of Marcangelo)) are killed in the film. Wenders arrives as soon as possible to film *Lightning Over Water* but seems to be wishing that he has come too late—what is the filming called which takes place after the filming ended? The reshoot— that is, that the whole film be as it were a reshoot/pick-up-shoot with Nick as revenant (one can imagine Wenders' frustration: why can't Nick do in *Lightning Over Water* what the character he played in *The American Friend* managed to do so well, be a revenant while still alive?). After *Lightning Over Water*, he went on to make *The State of Things* (1982), in which the film director in the diegesis is killed, and *Tokyo-Ga* (1985), a tribute to a dead film director, Ozu. On the contrary, Herzog delays arriving to the hospital where Lotte Eisner is dying, to postpone her death (he writes in *Walking in Ice*: «At the end of November, 1974, a friend from Paris called and told me that Lotte Eisner was seriously ill and would probably die. I said that this must not be, not at this time, German cinema could not do without her now, we would not permit her death... I set off on the most direct route to Paris, in full faith, believing that she would stay alive if I came on foot.»[207] Not to let her die before it is time both from the perspective of what is still outstanding in her life but also in terms of the services she could still render to German cinema (we witness here the taboo on unfinished business, which is a central theme in vampire films (Herzog's *Nosferatu*—))), and arrives in such an altered state that it is no longer clear who is in danger of not comprehending the enigmatic words of the other[208].

The mystical *die before you die* becomes the shallow die before you die of cryonics. Many people who have their bodies cryopreserved are really trying, most often without knowing it, to postpone undeath much more than to evade death-as-extinction. In this regard, there is a huge difference between being cryopreserved only after death has occurred (even if the interval between the death and the freezing was not long enough to cause irremediable damage) and being frozen before dying; in the former case the freezing followed by reanimation would not have short-circuited undeath.

Any definite quantity compared to infinity is zero, so that we the living are in the eyes of someone who experiences infinite time, such as the schizophrenic or the one on LSD, already dead, never were alive, never were but dead, and that's how we look, that is how infinite time changes us into ourselves as dead.

In Dreyer's *Passion of Joan of Arc*, Massieu asks Joan: "Your deliverance?" Joan replies: "My death!" *Vampyr* shows that death is no deliverance. *Ordet* as the deliverance from death. Then *Gertrud* as the coexistence of the two: death (old Gertrud says: "Have I lived? No") and, much earlier, resurrection (a younger Gertrud says to Erland: "You make me alive again")—only, in *Gertrud* we are dealing with the cheaper version of death, death as deadened life, as cheap as *dead labor*, rather than with death as undeath.

One can no longer say: "today, I lived a day too long." These words apply only if after death there is nothing, if one dissolves totally. If at all, one may say it on the day when one discovers one cannot die, for that, rather than any specific disaster, is the disaster per se.

Bataille writes that death cannot be experienced except through identification with a character in a fiction/spectacle. This is true, but not because death is the extinction of life and hence cannot be experienced, but because it is stolen, experienced by another, by the one who replaces one there, the double, hence by another character/other characters. That is, even when undeath happens to the one who died, it is in the form of spectacle, of which s/he is the spectator. And it is then the most difficult to accept to be a spectator. Maybe it is in death that we can experience the death of another, becoming the spectator of the spectator.

If anxiety is induced in consciousness from the unconscious, then when one dies, i.e. when consciousness totally disappears, there would be no anxiety, only the unconscious like an indefinite lapse. In which case *our* death can only be experienced by schizophrenics and some of those in altered states.

Murder in mystery novels reactivates a whole gamut of archaic beliefs, and this irrespective of whether the mystery story, for instance Doyle's *The Hound of Baskervilles*, explicitly invokes the supernatural:

— The communication with the dead: in Agatha Christie's *Appointment With Death*, at 4:15 Lady Westholm, in the company of the suggestible Miss Pierce, paused below the ledge, shouted up to Miss Boyton, and remarked to Miss Pierce: "Very rude just to snort like that." Nadine Boyton returned to the camp at approximately 4:40, sat on a chair next to Miss Boyton and had a conversation with her, leaving her at 4:50. Carolyn Boyton affirms that she returned to the camp, where her stepmother was, at 5:10, went up to the latter and spoke to her for a while. Raymond Boyton affirms that he returned to the camp at 5:50, went up to his stepmother, exchanged a few words with her, then went to his tent and afterward to the marquee. It is later revealed that the death of Miss Boyton occurred around 4:10.

— Being in two places at the same time (by means of a false alibi[209]), which echoes the primitive's belief in astral bodies and doubles: in Christie's *Thirteen at Dinner* (1933), Jane Wilkinson, who is identified by two witnesses, the butler and the secretary, as having been to see her husband at 10 p.m. the night of his murder (his dead body is found in the library of his London home; time of the murder: between ten and eleven at night), is also identified as having gone to a formal dinner party at the house of Sir Montague Corner at Chiswick that same night, arriving at quarter to nine p.m. and leaving at half past eleven p.m. (during the party she left the dinner table only for a few minutes in the company of the butler to answer a phone call).

— In primitive cultures, the name of the dead, and in some cases, even the names of the other members of the tribe, of animals and plants, was changed. In mystery stories, we encounter the change of name of 1) the dead: in Christie's *Murder on the Orient Express*, Poirot propounds two solutions to the murder. According to the first, the murderer joined the train at Belgrade or Vincovci, changed into a Wagon Lit Uniform, mortally stabbed Ratchett at quarter past twelve, then left the train before it became stuck in a snowdrift at half past twelve. The dead Ratchett changes into Cassetti, who is, according to the second solution, killed by the twelve occupants of the Calais-Stamboul coach, who are avenging the murders the latter committed. It is hence neither simply as the coach's other twelve occupants' red herring, nor out of humanitarian considerations on the part of Poirot and M. Bouc (the representative of Compagnie Internationale des wagons lits) that there are two solutions to the murder, since there would not have been a Cassetti on the train had there not been the first murder that changed Ratchett into Cassetti (Lumet missed a reconstruction flashback here: it should have shown the hypothetical murderer, "a small dark man with a womanish voice," accomplish the murder according to Poirot's scenario (this visual rendering would have imbued Poirot's first scenario with a bigger quotient of reality than its mere verbal relating)). Thus it is not at all accidental that one additional passenger was to take the train but didn't. It is a weakness in Lumet's film adaptation to have started with the section on the Armstrong story, since this later establishes Ratchett as already Cassetti even before he is murdered; it is appropriate that in Christie's book the Armstrong case is mentioned posterior to the murder (Lumet missed his second flashback here). The bad forgery perpetuated by Lumet makes of Poirot's first solution a bad counterfeit, at best merely a counterfeit induced by humanitarian, hence extrinsic, reasons. The change of the name of the dead also occurs in the form of burial under a false certificate; substitution of one corpse for another (Chesterton's *The Secret Garden*), etc. 2) The change of the name of plants: at the end of Ruth Rendell's short story *Means of Evil*, we are informed that the shaggy cap (*coprinus comatus*) was replaced with ink cap (*coprinus atramentarius*). 3) The change of the name of at least some of the survivors: in *The Maltese Falcon*, after the death of detective Miles Archer, Samuel Spade's female client's name changes from Wonderly to Leblanc to Brigid O'Shaughnessy.

— Tunneling in the locked-room mysteries: how did the murderer manage to get out of the room in which the murder happened although its door(s) and windows are found sealed from the inside and no footprints lead to it (Robert Arthur's *The 51st Sealed Room; or, The MWA Murder*; Chesterton's *The Secret Garden*; "Sapper"'s *The Horror at Staveley Grange*)?

— In primitive cultures there is no notion of natural death; the death of someone has been willed by another (whether human, dead, demon or god). Similarly, in mystery stories it is extremely rare for what seems to be obviously a suicide or an accident to be accepted as just that rather than as a murder. As in *Murder on the Orient Express*, the reason for Poirot's nondisclosure of the truth in Christie's *Appointment With Death*—Lady Westholme is the one who murdered Miss Boyton—to the police and the diegetic general public is not to be attributed solely to humanitarian reasons on his part, but must also be attributed to a structural reason (this time not pertaining to the diegetic world but there to influence extra-diegetic factors): although neither the police nor the general public and the newspapers doubt that Miss Boyton and Lady Westholme died of accidents (according to the *Evening Shout* Lady Westholme, M.P., died as a result of a tragic accident, the revolver she was using going off accidentally), the reader of Christie's novel, like a superstitious primitive, *knows* that these deaths have been willed and are in no way accidents.

There is a secondary elaboration to place this changing of the name (beginning from the end, from the found corpse, to then reconstruct what happened does not find its necessity in the procedure of deductive reasoning, for the latter can be applied, in a projective way toward the future, as we see in Poe's *The Murders in the Rue Morgue* during the walk Dupin has with the narrator, a close friend of his, as well as in many of the Holmes stories—but in forgery), the communication with the dead, the refusal to believe in a natural or accidental death, the taboo on touching the dead or anything touched by him/her (the avoidance of leaving any fingerprints), the presence of a person in two places at the same time, and tunneling (which can be accounted for by one of the solutions John Dickson Carr gives in the chapter titled "The Locked-Room Lecture" in his novel *The Three Coffins*) within an acceptable rational scheme, rather than leave its uncanny, archaic origination manifest. That it is a secondary revision is also shown by the fact that companions to mystery stories stop in their synopses of the plots at the presentation of the facts before the detective begins to solve the puzzle (their legitimate excuse is that they must not reveal the whodunnit).

Guilt:
We notice the conjunction of death with guilt, already in the Bible, although there it is twice covered-up/inverted, made to look as if mortality is due to guilt, and guilt is due to a specific, willed act. But guilt precedes any specific willed act precisely because mortality precedes guilt: it is because there is death and hence the unconscious that there is a guilt that has nothing to do with any intentional, willed acts. I, but also the dead and schizophrenics, in fact everybody, with the possible exception of the yogi—yoga works to burn, do away with the unconscious—am always guilty toward the dead and the schizophrenics, those who died-before-dying. Ghost and vampire do nothing but free associate, that is why they return-to/haunt life, the scene of crime both against and of the undead (the murderer but also the victim return to the scene of the crime).

This guilt is also encountered in cases where temporality becomes idiosyncratic: in James Cameron's *Terminator 2—Judgement Day* (1991) someone's invention of a very advanced computer chip results in the long run in a nuclear war that kills over three-billion people in 1997. A terminator is sent from the future to stop him in 1994 from finishing its development. When he hears the story, he decides to help the terminator to destroy it, but he is still guilty of the death of three-billion people: his change of one future will not alter the other one(s). I am guilty in 1994 for what I did in 1997, though I will not do it this time, though I may die long before 1997.

Matte:

The photograph of Syberberg and Herzog on page 24 of *Syberberg* (*Cahiers du Cinéma*, numéro hors-serie, 1980), of both the one who does everything in a studio, even to the second degree, since the studio often remains vacant except of the *front projection*, hence does not become a set, and the fiction film director who has an abhorrence of studio shooting, who stressed the most shooting in real settings (*Fata Morgana* was shot in the Cameroons; *Aguirre, the Wrath of God* in the Peruvian jungle; *Fitzcarraldo* in the Amazon jungle), which may at first seem idiosyncratic, almost a matte photograph, is in reality not idiosyncratic at all: if Herzog shoots in these natural settings it is not because they are real/truthful (Herzog told Fini to say certain lines he wrote as her own in his documentary *Land of Silence and Darkness*), not artificial, but because they create, through the hardships/complications/dangers that one undergoes in them, the right mental set-up (this is reinforced by delaying writing the dialogue to just before taking the shot, hence under the maximum of pressure, in a far-from equilibrium state). Otherwise there would be a contradiction between Herzog's insistence on shooting in natural settings and his hypnotizing his actors during the filming of *Heart of Glass*, for hypnotism is precisely the absence of context: «You move as if in slow-motion, because the whole room you are in is filled with heavy water [in *At Land*, Maya Deren intercuts shots of herself crawling on a table covered with plates to shots of her penetrating a thicket. Rather, she should have undergone self-hypnosis: "You advance on the table as if you are penetrating a thicket"—thus dispensing with the thicket shots. A cinema of overtones, superimposing the impression of a different movement on what one is seeing. An *as if* that no longer has anything metaphorical about it, but has to do with an *I feel, I have the impression*. Were one though to get entranced by the shot/scene, one would be prone to actually no longer just have the impression/feeling but to see the shot of Deren advancing in a thicket intercut or superimposed on the shot of her creeping on the table]... Under water you can move only with difficulty, although your body has become very light. You drift. You don't walk». Hypnotism is a keying/matting before the latter was invented («You see your partner, but you look through him, as you look through a window.» During one of the hypnosis sessions Herzog conducted prior to the filming of *Heart of Glass*, one subject said in answer to an inquiry concerning what he was seeing: «And every night the trees disappear altogether, and only the sleeping birds remain.»[210]) This is very clear in hypnotic phenomena such as positive hallucination (in Browning's *Dracula* the doctor looks in the mirror at Mina speaking to the vampire and sees her alone) or negative hallucination, whether they happen during the trance or posthypnotically. In *Heart of Glass* the actors hypnotized by Herzog most often act as if the other person(s) and objects at the same location with them are not present there, were matted later. This absence of context is achieved here not through video and film special effects (frontal projection, etc.) but through special effects (hypnosis) done with the psyche of the actor.

Magritte uses "matting" in *L'Empire des lumières* (1954): the lower part of the painting is at night with the lights turned on in the house (*day for night*?), while we see in the upper part of the painting a daylight sky with few white clouds (*Night for Day*?). Similarly, at one point in Bill Viola's *The Reflecting Pool* the pool is at night while the surrounding scenery is a daytime landscape. It is hence unfortunate that no vampire film shows the trap Harker's wife sets for the vampire—retaining him till (her) dawn—backfiring on her, the vampire standing in a nighttime part of the frame with his victim in a daytime part of the frame (Picasso's *Sleeping Nude*, 1904). If such an encounter has to be shown without the recourse to matting, the shot would have to be filmed during the *blue hour*, the brief spell between the close of day and the evening when one gets a Magritte-like coexistence of day and night in separate parts of the frame. While the vampire stands in the night and his victim stands in the daylight, there is the *blue hour*'s minute of silence between the moment night birds stop making sounds and the moment day birds start making them (are the birds commemorating the victim's death?): the victim of the vampire undergoes a minute of silence commemorating his death. This indicates the kind of sound track that one should have if one uses mattes instead of shooting the scene during the *blue hour*.

For horizon, the matte line.

The danger of the matte is that you can be transported like the Jews to Auschwitz, like the Jews to Palestine[211] (like the Palestinians out of Palestine then out of Israel[212]).

He got rid of the clean garbage strewn around in an ordered way that they call chairs, tables, closets. You see nothing in his apartment but the white walls and a few laconic books. But there remained, since he was a Stanislavsky actor, the imaginary object that he could evoke as if it were real and rehearse with it. So then he got rid of his acting.

In the near future we will encounter a proliferation of activities that seem one-sided because they are only later complemented, by means of matting, with what they are responding to or trying to initiate—as long as one of two people is telepathic, the two complementary activities do not at any point have to be within the same frame: the fight with an invisible bear in Herzog's *Heart of Glass*. We are certain to also witness the proliferation of this phenomenon's pathological version, which occurs when the first stage of the matting process is not followed by the complementary stage, and which will exactly correspond to the *vacuum activities* of animals (an idiosyncratic form of miming), which occur in the absence of the stimulus that usually elicits the corresponding normal activity: canaries (*Serinus canaria*) deprived of nest material will perform the movements of weaving material into a non-existent nest; starlings (*Sturnus vulgaris*) which have not caught flies for some time may go through the motions of catching and eating non-existent flies. The invisibility of the object or stimulus (for instance, a slap) and the silence that accompanies such invisibility reintroduce miming (not just, as in *Who Framed Roger Rabbit*, at the phase of the filming)—which one saw at the beginnings of cinema, in its silent phase—into modern cinema (Antonioni's *Blow Up*, 1967), and not, as in Chaplin's *Limelight* (1951), as a vestige and hence in an occulted form (the bug that is so small it is invisible)—and will do so increasingly in the future. Is what occurs to the photographer in the final scene of Antonioni's *Blow-up*, his following with his eyes a ball that does not exist and then throwing it back to the mimes who were playing a tennis match with it, a prophetic illustration of the aforementioned form of pathology? Or is it rather to be inscribed within the kind of meditative practices, such as T'ai Chi, that train one to trace what is, at least in the first stages of the training, intangible, for instance directing the breath/chi by thought through given paths through the body? Is it merely due to suggestion (we often hear in hypnosis phrases such as: "the tension in your body and mind is going down from head to neck to thigh to leg to floor")—in which case it would be as difficult not to follow this ball as to comply with the (waking) suggestion not to follow the soccer ball in Wenders-Handke's *The Goalie's Anxiety at the Penalty Kick*? If one leans toward the first alternative, it is that only after Antonioni's film camera follows the invisible ball does the photographer accept its presence. What applies to objects applies also to spaces; hence when in one scene in Toufic's *Night For Day* the black matte is not replaced by a shot, the ceiling remaining black, this is to be considered neither as an iris effect nor as a pictorial device to stress the horizontal (in *Potemkin*, Eisenstein used a black matte at the sides of the frame as a pictorial device to stress the vertical coordinate in the shot where the people of Odessa are shown descending the staircase). Increasingly, we will witness parts of the shot used as a black matte but not replaced by shots from other locations/times (denoting either the absence of off-screen or *presence*, both encountered in many altered states).

At present, the frame has so much that comes at one *out of the blue* (of the matte).

During the rehearsals of *Who Framed Roger Rabbit*, rubber figures of the animation characters were moved through the scenes in which they were to appear so that both the actors and the camera operator would know the exact trajectory of the animation character. «Then when we shot the scene, we didn't use the figure and the operator [and the actors] would have to imagine where the character was in relation to the dialogue, which was being delivered by an off-camera actor...»[213] Matting, which does away with the aura, since it does away with the context—making the far and the near and different temporalities intermingle—itself creates an aura, since the gaze of the person looking at the figure that is matted later is never centered but traces a circle of confusion. It is no longer only the cinematographer who experiences and knows how difficult it is to accompany someone in a pan, zoom or even a static shot (*Distracted*); the actor who has to interact within a shot with an element that will be matted later experiences and knows it as well.

Casey O'Connor's painting *Basic* (1989) shows four coffee cups, one in each of four quadrants. The cup and its plate in the upper left quadrant are in black, the background in gray and brown; the background in the lower left quadrant is black (the coffee cup is yellow); the background in the upper right quadrant is black (the coffee cup and the plate are yellow). This black adds one more use to the *very different* usages of the monochrome in painting (Mark Rothko, Francis Bacon, Barnett Newman, Ad Reinhardt, etc. (usages ranging from the purely abstract to the traditionally figurative)). What we are witnessing in this case is the transcription of (the first stage of) a process taken from film and photography, matting, into painting. It is a standard procedure to paint backgrounds that would otherwise cost a lot to construct. Because the use of paintings for the background means that the characters cannot penetrate the latter, this is bound, at least in certain instances, to secrete a content that revolves around a trauma and/or hysterical characters. Hence, in Alfred Hitchcock's *Marnie* (1964), the five different names (perhaps two of the different names Marnie used for her five impersonations—Marion Holland is one of the five—were Cindy and Sherman), social security numbers, and hair colors and styles of Marnie, her hypnoid states, frigidity, and the dissociation manifest both in the obvious back projections for her horse-riding, a procedure that separates her from the background, and during the scene of the robbery where the dissociation is displaced to the set, the screen cut in half by the wall of the office where the safe is, so that as we look at Marnie embezzling the money in one half of the frame while in the other half the maid cleans the other offices, it is exactly as if we were watching a multi-screen shot—an impression reinforced by the fact that when Marnie closes the heavy door of the safe, the maid is not alerted by the sound, does not hear it—up to having the strange impression of watching a parallel montage as Marnie walks in the direction of the other offices. It is quite clear that in the scene near the beginning of the film where we first see Marnie visit her mother, the background of the street where the mother lives is painted (the rear section of the two buildings to either side of the street and the ship (Marnie, when still a child, killed a sailor)),[214] Marnie returning to the site of what cannot be penetrated—a trauma. In the last shot, after the acting out, after reaching the trauma[215], Marnie and her husband drive into what was, at the beginning of the film, a painted background[216]. Hence the last section of Kurosawa's *Dreams* (1990)—where in the Van Gogh section the diegetic spectator literally penetrates into the paintings—succeeds in confronting the trauma of a nuclear holocaust. What is fishy about *Basic*, what haunts as a *presence*? The fish that is not matted into the quadrants to replace the black, but appears at the corner where the four quadrants meet. Two white spots, one at the upper left quadrant and one at the lower right quadrant form the eye of the fish; the background of the left edge of the lower right quadrant forms the major part of the fish's body. We witness here a confirmation that where the matte is not replaced there is a *presence*. More than the black of the matte or the *presence*, what draws us in this painting is the white in the ears of the cups, a white radically different from the representational one in the cups themselves (merely the color of their interiors).

Parallel Montage:
Two men are talking in a room. A painting can be seen behind them. Suddenly the painting becomes transparent, and we see the female lover of one of the men in the company of her girlfriend in the latter's apartment, which happens to be in a totally different section of the city. Then the camera dollies from the room through a corridor that is still part of the house where the two men are sitting and into a room in the woman's apartment, just as the two women

enter the room. One does not have to see the rest of Francis Coppola's *One From the Heart* to know that the two lovers, who we saw breaking up earlier in the film, are destined for each other. This contiguity and tunneling is an ironic twist to Bazin's proscription of montage (no parallel montage) when the simultaneous presence within the frame-as-cage would put at stake the life of one or both of the two protagonists, since it replaces the risk of death with the *till death do us part*[217]. In *Meshes of the Afternoon* the female character standing in a grassy space raises her foot in a first shot stepping on a sandy shore in the next shot then raises her foot again stepping into a grassy space in the following shot then into her room in a fourth shot. While Deren's steps join the outside to the outside, Coppola's screen joins the inside to the inside.

Death happens on two planes. Archaic societies had a minimal separation, differentiation between the two, hence to them any death is willed. For us there is a separation of the two, the reality/life realm (where death not only can be natural or accidental but most often is so) and the undeath realm; moreover, many of us who are not oblivious to the latter realm do not believe that on that plane everything is willed; even there the accidental predominates. We know now that *precision bombing* was an imprecise term to describe much of what took place in the Gulf War, since only 7% of the bombs dropped on the Iraqi forces in Kuwait and on Iraq were precision bombs. While we are highly impressed by the very high precision of the Tomahawk missiles fired from ships off-shore hitting their targets in Baghdad, we are much more impressed with Jacob Maker-Zoltan Abbassid-Cain moving in David Blair's *Wax, Or the Discovery of Television Among the Bees* (1992), despite all sorts of interim inaccuracies (that Jacob Maker is Zoltan Abbassid only *seems* to be an imprecision) and uncertainties (Jacob Maker suddenly forgets where he is, and, on several instances, is uncertain how much time elapsed between two occurrences; his assertion that he could not move beyond the perimeter of the acre is not very accurate, since the perimeter and the frame do not coincide (the black around the frame is an instantiation of the absence of off-screen; indeed, when the protagonist reaches the edge of the frame in instances where black surrounds the frame, there is either a dissolve to another frame or else the character acknowledges the limitation ("I couldn't go beyond the perimeter of the acre")), the latter extending slightly beyond the former: the protagonist could have taken one or two steps beyond the perimeter), from Cain's time through 1818 and 1919 to 1991[218] to reach and fire at an Iraqi tank at the exact second it was being fired at on another plane, that of reality/life (this superimposition of two causes for one effect is encountered also in Dreyer's *Ordet*: what is the source of the light on the wall? Is it the lights of the doctor's car or is it the negative shadow of the man with the scythe coming (from the beginning section of *Vampyr*) to claim Inger's life? And in the superimposition in the "+" of both Cain's sign and the target marker in the flight simulation machines). Only someone who has died before dying can achieve that precise registration of the two planes (those who consider that no one on the other plane is killed accidentally/naturally, but that every death is willed, can consider *Wax* to be Blair's hint that even in the case of the Iraqis who were killed by imprecision bombing their deaths on the other plane were precise). In comparison to this precision, the utter sloppiness of the American Forces' precision, since while they were precise on one plane they remain indiscriminate on the other plane. I am grateful to those who demonstrated against the Gulf War, but also and above all to Jacob Maker-Zoltan Abbassid, who killed two Iraqis on the other plane. Vengeance for the dead can happen at the reality plane, for instance through attacking American interests, and still would not account for the dead. "They were dead, and vengeance was their life." The vengeance of the dead for their total anonymity during their life as far as their enemy was concerned can take the form of destining someone to kill them on the other plane. *Wax* presents us with a parallel montage not to save (the parallel montage to save, which generally presupposes telecommunication (already in Griffith's *An Unseen Enemy* (1912), one of the two heroines locked in a room adjoining the one where a burglary is in progress succeeds in phoning her brother for help, setting in motion the high-speed chase to save them (the telephone plays the same role in *The Lonely Villa*); in *The Lonedale Operator* (1911), the telegraphist threatened by thieves locks herself inside the office and telegraphs asking for help, setting in motion the rescue by the train operator) had become impossible for the Iraqis during the Gulf War since all their telecommunications were either destroyed or neutralized/blinded (many of the wounded Iraqis in the bunkers in Kuwait died for lack of adequate medical care)) but to affirm and redeem the killing: a parallel montage to reach the dead in time to kill *him* on the undeath plane just as he is being indiscriminately killed on the reality/life plane—to be able to achieve this parallel montage, Jacob Maker had to make telecommunication possible again: the bee-TV. We will often find those who were on the point of disappearance going through a more extreme depersonalization to find a uniqueness to those who were treated as anonymous (a uniqueness which does not necessarily reside in, indeed often precludes, explicit peculiarities: the two Iraqi soldiers killed by Jacob Maker are quite singular even though having no names and even though we are provided with no specifics about them): Jacob Maker, and probably Blair himself, had to go through *all the names of history* [including Fat Boy, the first plutonium bomb] *are I*. Saddam is not Hitler[219], but Jacob Maker, a flight-simulation programmer in 1991, iis Zoltan Abbassid, who died in 1919[220]. In gratitude to David Blair, the video maker of the first adequate aesthetic response to the Gulf War, a kindred spirit, even if in a lapse "in gratitude" were to become "ingratitude," even if we were to betray each other on that other plane.

The undead has no mirror image:
In Georges Franju's *Eyes without a Face* (1959), Christiane, a young woman whose face was deformed as a result of a car accident, is to be given a transplant of the facial skin of another woman. She enters the room where the other woman is stretched anesthetized for the operation, and looks at her. Franju does not cut from the long shot from behind Christiane to an extreme close-up of her eyes and then to her pov of the face of the one lying anesthetized. Her pov would have shown her her mirror image. What we are witnessing here is the prohibition against showing a mirror image of the vampire (there is a second scene where we also witness this prohibition: the woman whose facial skin has been taken, and who is covered by bandages, manages to flee the room in which she was imprisoned and wanders in the house. One then expects that she would encounter Christiane,

who at present has her face, seeing her (negative) mirror image; the two women do not meet), this indicating that the film is a vampire film, not just in a general sense (the vampire as one who parasitically drains another) but in a very specific sense (the vampire as an undead that drains the living). But it is clear that Christiane is not an undead. Has a certain logic led us astray? Then one suddenly remembers that at the beginning of the film the disfigured corpse of another woman was passed as Christiane's corpse; this was followed by the scene of Christiane's fake funeral, with the other woman's dead body buried in a grave with Christiane's name engraved on the tombstone.

The vampire has no mirror image even in the form of body-image, hence he does not and cannot have a *phantom limb*.

The vampire, who is excluded from being fixed on the cornea or on a photograph, hence who is deprived of the upside down facet to those who have an image, "lives" at times upside down (Badham's *Dracula*)(the return of the repressed?).

At no point did their [many, if not most, non-posed photographs] referent really exist:
Looking at many, if not most, non-posed photographs (even those that were not altered, digitally or otherwise), he knew now that at no point did their referent really exist, at no point did they belong to (the film of) life. He knew that they were equivalent to film posters that show a shot the spectator will not see in the film (most professional productions hire a still photographer to take stills during rehearsals and/or film takes (the film take during which the still was taken may not be the one included in the film)—this is easier and cheaper than making an enlargement of a frame from the finished film. These production stills are used as illustrations for magazine articles, in film stores as 8x10 glossy photographs, in books on cinema (for instance, in the script *The Cabinet of Dr. Caligari* (New York: Simon and Schuster, 1972) «most of the stills are production stills» (p.4); Seymour Chatman's *Antonioni: or, The Surface of the World* is among the few exceptions that use only frame enlargements), and many film posters are made from them). Is all of Marker's *La Jetée* (with the exception of the first and the last shot, in which the protagonist

is shot and dies) made of these posters that don't exist in the film of life? Is that the main character's way of fooling the experimenters, of not reliving his past, but something else, something new?

What does not resemble me looks exactly like me/what looks exactly like me does not resemble me:
If, as in *The Student of Prague*, the double is one's mirror image that has been stolen from one, there is no reason any longer for one to see doubles only in people that others find extremely similar to one. Because we no longer have a mirror image, anybody can be us, or rather we can be anybody (for anyone reciprocally to be us s/he has to have lost his/her mirror image). Edgar G. Ulmer writes that the scriptwriter Hans Ramo, not Max Schreck, played the role of Nosferatu, although the film's credits list Max Schreck for that role; in Fassbinder's film *Despair* based on Nabokov's novel by the same title, the protagonist finds a double who according to the other characters and to the spectator clearly does not resemble him, while he himself thinks that he is identical to him (this is not due to a lack of discernment, for in Nabokov's novel it is the wife, not the husband, who «mixed dates, names, faces»[221]). The same in the case of the vampire, who has no mirror image: in Herzog's *Nosferatu*, the driver of the coach which transports Harker from the bridge to Nosferatu's castle does not resemble the Count, though they are the same person (in such cases and in cases of possession, for instance the final and total possession of Norman by his mother in the prison in the last scene of Hitchcock's *Psycho*, cinema averts the criticism that it embodies the character whom one was otherwise free to imagine). In Duras' *Son Nom de Venise*, the hand-held camera (without a steadycam) moves along the building and along the walls of the different rooms, like a person returning to a place of old (Nicholas Ray's *The Lusty Men* (1952); Wenders' *Kings of the Road*), except it returns to a different place, not the palace of *India Song* (château Rothschild) now older, more ruined, but a different palace, also in ruins.

These days he often mistakes one actress for another, for instance Lara Flynn Boyle of *Twin Peaks* for Winona Ryder. That phenomenon disappeared only to be replaced by his being gazed at by people in the street, as if they were mistaking him for someone they knew, maybe from TV or film (when in fact he was a totally unknown filmmaker).

The fear of the encounter with the double is in large part the dread that others will not recognize the similarity, hence the fear of a *sous-entendu* metamorphosis: if the other is my mirror-image but others do not seem at all to recognize the startling exact likeness—in Dostoyevsky's *The Double*, both the clerks in the office where Golyadkin works and Golyadkin's servant Petrushka show no sign of astonishment or fright at the uncanny resemblance between Golyadkin and Golyadkin (who moreover have the same bald patch and are dressed in the same way); one of the clerks at first speaks of a family resemblance—I must have become different-looking and different. The dread of the encounter with the double is also the dread of the indefinite extension of responsibility, which is a facet of the unconscious: other people's strange failure to notice the uncanny resemblance when my double and I are together is conjoined to their mistaking him for me when we are in different locations—I am responsible for what the other did. The latter instances also reinforce what is implied by the former instances, for if others keep ascribing to me the responsibility of acts I never performed, this must signal that I have metamorphosed, am no longer my traditional self.

Non-embodiment/Indefinite embodiment:
Cinema, this art linked so closely with embodiment/incarnation, as well as photography and figurative painting, has secreted a countercurrent interested in undoing the explicitness, the definite embodiment that the image entails. This is clearest in films dealing with Islam, with its prohibition of the representation of the prophet (and for the Shiites, of the imams as well), and certainly not necessarily in the simplistic form this prohibition assumes in Moustapha Akkad's *The Message*; or with Jewish religion, with its prohibition of the representation of Yahweh (Straub-Huillet's *Moses and Aaron*). But forms other than the aforementioned all-or-non strategies exist for *undoing*, fissuring embodiment/incarnation:

— Reincarnation: at one point in Annette Barbier's documentary *Women's Movements* (1989), we see the scriptural comment of an on-screen woman to being informed that the videomaker wants to take her picture: "look at this incarnation I am in [!]" India, this huge factory of films, is also the land in which re-incarnation is believed: given a long enough span of time, I can be in myriad looks/lives.

— Remakes. Since a character can be played by different actors (exception: Bresson's models—), something that becomes especially manifest in the case of remakes, Bunuel has two actresses play the female protagonist of *That Obscure Object of Desire* (1977), this making of his film a remake within the same film (a reflexive film), although in a manner different from the one one can expect in a film adaptation of Le Fanu's *Carmilla*.

— Doubling: *Persona*; in *Despair*, the husband and the man he thinks is his double do not look alike: it is as if we are witnessing a remake within the same film, each of the two actors playing the lead role in one film, with Hermann's double in both films looking, as in *The Student of Prague*, exactly like Hermann.

— Forgery: in Billy Wilder's *Fedora*, Fedora can look at her corpse, oversee her funerals, making sure that the physical image of the ageless Fedora remains identical with itself, only because 1) she no longer looks like herself *or how she would have looked when old* (a Nancy Burson composite would have provided us with a very good approximation of how Fedora would have looked when old had she aged naturally), due, in the book, to the deleterious cumulative effect of the injections to prolong her youth, and, in the film, to a disastrous youth-prolonging operation; 2) she is no longer Fedora, since the beginning of Antonia's counterfeit of her is simultaneous with her counterfeiting Countess Sobryanski (who is dead); 3) according to the book, she has trouble seeing (p.59)—this stipulation, this precautionary measure resorted to by Tyron even though nothing would be eliciting it were Fedora looking at the corpse of her daughter Antonia either favors the other interpretation, namely that Fedora is looking at a double or at her own corpse, or indicates the degree to which the slightest, remotest *possibility* of their transgression immediately reactivates taboos. Once more a sort of remake, and indeed we know that Billy Wilder thought of calling *Fedora*, *Fedora II*.

— The refusal of re-creation. Duras' films span a spectrum from the indefinite embodiment, with, in *India Song*, the actress Delphine

Seyrig not incarnating Anne-Marie Stretter but standing as actress next to the latter's photograph (does this maintenance of the image of the dead in *India Song*, which amounts to a forgery, lead to a more extreme forgery, that of the whole image track of *India Song* in *Son Nom de Venise Calcutta Desert*, indeed to the forgery of *India Song* by *Son Nom de Venise Calcutta Desert*?)—the Indian cycle—to the non-embodiment in *Le Camion*, 1977, as we move closer to the Jewish motif, for instance with *Aurelia Steiner—Melbourne* (1979), and *Aurelia Steiner—Vancouver* (1979).

— The 180° over-turn (Magritte's *Reproduction Interdite*).

— The non-appearance of the vampire in the mirror in vampire films, and the suspicion this induces that one is at other times not seeing the vampire but having a positive hallucination of him.

— Disappearance, as in the top photograph on the jacket of Jalal Toufic's *Distracted*: though we see Toufic in the company of Peter Rose and a woman, the caption reads, "Peter Rose and an unidentified person."

— The masks produced by the fear-induced swish pan/tilt, whether frozen as in Bokanowski's *L'Ange*, blurred/fluid as in *Jacob's Ladder*, or both as in Meatyard's work.

Bifurcation versions/filiation/remakes:
Some of the film versions of Stoker's *Dracula* and Le Fanu's *Carmilla* are bifurcation branches, Stoker's *Dracula* and Le Fanu's *Carmilla* not being the origins, but only two versions. While others are to be seen in terms of filiation (for instance to Stoker's *Dracula*). Herzog's *Nosferatu* (1979) is part bifurcation, part filiation (choosing to have a genealogy with a bastard film, a film banned for transgressing the copyright's aura, Murnau's *Nosferatu*, 1922). Filiation can be replaced not only by bifurcation but also by déjà vu in the same book or film: the second female victim of Carmilla should be the one to have a déjà vu feeling—in Roy Ward Baker's film *Vampire Lovers* (based on *Carmilla*), either the exact same shots (especially the inserts and cutaways) that were used in the first section in which Carmilla encounters her first victim should have been used when she encounters her second victim in the second part of the film, with the actresses playing the victims keyed in; or else the same shot should be filmed

twice, once with the actress playing the first victim, a second time with the actress playing the second victim. Or rather the shots in each section should begin in the latter mode to be replaced, past the first attack of Carmilla on her victims, with those in the former mode, with the victim becoming close to a Dreyer character, she and those present not looking in each other's direction or doing so rarely—while the amnesiac vampire Carmilla, who went through both episodes, doesn't have any déjà vu sensation, for otherwise this mirroring of the two parts would constitute a mirror image for the vampire. A kind of remake, *Carmilla II* takes place alongside *Carmilla I* within the same film, *Carmilla*.

Why make another version of *Nosferatu*?

There has been an absence of a continuous tradition in German cinema: between the expressionist period and the New German Cinema of Rainer Werner Fassbinder, Werner Herzog, Alexander Kluge, Hans Jürgen Syberberg, Wim Wenders, et al. there is the black hole not only of the Nazi era, but also of the period of reconstruction that followed it, which in the domain of cinema was almost totally controlled by Papa's Kino, filmmakers who began to make films under Goebbels and continued to dominate film production up to the late 1960's. The New German Cinema directors felt the need, some more strongly than others, to reestablish a link with the pre-Nazi filmmakers: Wenders' *Kings of the Road* (1976) begins with the actor Rüdiger Vogler interviewing an old cinema organist who used to accompany films in the silent era; Herzog remakes Murnau's *Nosferatu* («we are trying in our films to build a thin bridge back to that time»[222]); Wenders dedicates *Paris, Texas* (1984), and Herzog *Every Man for Himself and God Against All* (1974) to Lotte Eisner, the critic-historian who wrote *The Haunted Screen* on German cinema from its inception to the late nineteen twenties («Lotte Eisner's interest in our fate... built a bridge»[223]). The first motif of *Nosferatu* («and when he passed the bridge, the phantoms came to meet him»), the bridge, has been found (the filming of Joe Levine's *A Bridge Too Far* in Delft had just finished when Herzog came to film *Nosferatu*, a film about someone who crosses a too far bridge. Coincidence?).

The second motif is the phantoms. In a letter he sent Eisner in 1976 (*Nosferatu* was released in 1979), Herzog wrote: «Fritz Lang died... I believe no one really knew that he was still alive... they chased Fritz Lang so far away from us, that he was no longer among the living, but rather a rumor. You were among those who kept urging me to go see him, but I never really dared because... he had already become a spirit to me.»[224] Fritz Lang was not the only director who had become a phantom in post-war Germany. But there are also other kinds of cinema phantoms: nine out of the twenty-one films made by Murnau are lost, and some of the remaining ones are incomplete (Bazin writes about the mummifying/embalming and preservative function of film.[225] Film images preserve, but films themselves were for a long time not preserved.[226]) *Nosferatu* was banned because it did not receive the authority of Bram Stoker's widow, detainer of the copyright of *Dracula*: news of the film reached her only two months after its release by the Prana Company of Berlin in March 1922. A legal action was directed against it for infringement of copyright. In July of 1925, a German court decreed that all the prints must be destroyed. Most of the prints subsequently disappeared, but the makers managed to steal the negative abroad. *Nosferatu* was for a time a phantom. The film was shown again, in London, on December 16, 1928, reaching American screens a year later. A bridge had to be created to the directors who had become phantoms, but also to those of their films that had become, permanently or temporarily, phantoms.

M.-L. Potrel-Dorget points to the alternation of the figures of superman and under-man in Herzog's films:[227] Stroszeck as superman in *Signs of Life* (1968), the blind-deaf (and in one case, the blind-deaf-mute) as under-men/-women in *Land of Silence and Darkness* (1971), Aguirre as superman in *Aguirre, the Wrath of God* (1972), Kaspar Hauser as under-man in *Every Man for Himself and God Against All*... and then the alternation of Murnau's Nosferatu-as-superman and Herzog's Nosferatu-as-fetus.

Herzog succeeded in introducing sound into what was a silent *Nosferatu*: music-over is heard telepathically, *over*heard by the people in the town square who dance to it and not to the inaudible music being played by the musicians in the diegesis.

Herzog must have wanted to make a color version of Murnau's black and white *Nosferatu* (but is Murnau's *Nosferatu*, which contains shots in negative footage, a black and white film? The white of negative footage is unanalyzable into colors (one more unanalyzable phenomenon in tales of vampires); it is itself a color): white is rendered as a color by Herzog («Newton composes and decomposes light and makes colors the result of this decomposition... against Newton, Goethe affirms that... colors are not contained in the light»[228]), rather than, as in most other color films, as a summation of colors: it intensifies gradually on Kinski's face until it becomes lymphocyte's color. He failed in rendering the color red of erythrocytes.

Herzog presents a different model of the plague than the one in Murnau's *Nosferatu*. In *Discipline and Punish*, Foucault writes about the presence of two models of the plague each answering to a different political project. One is that of «suspended laws... bodies mingling together without respect... in a sort of collective festival.» We have all sorts of intermingling in vampire films:

— the living dead, the vampire, who is one form of undeath (the cross which the burgomaster draws on doors to distinguish the dying/dead from the living in the plagued city in Murnau's film is prefigured by that other cross given to Harker by the woman in the tavern to defend him against Nosferatu, the living dead).

— the dead living, the mad, those who *died before dying*, who are another form of undeath.

— the mixing of the dead and the living in the plagued city.

In the second model, «everyday... the syndic... stops before each house: gets all the inhabitants to appear at the windows... If someone does not appear at the window, the syndic must ask why?... each individual is constantly located, examined and distributed among the living beings, the sick and the dead—all this constitutes a compact model of the disciplinary mechanism... Against the plague, which is a mixture» (unpleasant rumors circulate about Renfield at the beginning of Murnau's film—rumors, hence already the motif of contagion, hence of the plague to come), «discipline brings into play its power, which is one of analysis.»[229]

The first shot of Murnau's *Nosferatu*: a panoptic vision from the tower dominating the city. Murnau's *Nosferatu* is inscribed within the disciplinary model of the plague (the other model can be found in his *Faust*, 1926). Herzog opts for the second model, the plague as festival/carnival/anarchy.

But viewing Murnau's *Nosferatu* within the disciplinary model is only partially right (the mixing that the plague introduces and which Murnau's film deals with propagates itself to a mixing of the two models of the plague in the film), since the city is ultimately saved by Ellen's sacrifice (as in Herzog's *Nosferatu*), and not by the disciplinary measures. The plague as carnival introduces inversions («the chaste man performs sodomy upon his neighbors. The lecher becomes pure. The miser throws his gold in handfuls out the window...»[230] and in prison Renfield sucks the blood of flies), until everybody becomes undifferentiated, so that one person has to be sacrificed, this sacrifice making him singular, hence reintroducing differentiation thus doing away with the plague. Rather than being determined by what differentiates him from others, the choice of the one to be sacrificed is what makes of him singular[231]. Or rather/else the choice falls on the one who was already, prior to the appearance of the plague, telepathic and somnambulistic (Harker, who is charged by his employer to take the ground plan of the house to Nosferatu in Transylvania and to get his signature on the ownership papers, is, through a parapraxis, the messenger of a message he was not asked to give, Lucy's photograph—he sacrificed her), one who differentiated herself/himself from the normals, from those who had restricted spectra, precisely by being the undifferentiated.

In *l'Espace Critique*, Paul Virilio writes about three kinds of windows that followed each other historically: the first window is the door; the second is the illuminating opening in the wall, which was not present in all periods of history but was introduced relatively late; the third is the TV screen which introduces a false day that opens not onto the near space, but beyond the perceptive horizon. It is here that one can say that Herzog has failed, in so far as he did not try to create a Nosferatu that lives in the age of TV (for this it is not enough, as in Tom Holland's *Fright Night* (1985), to show a TV), where the opposition between natural day and natural night is challenged by this false-day of TV, which, by opening onto what lies beyond the perceptive horizon, abolishes the relevance of the bridge («and when he crossed the bridge, the phantoms came to meet him») and the distance-differentiation it establishes between the space of the vampire and the space of the city.

Re-creation and period:
Between the usual re-creations (studio sets) that we see in many films, and the radical refusal of any re-creation in Duras' cinema (*Le Camion*—) and theater (*The Malady of Death*), are the films that at one point raise the question of whether what the character is experiencing is something objective or a hallucination: in these films we have something intermediate between re-creation and its prohibition (a prohibition that accounts for the recurrence of ruins in Duras' cinema):

— The castle exists in the mind in Herzog's *Nosferatu*, so that we see flashes of the ruined castle even as Harker lives in a more or less restored castle.

— The film set of Syberberg's *Parsifal* is a giant version of Wagner's death mask. So that all the film takes place in the head of Wagner (with Parsifal's question: "have I dreamt it?"). This goes hand in hand with the absence (of the re-creation) of the world in the studio. The studio remains empty except for the frontal projection, which does not recreate but quotes documents or hallucinates settings.

Many of the things that Dreyer reproduces from a previous historical period are those that have had a revival or are still the same hence/or are in fact the least characteristic: «I had given the English soldiers who attended the trial against Joan of Arc steel helmets to wear, and several critics resented that. But the truth is that the fifteenth century's soldiers actually wore steel helmets that were exactly like the ones English soldiers wore during the First World War. The same critics also made a fuss because one of the monks in the film wore horn-rimmed glasses, which, in 1927, were very much in fashion. But I could produce miniatures that prove that the people in the fifteenth century wore horn-rimmed glasses just like the ones that were used when the film was made.»[232] If we add to this that Dreyer through the abstraction and simplification that he advocated and practiced made it more difficult to have many indices to clue one to the period in question, it is not strange that this same director made a film, *Vampyr*, about one who subsists from one historical period to another.

As an indication to the spectator that at that point in the film s/he is dealing with an earlier historical period, many color films revert to black and white (most probably because black and white preceded color in film history). It would be more appropriate to use for the contemporary section(s) filters that allow the simulation of the colors that would have resulted from the gradual fading of color film (for instance, blue and green fading result in an effect of magenta or pink), reverting to the more intense colors for the sections that are in the past.

Am I dreaming?
The vampire does not dream, this excluding the possibility of the *mise-en-abyme*—seeing oneself simultaneously in several positions—found sometimes in dreams (the vampire has no mirror-image). In vampires films and books the victim of the vampire, of the one who does not dream, feels and thinks past his encounter with the vampire that he is always dreaming.

Am I dreaming? It suddenly struck him that the Freudian way of interpreting a dream—«whenever my own ego does not appear in the content of the dream, but only some extraneous person, I may safely assume that my own ego lies concealed, by identification, behind this other person»—could apply to his present case: it could well be that he himself was just the substitute by identification (through a common element) of the dreamer, and this to evade the censorship of an agency of the latter's psychic apparatus. In which case, it is that other who would wake-up.

Am I Dreaming? is less interesting as a formula for dissociation than Harker's words to Mina before he leaves to Transylvania in Murnau's *Nosferatu*: «Nothing will happen to me.» Is what happens to him later really happening? In Transylvania, «the land of phantoms,» he encounters only what cannot be met, phantoms, with the consequence that all that happens to him did not happen; i.e., in accordance with the above definition of Transylvania, Harker himself becomes a phantom since a phantom is by definition one to whom nothing ever happens. This thanatosis that life can become, and not because one has become a witness, for the witness/master/guide/reference—needed when «nothing will happen to me» is, as always, inverted, becoming: everything is happening to me (death's/ schizophrenia's overinclusion)(the master/guide knows that, as with the hypnotized person who is registering no pain in the hypnotized hand immersed in ice-cold water while his second hand is reporting out-of-his awareness in automatic writing ascending intensity of pain, *nothing will happen to me* **is all along** *everything is happening to me*, including the lapses and the absence of time (that undo the present, the *is* in *everything is happening to me*))—on the contrary is in the greatest danger: the master is the other *hidden observer*, hence feels even more pain than the disciple, who may be feeling no pain at all, having the impression that nothing is happening to him; but detachment applies to the master since, as the *hidden observer*, he knows that there is another realm besides the one where the hypnotized is at that moment—not that what is going on in hypnosis is false.

After all this is only a dream. The writer/witness/master/guide/ guard would say: *after all this is only reality*—a writer is concerned mainly with and about the coupling of the two *after all this is only* according to most others: *words, words, words (after all this is only writing)* and *after all this is only a dream*.

Reality-as-filmic:
Whereas in the vast majority of cases films imitate/(re)present a reality that is prefilmic, Jalal Toufic's *Night for Day* is simultaneously autobiographical and automediatic because the filmmaker lives, or at least lived for a while, in a reality that is itself filmic. The first forty minutes of *Night for Day*, in which the main character is played by Elliot Cutler, turns out to be a film being shot by the second section's main character (played by the director). While the first section is devoid of any special effects and is edited smoothly, its shots being cut on movement, the second section contains special effects (fastforward of interview—) and jump cuts.

«Il n'arrive plus rien aux humains, c'est à l'image que tout arrive.»[233] Through the following features the character reaches the point where the diegetic world itself functions according to the rules that operate in the film universe, this making events still happen to humans since the latter are becoming a quasi film image:

— The immobilization of the pov caused by fear (similar to hair standing on end, to the blocking of the scream, and to the gesture of the ship's captain in Murnau's *Nosferatu* who binds himself to the wheel of the Demeter after all his crew has died, thus reproducing voluntarily the involuntary immobilization that fear creates) or by a state of trance/fascination results in a frame. The main character in *La Horla* stops walking, then notices, on looking in both directions, that he cannot differentiate between them, so that suddenly the two become doubles of each other separated by a labyrinth. One may object that all the character had to do in order to know which of the two directions he came from was to look, if the road was not paved but sandy, at the footsteps he must have made. But fear immobilizes the pov, the person no longer able to look at the ground, continuing to look parallel to the road—except if fear induces a dissociation of the person, hence a dissociation between the immobilized pov and a new pov, the latter framing the footsteps; but even in that case the dissociated component of the person will, like a corpse, have no pov.

— The lapses of time in epilepsy,[234] hypnosis (the hypnotist may use the tap of a pen against a hard object as signal for the subject to come out or revert to trance. He can thus abruptly return the subject, whom he has earlier brought back from the hypnotic state, and who is then in a particular room at a specific time of the day, for instance, evening, to the trance state, conduct him to a totally different location, and there tap his pen an hour or so later when it is already night, the subject experiencing a jump cut between the two locations-times. Due to amateur editing, there were jump cuts in John G. Watkins' video *Hypnotic Phenomena*, so that one suddenly felt that oneself as spectator may be undergoing hypnotic lapses), schizophrenia, LSD trips, and undeath permit editing in reality (editing in film started with the blocking of the film strip in Méliès' camera). While in many a Morissey-Warhol film flash frames at the end of the shot were left in the film, in Herzog's *Heart of Glass* it is the frequent closing of the eyes of the hypnotized/somnambulists, after they say their lines, that is left in the film.

— As in film, where sometimes in the case of cuts on movement the last few frames of the action of the first shot are repeated in the second shot in order to obtain a smoother cut, reduplications occur in reality-as-filmic and have the same function. Such minimal repetitions, which usually hide cuts in duration, are themselves sometimes though noticed by the person in an altered state.

— Once one gets to immobilizations—in Roman Polanski's *The Tenant*, the other tenants in the building where Tralkovsky "lives" stand still for hours (actors playing a dead person have to be immobile for the length of the shot; the actors in *The Tenant* standing immobile are playing dead, whether they know it or not). He is driven by them into becoming obsessed about not making any noise (he cannot even move his furniture) so that they will not complain, hence obsessed with reaching a state of *dead silence*. For that he has to become *dead still*, becoming like them—as the photograms of time (and not merely at Vertov's film photogrammes in *Man with a Movie Camera*), time can be reversed: the shot of the person covered with bandages in the hospital near the end of the film is the same shot as the one near the beginning of the film: in both, it is Simone Choule who is bandaged in bed looking at Tralkovsky and Stella (the man who at long last went to Choule's apartment to tell her that he loved her, only to be told by Tralkovsky, the new tenant of the apartment, that she had committed suicide, may still tell her in the future that he loved her). If *Encephalitis lethargica* is such a purely cinematic subject it is because it confronts cinema with what is essential to it, not motion (*motion pictures*) but real immobilization, an immobilization which affects time directly, making possible fastforward and other time-idiosyncrasies, i.e. the lapses and other time idiosyncrasies then pertain not only to the time and speed of narrative (Gerard Genette, *Figures III*) but also to the time and speed of story. Every time cinema deals with true immobilization it becomes reflexive, for when true immobility is reached reality itself begins to function in cinematic terms. This seems a more intrinsic way of being reflexive than the more traditional way in which cinema has been self-reflexive.

— I was sitting in the #30 bus in Milwaukee. His tongue moved on his thin lips in a quick gesture. But I also saw-felt for a split second a lizard's tongue moving. Was it a superimposition of a lizard's tongue on the man's tongue or was the man's tongue replaced by a lizard's tongue for that split second? The phenomenon had nothing to do with a metaphor; nor did it function subliminally, for

I did not just sense it but also saw it. A flash frame of the lizard's tongue moving outside its mouth was cut into the sequence of the man's tongue moving over his lips. A flash frame that existed not in a film but in the world. *Kinematic vision* (during which the person perceives (in) stills) occasionally occurs in acute psychoses and in some cases of migraine auras and epileptic seizures and in the case of those suffering from *encephalitis lethargica.*

— Hypnosis is in part a form of matting: positive and negative hallucination, post hypnotic sequelae.

— Most people are mere extras, but whereas their presence in film contributes to making the spectator accept the world portrayed in the film, their presence in the world contributes to the feeling of unreality of schizophrenics and of those undergoing a bad LSD trip or who have undergone one and are suffering from anxiety and/or flashbacks.

— Beverly leaving the public phone in *Dead Ringers* (1988) and walking back to his apartment to commit suicide is moving away from the spectator, leaving him behind, as if leaving the cinema theater in which the spectator remained.[235]

In Bergman's *Persona*, not only does the frame of the screen crack in the middle and burn, and the sound go backward (as during film editing), but also what takes place in the scene where Alma removes a snapshot of Elizabeth's son from under her hand and talks to her about her relation to him is repeated twice, with Alma uttering the same words in an identical delivery, once with the camera on Elizabeth, a second time with the camera on Alma—it is a standard procedure when filming angle/reverse angle scenes to shoot with the camera first on one actor, then on the other, then to intercut the two set-ups; but here the two takes, from opposite angles, are not intercut but added. Not to consider this presence of filmic elements as an extra-diegetic self-reflexivity; rather, as in (other) vampire films, these elements belong to the diegetic world, a diegetic world where self-reflexivity is both absent, with respect to the protagonists—the mixing of faces (and in vampire films, the absence of mirror-image)—and present, since the diegetic world itself functions in cinematic terms.

Dissociation sometimes permits one to observe the edited film that one is in. The fragments can be (re)edited only in this dissociated state, but that means that the dissociated self has to be not only passive (hence the limitation of hypnagogic states and of many a meditative state, unless one (re)edits the film through the master) but also a participant. Where is one then? Unlike Bazin, who wrote, «there are no wings to the screen. There could not be without destroying its specific illusion, which is to make of a revolver or of a face the very center of the universe,»[236] we have to write that one is then in the wings, wings that strangely enough function in cinematic terms.

The world has a becoming-cinema in certain altered states, the set itself becoming a quasi-edited image, but with the introduction of digital editing (paintboxes, etc.) the image itself in the form of the chosen take is no longer already part of the film but remains part of the set, since the colors of any of its elements can be altered and things layered and keyed into or out of it without any generational loss. In the contemporary world the set moves toward the image, toward an image-becoming and the image moves toward a set-becoming.

Film is asymptotically moving toward the real (if cinema is moving (with the addition of color and sound—) toward becoming total cinema (Bazin), what about Baillie's superimpositions? Are they part of total cinema?), that is toward the film becoming reality. It is because in altered states and undeath reality is filmic[237] that film cannot become reality, for otherwise we would be dealing with the double, hence with the possible death of reality.

The suffix *er* either denotes the person who does a specified action or is used to form the comparative degree of adverbs and adjectives. In certain situations though the two are linked: in vampire films, the harker is the one who cannot hark except if he harks more than others, but also more than himself (by being telepathic), but also the one who if he stopped harking would lose his name and his being a subject. Thus the irony in the name of Harker.

In Bram Stoker's novel, the fog around the ship transporting Dracula («only God can guide us in the fog, which seems to move with us») is not foreign to hypnagogic states: «Landscapes, like faces, usually have a "cloud accompaniment" in the shape of cloud formations»[238] from which they emerge and into which they disappear (the fog as matte). Neither are the many out-of-focus povs of Harker in Herzog's *Nosferatu*. One of these begins on an out-of-focus gypsy who is brought in-focus just before the subjective camera pans to another gypsy sitting at a closer plane. The shot is at that point out-of-focus. First the background behind the latter gypsy becomes in-focus, only then does focus shift to the foreground plane where the gypsy is sitting. It is clear that these out-of-focus instances cannot be explained by the rack-focus structure and are different from the haptic shots we see when, as in Morissey's *Flesh* and *Trash* and in many of Jalal Toufic's videos, the camera (often with a telephoto lens) pans and tilts mostly in continuous close shots from one object/subject to another (coming in and out of focus). They rather indicate the entry into a hypnagogic state.

Grace of what is both marionette and god,[239] of the undead (whose bodies are as inanimate as a marionette, and whose minds dwelling in the Bardo state have the powers of God) as they dance in Roman Polanski's *The Fearless Vampire Killers*.

It is not the image that Krzysztof Wodiczko projects on the memorial that is the ghost, it is rather the latter, the memorial, that is the revenant. Wodiczko showed *The Homeless Projection* **in** a New York Gallery instead of his proposed site of Union Square (where it was supposed to be projected **onto** buildings[240]). This exile from exile: what should have been projected on the outside is now put inside a gallery (home as the exile from exile); the gallery in which the projection is installed becomes a Christo wrap of the projection.

In Bergman's *Wild Strawberries* the father's watch ends up having no hands; this may explain the provenance of the handless clock in the son's dream. On the other hand, it could be that the father's watch lost its hands in real life so that it could appear thus in the dream. Some of life's accidental happenings occur because they will be needed in the dream (most of what appears in dreams has no such provenance, since images can be metamorphosed by means of condensation and the other processes of the dreamwork).

A friend of John Corbett took LSD and felt at one point that she had a revelation. She wrote it down. When she woke up the next day, she remembered that she had written down a deep revelation. She looked for the piece of paper and found out to her disappointment and surprise that she had written: "There is a strange smell in the room." But wasn't that a koan (on being asked why Bodhidharma came to China, Joshu said: «An oak tree in the garden»)? Wasn't what she experienced in the altered state a satori?

I am speaking on the phone to John Corbett. Suddenly, it hits me that he is speaking to me with *my* voice. Horror. I say to him "speak to me with your voice." He says, "but I am doing that!" It is still my voice.

If you see yourself hitchhiking on the highway pick yourself up.

One got *lightly* hypnotized, with one hand asked to write out of awareness: what was being consciously written with the right hand belongs to the double, one discovering later what one oneself thinks by reading what the left hand had written out of awareness.

The empty-looking city asleep at dawn in the beginning section of Vertov's *Man With a Movie Camera*: as if under quarantine. Even more empty are the cities in the dreams of those asleep in such a city (the dream sequence in Bergman's *Wild Strawberries* and in Bunuel's *The Discreet Charm of the Bourgeoisie*), where the dead-as-undead finds himself as the only survivor.

She's speaking to me. She interrupts herself: "I am talking to you and you seem somewhere else, like a zombie." Wasn't there in that most famous love story, *Romeo and Juliet*, mention of the undead?

The *dead water* of Wismar's canals in Herzog's *Nosferatu* more still than the bridge over it (the bridge more stagnant than the water under it).

He looked back at the road and it had dwindled like a rivulet that had almost totally dried.

Behind the turned-on TV, the window, and behind the window, the snow in the wind. I, body and mind, am the mind of this building where I am now: I am not shielded by a window and walls from the outside world, but am in contact with it (the walls like frozen limbs).

In Milwaukee's Museum of Science, one can stand in front of a machine that constructs out of one's face two different faces, one fatter than the other, each formed by joining one side of the face to itself inverted left-right. If one were to see one's double s/he would not look like oneself, but would have either of the aforementioned two faces.

He could see the moon moving up the sky—in time-lapse—like a rocket.

The vampire did not do any obscure, intriguing thing in response to someone's conceited: "I can see through you"; only, the person's vision suddenly tunneled through the vampire. One interesting way of responding to a falsity said in figurative language: literalize it. The meaning of the aforementioned expression was no longer "I understand you" but "you are translucent."

Sunrise: the close-up of the maid shouting that the wife has been found alive echoes the face of the city woman being strangled by the husband in a medium shot—especially since the maid's two hands, cut by the frame a little above the wrist, hence appearing not to belong to her, encircle her face (forming a resonating funnel for the shout) and seem to be strangling her. It is this substitution of the face of the maid with that of the woman being strangled (again the theme of sacrifice, which we find in Murnau's *Nosferatu* and *Faust*), and not her shout, or not her shout alone, that stops the man from fully strangling the city woman, saving the latter. This could not have ensued without the man somewhat sensing the framing.

The world depends on the questions asked. Sorcery and everyday life ask different questions since they deploy different measurement apparatuses: the body-as-organism in everyday life and the body-as-egg with light filaments in the sorcery world of Castaneda's don Juan. But *the world depends on the questions asked* becomes fully deployed only in the latter case and cases of the same nature, such as yoga. In yoga there is a concentration on withdrawing from the world: the elimination of all psychosensory events whether they be exteroceptive or proprioceptive (similarly, all internal monologue should stop in Zen and in don Juan's system). This absence of measurement-observation puts one in a state similar to that of the quantum system between the source and the detector, i.e. prior to the measurement-observation. This leads, as in the case of the quantum world (especially in John Archibald Wheeler's delayed choice and participatory universe model), to a dependency of the result on the experimental apparatus. By working, the slave objectifies, changes and humanizes the world (Kojève), but the master/guru/guide/sheik creates another world.

To J. and T. on their wedding day: perhaps the dead need the living so as not to be imprisoned in an eternal madness. So live long; so judge for yourself which is the least detrimental: not bringing to the world a child, who may have to go through the Bardo state maybe endlessly, or bringing him to the world, for maybe the living are what still permit the credit of reincarnation and hence the possibility that in the long run one would be exempted from the cycle of rebirth-redeath, and maybe if the nuclear holocaust were to kill everybody, it would mean not the obliteration of the soul/ka/shadow/consciousness-flux, but only, which is the scariest, obliterate the possibility of credit-reincarnation.

I wish you a happy life, that is I wish each of you not to become a survivor. Happy couple life, for one will live both absolutely alone and penetrated by everything/everyone enough in death-as-undeath.

If I am to attempt suicide it will be by eating a small puffer fish.

The End of the World: a story that follows six or more characters, all unknown to each other, who commit suicide within the same time period. The story has to give the impression of an end of the world since all those the reader ends up knowing kill themselves. For there are sub-temporalities within time: the end of the world is simultaneous with the continuing world.

Eternity is not possible as long as any refractory period, during which the nerve cell cannot react to a stimulus after it has just been subjected to one, exists.

The testament is to maintain the idea that the dead have a will. It may be that the legal system exists more to give a will to those who no longer have one than to institute laws for the living. All testaments are forged.

In death the body is reduced to weight, as if all of it has become a center of gravity. Cadaver: *cadere*, to fall. This fall is its grave (*tombe*: 1) *fall*; 2) *grave*). Nonetheless, the light flooding the room in Dreyer's *Ordet* manages to make this extremely heavy body, the corpse, and the coffin on which it is lying, float.

One way of averting being surprised is to reach the stage of rushes, since rushes contain no jump-cuts.

In the absence of either Dzogchen self-liberation, which presupposes non-discrimination, or Lyotard's occurrence, one either accepts the law of karma as supreme, or one refuses such a law by intentionally and at the price of extreme artificiality disconnecting the effect from the cause, establishing the realm of the arbitrary, so that for instance one is nice to people who are bad to one, and not from forgiveness, for the latter still inscribes the act in a causal chain. To someone who does good things for us we may link to them with good or bad things.[241] It is as if one has to get to this (frequent) change in the sign before the double (Freud: «reversal, or turning a thing into its opposite, is one of the means of representation most favoured by the dream work...»[242]). Becoming a simulacrum of the double. It is this way that one's friends, who due to bifurcation were no longer one's friends, become temporarily once again one's friends. And the question is:

how far and for how long can one try to disconnect the normal associations before one finds oneself sinking into an altered, fascinated state where things, images and words link on their own?

Beyond the extreme is exaggeration; exaggeration is the total non-freedom from the extreme: *dead certain.*

There are stages and we do not have to continue to go through or undergo them: the stage of being rebels with *and* without a cause; the stage of being sensitive to those who are passing through a far from equilibrium state and hence need our help in their depersonalization; the stage of freedom, where the connections between events have to become arbitrary.

"You only talked about it, I *only* did it." Only someone free can understand the second *only*.

Talk is cheap, i.e. stop your on-going interior monologue.

In *Truly, Madly, Deeply* (1991), unbeknownst to the filmmaker, the fact that the dead have no individuality, or a larval one that is penetrated by many others, is inscribed in the film in the form of having the dead person gradually bring back with him an ever-increasing number of the dead.

Rick Silverman cut a hologram of a vase into three pieces, which he then put next to each other producing *Rough Cut* (1979); each of the three sections can reproduce the whole. It is as if Arman's *coupes*, for instance *Ascent into the Sky*, 1961, *Virtuosity*, 1961, *Dividend*, 1962, *Treatise on the Violin*, 1964, were a premonition of the coming of the holistic holograms and a precocious attempt to deal with, resist, their totalizing propensity[243]: since the hologram cannot be divided into pieces which do not contain the whole, one has to slice the object beforehand.

In the same way that it permits one to have control over the body's autonomous system (heart rate, blood pressure—), yoga permits one to control to a large extent the otherwise autonomous operations of the mind in altered states, when the unconscious comes to the surface: death is the unconscious come to the surface. One has then to rise to a new surface (a la postmodern columns that come down from the ceiling but do not touch the ground in Robert Mittlestadt's R. Mittlestadt Duplex, San Francisco (1975-9)): asked how it feels to have attained satori, D. T. Suzuki answered, «just like ordinary everyday experience, except about two inches off the ground!»

What would we do without Richard Foreman's strings, we who are blind to perspective and its virtual lines that have a similar function to the umbilical cord that divers maintain with the world above water?

As a counter to the loss of perspective, he used to stand for long periods in front of the southwest facade of Hiromi Fuji's Todoroki House, Ichikawa, Chiba Prefecture.

For space to come to the fore in relation to time, it must either be devoid of ether or become flat, for perspective has a relation, even if potential-virtual, to time.

Vision in terms of perspective did occasionally return, but most of the time his vision alternated between the two extremes: absence of ether (the utter clarity when perspective is neutralized—haze masks perspective since it flattens, but perspective itself is a sort of haze); seeing things as if through a glass.

Michael Powell's *Peeping Tom*: as if the voyeur had to commit crimes or adultery so that someone would assign a detective (that other peeping Tom) to follow him. The shadow needs a shadow to follow him in order to exist in its own right.

The vampire in the coffin on the ship in the storm (Badham's *Dracula*): one would have liked to see traced on the coffin the word "Fragile."

Only very rarely does acting become counterfeiting. For this to occur the actor must no longer be someone who plays different characters while having one role only, that of actor.

We are unique only in death, i.e. precisely when we are penetrated by everything else, confused with everything else. Even in death we are not equal (yoga master—).

Those who are not *fast asleep*, those who maintain themselves in an intermediary state whether it be hypnagogia or lucid dreaming are *fast* (the ability of don Juan and some yogis to be simultaneously in two different locations).

Perhaps every effect is caused by a posthypnotic suggestion: the deployment of the cause-effect scheme would then presuppose a universal hypnosis (someone may think he is not in trance when in fact he is: for instance the hypnotist taps the table with his pencil (the cue for the posthypnotic suggestion) and says to the skeptic: "try to raise your hand from your lap"). Miracles happen when the posthypnotic suggestion is canceled (whether the hypnosis itself is cut or not) or replaced by another suggestion.

At the speed of light time slows down to zero; light, the eternal, is what can kill the non-aging, the vampire.

The running heroine of Meshes of the Afternoon is unable to reach the mysterious walking figure. This framing effect can be viewed either as due to her running within one of the myriad frames of a joiner (the three Maya Derens sitting around the table form a joiner), or as due to the fact that the gloomy, mysterious figure has become a figure of light, since, like light, it remains at a constant speed in relation to the one following her however much the former increases her speed[244]. In both cases an underscoring of frames (frames of reference or frames of the joiner).

How is it some manage to live, instead of survive, with the realm of undeath in them? How is it we often manage in the end to move these objects that are outside of time—the flashing light on the video a sort of palinopsia—immobile (one has the impression that the deliberations of billiard players, the cue held in the hand for a long time, are not a mark of how best to hit the ball, but a translation of the immobility of the balls)? How is it conceivable that the singularity of a black hole, where all the laws of physics no longer function, where space and time become inoperational, could so easily be disposed of through a process within the laws of physics, radiation, which results, at the end of a long process of evaporation, in the black hole's explosion and hence the singularity's disappearance?

In Fassbinder's *Despair* Lydia walks from the bedroom through a corridor lined with glass quadrants that seem to compose one long mirror, her reflection appearing in the first quadrant. When she reaches the third quadrant she looks to her right. The camera pans slightly to reveal her husband standing looking at her. We think that we are looking at his reflection in the mirror and hence that he is standing to the same side of the glass as she is, only to discover as he crosses behind the glass and joins her that the glass of the last quadrant is transparent and not part of the mirror. Having reached the corridor, he looks at her for a second, then looks furtively off-screen to what would have been his position if what we had seen previously had been his reflection in the mirror; Lydia leaves frame left to the bathroom. Superposition of two reasons for his sideway look: either as an order to Lydia to go to the bathroom to finish freshening up, or to look at himself. If the spectator is to be drawn into the film it is neither simply through identification with the characters, nor even through the more elaborate version of identification, the structuring of the film around the spectator in Hitchcock's suspense (which led to the character becoming a spectator in *Rear Window*), but by the objective status of this impression/fluctuation: the audience's (programmed) mistake, that of taking the transparent glass for a mirror (in a later scene that same glass quadrant functions as a mirror), has consequences in the film. This certainly won't be achieved every time the spectator misunderstands what is going on in the film, and is one criterion by which to judge whether the spectator has become part of the film. One must point out that the latter situation most often occurs when identification is no longer possible (for instance in cases where the character is a schizophrenic, or someone going through an out-of-the-body episode, for the latter can no longer identify with the body/image: a construction worker who had a near-death experience following cardiac arrest said, «I recognized me lying there.... [it was] like looking at a dead worm or something. I didn't have any desire to go back»), hence the humor in the real-life episode when an armed man in a cinema theater in West Beirut fired his gun at those trying to kill Stallone in the film, for this attempt at interfering in the film diegesis was made while identification was occurring.

Edvard Munch's *Evening on Karl Johan*, 1892[245]: although the figure in the background continues to walk into the distance, he continues to face the figures in the foreground plane staring ahead. He can feel his legs walking but all he can see are these faces staring at him; his walk does not extricate him but on the contrary implicates him all the more since the more he walks the more numerous the faces staring at him become. Hence the intuition the spectator has that the mask-like faces are not looking at him/her, the spectator, but are staring at the one who is in the background. Between the spectator and the faces facing him in the foreground is the one walking in the background.

La Rochefoucauld wrote that neither death nor the sun can be looked at directly. The living cannot look for long directly at the sun, but the undead can: Daniel Paul Schreber could do it for minutes on end.[246]

Prologue: An 18-year old woman with an ancient Egyptian face (the two fish-like eyes, forming the two halves of the sign of eternity, etc.), Natasha Uppal, is asked to act in *Night for Day*—basically to do a photocopy degeneration of two photographs of herself[247].
Three years later: Looking at her *Site*, 1991 (the French title should be *Ci-gît*), one can discern several features that recur in films about the undead. The telepathic correlation between what is not *inter*acting: the drop-like points on the superimposed glass panes are washed by the water from another plane. The uncanny immobilizations of the camera movement: the tilt that suddenly stops on a few metal bars, with no residual movement (no conservation of momentum, hence

the unnaturalness of this freezing of movement (technically achieved by a Fairlight freeze))—

During his life, he used to think it was his movement nearby that made the cicadas cease their sound. He knows better now; not because when he moves they do not stop making sounds—as a vampire he not only does not have a mirror image, but he also does not have an aural image (the first time the non-ceasing of the sound of the cicadas despite his movement nearby happened he was startled, but this prepared him a little more for the absence of his image in the mirror)—but because, now, lying undecomposed in the earth, he hears both the cicadas and the grating sound of the time-lapse movement of the dry leaves and flowers on the ground («Fallen petals rise / back to the branch—I watch: / oh... butterflies!» (Moritake); to the undead the dry leaves and flowers keep fluttering even after they fall to the ground). The sudden freezings of the dry leaves and withered flowers on the ground, of what is immobile from the perspective of the living but fluttering frantically according to the undead, giving the dry leaves and flowers the appearance of wallpaper, both produced not normal silence (heard by the living passers-by) but the diegetic silence-over, and made the strange fluttering of what is moved by neither wind nor earthquake possible[248] (like a chicken whose head has been severed and whose body is still moving frantically, or a heart still beating in a fresh corpse, but for different reasons, non-biological ones, the whole corpse continued to have a jerky movement long after death had occurred, for it existed in a time-lapse temporality). A passer-by walked by the fence to the other side of which were the aforementioned dead leaves and flowers; in her house she looked at the wallpaper, saw it become animated and heard diegetic voice-overs issuing from it (Bergman's *Through a Glass Darkly*, 1961). Openings in the ground open not onto the sky, trees, electricity poles, i.e. not onto the world, but onto negative colors.

Passing the swinging tires (a child must have been playing here a short while ago), he, an undead, looked up at the sky, seeing the swaying of branches, their blurring, fusion into white patches. The continuing sound of the cicadas over the shot of the swinging tire is not an extra-diegetic sound-over but a sound that localizes one of the dissociated components of the undead: while walking near the swaying tires, he is still under the earth and the dry leaves. The sound of the swinging tires persisted as a refrain, a diegetic sound-over, in the head of a living passer-by.

Due to a sort of binocular suppression, you see the field of vision of only one eye, while the other one remains black, but in the former field are two frames of a static view taken from slightly different angles, inducing not an effect of depth (nor of a passage of time, as in Hockney's joiners) but one of a flat ecstasy (*I am beside myself* with vision).

Afterword: Are we dealing with a promising young filmmaker? The young filmmaker made no promise whatsoever. Artists and writers, whether young or not, do not make promises. At most, we can speak about a writer promising us... a second or third edition. (Are we dealing with a promising film, i.e. one that merely announces a sequel? No.) Not promises but postponements and anticipations, out-of-sync (faster or slower than oneself). If at all it is their just arrogance, by its exactness, sobriety that makes us feel concerned and somewhat sad for some young writers, filmmakers and artists, for it announces the modesty they will evince *if* they later do better, much more demanding work (not to take the former arrogance as itself received from this latter stage; it is rather part of the charm of youth that one can have such just arrogance about relatively little), whereas we feel, not pity, only revulsion for the youthful arrogance that is off, implicitly promising so much. In these first books and films, we find both receptions from the future (quicker than oneself) and anticipations (often of rather mediocre quality) of these receptions from the future.

One of the dangerous repercussions of the state of betrayal is the temptation one has thence forth to feel any change that does not reach both betrayal and a defense against it as a sort of stagnation, as a lukewarm state.

After-life, as in Sherrie Levine's *After Walker Evans,* since the recently dead does not know at first that s/he is dead.

The link between the writer and the amnesiac version is to allow both to elude the constant linking of ideas on their own. In the latter's case, a linking clearly experienced in the modality of imposition: paranoia/possession by the double; in the former's case, a linking that takes the form of the deduction of intelligent objective thoughts from each other by a scholar who speaks mostly in generalities (because s/he is not receiving from someone who has experienced, among other things, *all the names of history are I*). This link is a creation-reception.

On Saturday, November 16, 1991, I discovered that although the size of the *(Vampires)* file was 650K, when I opened the file it was empty. On November 20, Peter R. Schnack, a University of California at Irvine Macintosh Support Specialist in the Office of Academic Computing, tricked the computer into reading the file as a text file, and indeed it appeared as a large text file. The non-appearance on the screen of the 650K-file *(Vampires)* echoed the vampire's non-appearance in mirrors.

Notes:
1. Hellemans Alexander & Bryan Bunch, *The Timetables of Science: a chronology of the most important people and events in the history of science* (New York: Simon & Schuster, 1988). Enzymes and other factors (temperature—) could accelerate the rate of chemical reactions, but with recombinant DNA this fastforwarding can be done at the level of the whole organism (will childhood be bypassed or at least fastforwarded?).

2. Norman F. Dixon, *Preconscious Processing* (New York: Wiley, 1981), 70.

3. A middle-ground had to be reached between delaying publishing *(Vampires)* to give more chance for *Distracted* to be read, reviewed and acknowledged so that the telepathic connection between the two should not be obscured, and minimizing the temptation such a delay would provide to continue editing.

4. Stairs also function as trance deepeners in vampire films and in *Last Year at Marienbad*: "As you go down the heavily carpeted stairs, you are going deeper and deeper into trance."

5. *Webster's Third New International Dictionary of the English Language Unabridged*, s.v. "caution": *Caution*: «Precaution (a surgeon taking the ~ of sterilizing his equipment).»

6. Nothing in the *opening scenes* in vampire films indicates that it is the vampire that makes the door open—doors open on their own to receive the visitor in both Murnau's and Herzog's *Nosferatu*, Stoker's *Dracula*, etc.—rather than the visitor; whether the vampire is translucent or whether the victim-visitor's vision already tunnels through him. Not only this, the future victim of the vampire is in many cases the first to drink blood: in Browning's *Dracula*, Harker accidentally cuts his finger then proceeds to lick his blood. The person is already becoming a vampire, invested with the powers and weaknesses of the vampire even before he is bitten by and loses blood to the latter, indeed in many cases even before he meets him. These idiosyncrasies of behavior indicate that a *false threshold* was crossed by the visitor prior to his first encounter with the vampire; in which case the sucking of the blood of the victim by the vampire is an occultation of where the threshold is, merely the apparent threshold. Hutter's downplaying of the two punctures he finds on his neck the morning following his first night at the vampire's castle, reducing them to the bites of flies or spiders, is to the point. Another way of considering these idiosyncrasies of behavior is to view them as part of the inversions that announce the plague and that the latter makes widespread. In which case this would confirm the historian's words, which begin Murnau's film: «J'ai longtemps cherché les causes de cette terrible épidémie et j'ai découvert à ses origines puis à son apogée les figures innocentes de Jonathan Harker et de sa jeune épouse Nina.»

7. Larry Weiskrantz, "Neuropsychology and the Nature of Consciousness," in *Mindwaves*, ed. C. Blakemore & S. Greenfield (Oxford: Basil Blackwell, 1987), 313-4.

8. For an example from the field of physics: at atmospheric pressure and below 100°C, H_2O exists as liquid. For a temperature over 100°C, H_2O exists in

its vapor phase. At 100°C at atmospheric pressure, a phase transition occurs: an abrupt change in the density takes place (the vapor is one thousand six hundred times less dense than the liquid). The boiling temperature (Tb) depends on the atmospheric pressure: it increases smoothly [hence, the phase transition can be made less abrupt] until at P=218 atmospheres, Tb=374°C. The latter temperature and pressure is the *critical point*, where the difference in densities between the liquid and vapor phases on either side of the boiling temperature vanishes. Critical point means no surprise, no catastrophe (in the sense René Thom gives that word).

9. For an example from the field of biology: many insects avoid freezing by undercooling, a physical phenomenon by which the body fluids freeze at a temperature well below 0°C. This state is precarious, since undercooled water is metastable with respect to ice and becomes increasingly so with decreasing temperature.

10. Bram Stoker, *Dracula* (New York: Bantam Books, 1981), 11.

11. Gregory A. Waller, *The Living and the Undead: from Stoker's Dracula to Romero's Dawn of the Undead* (Urbana: University of Illinois Press, 1986), 32. (Death before) death can only be undergone by one person alone—but, so as to be able to come back from this non-local realm, that person has to have an outsider (reality begins only with two (not counting one's multiple personalities and/or the double)), whether s/he be the *hidden observer* or another.

12. Ibid.

13. In one of the earliest shots of Murnau's *Nosferatu* Harker's wife is seen playing with a cat (she plays with two cats in the beginning of Herzog's *Nosferatu*). Is the presence of cats due to their propensity to sit on the open book one is reading or the paper one is writing on?

14. Unfortunately, this strategy often backfires, playing into the hand of the vampire: it is precisely by writing letters and hence no longer belonging to the present that the victim enters into contact with the vampire, who himself does not belong to the present.

15. Matthew Edlund, *Psychological Time and Mental Illness* (New York: Gardner Press, 1987), 81.

16. Walter Benjamin, "The Work of Art in the Age of Mechanical Reproduction," in *Video Culture*, ed. John Hanhardt (Rochester, New York: Visual Studies Workshop Press, 1986), 43-44.

17. Alain Robbe-Grillet, *For a New Novel* (Evanston: Northwestern University Press, 1989), 152-3.

18. Ibid., 152.

19. Andre Bazin, *What is Cinema?* vol.I, trans. Hugh Gray (Berkeley: University of California Press, 1967), 107. Both in cases of multiple personalities with amnesiac barriers between them and of psychogenic fugues, one cannot always affirm that when a character leaves the frame he continues to exist, since his leaving the frame may coincide with his leaving one of his personalities.

20. Margiad Evans, *A Ray of Darkness*.

21. Bazin, *What is Cinema?* I:97.
22. Alain Robbe-Grillet, *La Maison de Rendez-vous* and *Djinn*, trans. Richard Howard/Yvone Lenard and Walter Wells (New York: Grove Press, 1987), 158.
23. Alain Robbe-Grillet, *Angelique: ou, l'enchantement* (Paris: Editions de Minuit, 1987), 38.
24. R.D. Laing, *The Divided Self*, 2nd ed. (New York: Penguin, 1965).
25. This facet of the fictional world of vampires cast the right actor for the role despite the incompetent director in the diegesis, who uses the actor he had earlier fired only once the latter has become free from his claustrophobia. The actor's stupor-inducing claustrophobia is a parapraxis of the fiction. A lot of "accidental" things are induced by the logic/necessity of the fiction but are discarded through the various sieves of the different stages of the production of a filmed fiction.
26. Michel de Certeau saw these words in a bathroom in a movie theatre.
27. Ingmar Bergman, *Persona and Shame*, trans. Keith Bradfield (New York: Grossman Publishers, 1972), 58.
28. Lewis Carroll, *Alice's Adventures in Wonderland & Through the Looking-Glass*, (New York: Nal Penguin, 1960), 16.
29. The narcissism in the shot of the inexistent mirror resides in that the index that Groucho looks at in order to ascertain whether he is looking at a mirror image of himself or whether an impersonator is miming him is his person only rather than the other objects in the hypothetical mirror. Or rather one should view this fixation not as indicative of narcissism but as induced by the fascination and slow-wit that takes hold of one in such situations.
30. «My Devil had been long caged, he came out roaring,» Robert Louis Stevenson, *Dr. Jekyll and Mr. Hyde* (New York: Nal Penguin, 1987), 115.
31. Ibid., 102.
32. Carroll, *Alice's Adventures in Wonderland & Through the Looking-Glass*, 26. In the LSD trip, one was replaced in the moment of surprise or lapse—the secretiveness of the transition from the normal to the altered state and vice versa—by the *dead ringer*; hence the fact that one's friends did not recognize one in the immediate aftermath of that moment (did one merely hallucinate that they did not?). Yoga makes it possible for the yogi to go through phase transitions without the lapses/swoons/unconsciousness that occur then and that permit possession and doubles. The yogi has no double, that is he manages, through psychomental withdrawal, to be absent from absence, to make his double absent, becoming/liberating the astral body.
33. Helmut Schmidt, "Evidence for Direct Interaction Between the Human Mind and External Quantum Processes," in *Mind at Large*, ed. Charles T. Tart, Harold E. Puthoff, Russell Targ (New York: Praeger Publishers, 1979), 211-3; Jahn and Dunn also found that some subjects had inverted results when they tried to influence random processes in a given direction, see Robert G. Jahn & Brenda J. Dunne, "Consciousness, Quantum Mechanics, and Random Physical Processes," in *Bergson and Modern Thought: Towards a Unified Science*, ed. Andrew

C. Papanicolaou & Pete A.Y. Gunter (Chu, Switzerland: Hardwood Academic Publishers, 1987), 277.

34. Another subject, K.G., had a positive scoring tendency: 52.5%. The odds against random fluctuations creating the difference between the results of K.G. and R.R. is more than 106 to 1.

35. Sigmund Freud, *The Interpretation of Dreams*, trans. and ed. James Strachey (New York: Avon Books, 1965), 357-8. The italicized "does" is Freud's; the two other instances of italicization are mine.

36. Ibid., 226.

37. Stan Brakhage, *Film at Wit's End* (New York: McPherson and Company, 1989), 104.

38. See Chapter 2, "The Michelson-Morley Experiment," in *The Relativity Explosion*, Martin Gardner, 2nd ed. (New York: Vintage Books, 1976).

39. The Kennedy-Thorndike experiment (1932) disproved the Lorentz hypothesis, «which gave a correct answer (the Lorentz-Fitzgerald contraction) by assuming an incorrect condition (the existence of the ether).»

40. Marguerite Duras, *Marguerite Duras*, contributors, Joel Farges et al., trans. Edith Cohen & Peter Conner (San Francisco: City Lights Books, 1987), 87.

41. Ibid., 103.

42. Ibid.

43. Deidi von Schaewen, *Walls* (New York: Pantheon Books, 1977).

44. «Nearby objects (many out of "view" of the patient's body) could often be seen (cardiac monitor behind the patient's bed, etc.)», Michael B. Sabom and Sarah S. Kreutziger, "Physicians Evaluate the Near-Death Experience," in *A Collection of Near-Death Research Readings*, compiled by Craig R. Lundahl (Chicago: Nelson-Hall, 1982), 150.

45. Andreas Mavromatis, *Hypnagogia: the unique state of consciousness between wakefulness and sleep* (New York, Routledge & Kegan Paul, 1987), 20.

46. Carl Theodor Dreyer, *Four Screenplays* (Bloomington: Indiana University Press, 1970), 101. The expression «the dead eyes of a blind person» is a metaphor made out of two terms that apply literally to the subject of the statement, since the blind person in question is dead, hence is another version of the literality of the figurative in the case of the undead and schizophrenics (see the section "Death," page 170).

47. B.W.Halstead, *Poisonous and Venomous Marine Animals of the World* (Princeton: Darwin Press, 1978), 714.

48. Wade Davis, *Passage of Darkness: The Ethnobiology of the Haitian Zombie* (Chapel Hill: The University of North Carolina Press, 1988), 156 and 159.

49. Ibid., 112.

50. Bazin is wrong when he writes «Montage plays no more of a decisive part in *Nosferatu* than in *Sunrise*», in *What is Cinema?* I:27.

51. *Edward Hopper*, text by LLoyd Goodrich (New York: Harry N. Abrams, 1989; originally published in 1970), 129. The at-an-angle look does not always denote matting/layering: in Godard's *Hail Mary*, Mary, who is looking in the

direction of the ground while sitting perpendicular to Joseph who is looking at her, answers his "regarde moi" with "je te regarde". Does the space between the two have positive curvature (Godard writes in "Vu par le boeuf et l'âne", *Le Nouvel Observateur*, January 6, 1984, p.14: "L'univers est courbe comme le ventre de toutes les mères?")?

52. For an interpretation of this scene/procedure in terms of fetishism, see Roger Dadoun's article "Fetishism in the Horror Film," in *Fantasy and the Cinema*, ed. James Donald (London: British Film Institute, 1989).

53. Sergei Eisenstein, *Film Form*, trans. Jay Leyda (New York: Harcourt, Brace and World, 1949), 197.

54. This paragraph was written in 1990 (Library of Congress copyright for the first version of *(Vampires)*: TXU 468-283, 3/13/1991). It was interesting to see a confirmation of this "povs between us" in *Until the End of the World*, released in the U.S. end of 1991, where a scientist succeeds in designing a camera which when coupled to a computer allows a blind person to "see" a simulation of a referential image on the condition that the latter be remembered by, seen in the mind's eye of the one who recorded it for the camera.

55. Constantin Stanislavski, *An Actor Prepares* (New York: Theater Arts, 1948), 26-7.

56. Jean-Paul Sartre, *Nausea*, trans. Lloyd Alexander (New York: New Directions Books, 1964), 10. Later, Sartre will write in *Being and Nothingness* (trans. with an introduction by Hazel E. Barnes. New York: Washington Square Press, 1956), p.583: «we hope simply that we have shown that the will is not a privileged manifestation of freedom but that it is a psychic event of a peculiar structure which is constituted on the same plane as other psychic events and which is supported, neither more nor less than the others, by an original, ontological freedom... freedom is one with the being of the For-itself.» It seems there is always an encounter/experience (even if it is a *gedanken* experiment) that reveals to one how unfree one is, inciting the search for freedom.

57. Caro W. Lippman, "Hallucinations of Physical Duality in Migraine," *Journal of Nervous and Mental Disease* 117 (1953), 347. The same applies in the case of Virginia Woolf's Rhoda in *The Waves*.

58. To check that the induction was successful the hypnotist may challenge the hypnotized person to raise his arm up from his lap or to separate his two hands.

59. Ernest R. Hilgard, *Divided Consciousness: Multiple Controls in Human Thought and Action*, 2nd ed. (New York: John Wiley & Sons, 1986), 100.

60. Sartre, *Nausea*, 9.

61. Once more, the vampire asked his hypnotized victim: "where are you now?"

62. In the latter case, the victim will probably have the illusion that he underwent a lapse, missed something, and hence that it could have been otherwise, but how can one miss what takes no time (the vampire, like a subatomic particle, has no trajectory)?

63. J. Sheridan Le Fanu, *In a Glass Darkly* (London: Eveleigh Nash and Grayson), 412.

64. Tunneling in cinema often requires quite a technical prowess, or an intricate coordination and/or an exacting matching in the rhythm of the movement in the two shots to either side of the barrier in order to form a seamless pan or zoom or tilt: the tunneling through the glass of the roof of the nightclub in Welles' *Citizen Kane*; the movement through the window bars in the shot near the end of Antonioni's *The Passenger*; the pan in Tarkovsky's *The Mirror* from the wife to the daughter to the mother in the background to the wife again now holding the son in the distant background. But it can be shown with as simple a device as using the sound of the banging of a door to indicate that although the person has closed the door we, now to the other side of the door, continue to see him (the latter shot, which appears in Hitchcock's *Stagefright* (1949), does not function there as a tunneling, but is an instance of an aesthetic where the sound and the image must not become redundant).

65. Roland Barthes, "The Third Meaning: Research Notes on Some Eisenstein Stills," in *Image, Music, Text*, essays selected and translated by Stephen Heath (New York: Hill and Wang, 1977).

66. Dreyer, *Four Screenplays*, 84 and 85.

67. Oliver Sacks, *Awakenings* (New York: HarperCollins Publishers, 1990), 112-113.

68. Le Fanu, *In a Glass Darkly*, 412.

69. Oil on canvas. 72,5 x 100 cm. Munch Museum.

70. Oil on canvas. 164 x 250 cm. Rasmus Meyers Samlinger.

71. Drypoint, etching and aquatint, 28.5 x 33 cm. Oslo Kommunes Kunstsamlinger.

72. Andre Bazin, *What is Cinema?* V.II, trans. Hugh Gray (Berkeley: University of California Press, 1967, 1971), 35.

73. Gilles Deleuze, *Cinema 1: The Movement Image*, trans. Hugh Tomlinson and Barbara Habberjam (Minneapolis: University of Minnesota Press, 1986), 33-4 (my italics).

74. *Kino-Eye: The Writings of Dziga Vertov*, edited with an introduction by Annette Michelson, trans. Kevin O'Brien (Berkeley: University of California Press, 1984), 41.

75. Bazin, *What is Cinema?* I:50-52.

76. "La Horla," in *The Dark Side of Guy de Maupassant*, a selection and translation by Arnold Kellett with introduction and notes; foreword by Ramsey Campbell (London: Xanadu, 1989), 76.

77. Stephen G. Gilligan, "Ericksonian Approaches to Clinical Hypnosis."

78. The undead, who can tunnel through obstacles, cannot tunnel through the earth on which she is standing in Andrew Wyeth's *Farm Road*. The victim saw the undead transfixed and walked away nonchalantly.

79. *Great Short Works of Fyodor Dostoevsky*, with an introduction by Ronald Hingley (New York: Harper and Row, 1968), 33.

80. Ibid., 38.

81. Michel Serres, *Statues: le second livre des fondations* (Paris: Editions François Bourin, 1987), 114.

82. Looking at the street from the cafe: this is the third homeless person to search in the same garbage can in the last five minutes; he is searching the same top three bags. The second homeless person had found an empty can that the first one had skipped. The garbage discarded by one homeless person is visited, as still not useless enough, by a second, then a third homeless— Something almost Buddhist in this gradation in nothing. A society that makes those it does not recycle, the homeless, recycle what it missed recycling.

83. Philippe Ariès, *Western Attitudes Toward Death: From the Middle Ages to the Present*, trans. Patricia M. Ranum (Baltimore: The Johns Hopkins University Press, 1975), 47.

84. Anders Stephanson, "Regarding Postmodernism—A Conversation with Fredric Jameson," *Social Text* 17, Fall 1987, 30.

85. IV, ii, 295-330. It may be Brutus' mistake to have told Varro and Claudius to sleep despite their offer to watch with/over him; though most probably, like Lucius, they also would have fallen asleep shortly afterwards.

86. Luke 22:41. How incisive is the laconism of this *a stone's throw*.

87. Matthew 26:36-45.

88. Hilgard, *Divided Consciousness*. The phenomenon of the hidden observer shows itself as covert hearing in hypnotic deafness.

89. Jalal Toufic had already wondered in *Distracted* (Barrytown, NY: Station Hill Press, 1991), page 61, in relation to the attempt to exclude the parasitical, how to film a close-up of a room.

90. A. Deikman in Mavromatis, *Hypnagogia*, 113.

91. Sergei Eisenstein, *Film Essays, with a lecture*, ed. Jay Leyda (London: Dennis Dobson, 1968), 150.

92. The falling in this painting is different both from the sliding of the meat from the bones in many Bacon paintings and from instances where the life and thickness is transferred from the person to the shadow—we find a beautiful example of that also in Coppola's *Dracula*, where the shadow of the hand of Dracula, of the one who does not appear in mirrors, knocks the inkpot over Mina's photograph—for instance in the middle panel of *Triptych* (1986-87), where the hands of the person sitting on the chair are not painted, or rather are overpainted (almost a la Arnulf Rainer): this transference is a vaccination against a fall (the chair has only two visible legs), hence a minimal fall.

93. Paul Barber, *Vampires, Burial, and Death: folklore and reality* (New Haven: Yale Press, 1988).

94. Alain Robbe-Grillet, *La Maison de Rendez-vous*, 141.

95. Alain Robbe-Grillet, *Last Year at Marienbad*, trans. Richard Howard (New York: Grove Press, 1962), 20.

96. Bergman, *Persona*, 29-30.

97. Raul Ruiz/Jean-Louis Schefer, "L'image, La Mort, La Mémoire: Dialogues imaginaires," *Revue Ça Cinéma* 20 (1980), 53.

98. Fear manifests itself in the section on LSD in *Distracted* (pp. 186-199), where being in a hurried time is relayed by the swish pan induced by fear.

99. The mask does not necessarily indicate a swish pan induced by something scary in the area of the body that is covered by it, but could be a swish pan that relates to the manifest parts: while you are staring at a non-masked area, seeing its minutest details, the adjoining mask signals that you had already, all along, done a swish pan of averting. An *aparté*: a "what am I seeing?" that is copresent with the seeing.

100. *Therefore* knowing that while in *Lucybelle Crater and her 40 yr old husband Lucybelle Crater*, 1969-71, Meatyard is behind the male mask and his wife Madelyn is behind the female mask that recurs in the other Lucybelle Crater photographs, in *Lucybelle Crater And Close Friend Lucybelle Crater In The Grape Arbor*, 1971, he is behind the recurring female mask, while Madelyn is behind the male mask, does not allow us to deduce that the mask plays at least in this instance the role of hiding the identity of the one behind it (therefore such a switching cannot function as an occultation, a masking of the real significance of the mask behind the traditional role it has, that of hiding what is behind it). Such knowledge remains merely anecdotal, gossip.

101. Hence these masks have little to do with those in the work of Cindy Sherman (an admirer of Meatyeard), which are hysterical; if we do not consider the masks in Meatyard's Lucybelle Crater series as produced by the fear-induced swish pan, but view them as pertaining to those shown in the photographs, the indistinguishability between the latter is psychotic (no mirror-image) rather than, as in Sherman's Historical Portraits series, hysterical.

102. The words in italics in the brackets are my additions to the captions that appear in *Ralph Eugene Meatyard: An American Visionary*, ed. Barbara Tannenbaum (New York: Akron Art Museum and Rizzoli International Publications, 1991).

103. Patricia Highsmith, *Ripley's Game* (New York: Penguin Books, 1974).

104. Hence the beauty of finding what in Bacon's work functions, in its overall effect, in the manner of traditional mirrors, namely the circles (see the section "Pain")—indeed, the blue of the circle around the head of the right figure in Bacon's *Studies from the Human Body* (1975) is identical to that of the adjoining mirrors—inside the mirror, which in Bacon's paintings does not have a reflecting role but a pinning-absorbing role (or rather the mirror can have both functions, as we see in the right panel of *Triptych Inspired by T.S. Eliot's Poem "Sweeney Agonistes"*, 1967: the man on the phone has been totally absorbed in the mirror, while we see the feet of one of the lying men and the edge of the bed reflected in the mirror) in the left panel of *Triptych*, 1987.

105. Mavromatis, *Hypnagogia*, 20.

106. Not even by temporal blocking; in Robert Wilson's theater the spectator is momentarily distracted from some of the simultaneous different happenings only to suddenly (Wilson creating jump cuts through the simultaneity of different

continuous actions) remember that other happenings are taking place as well (it is changes in the unattended stimuli that alters the suppression (almost a study in *binocular rivalry*)), this temporal blocking creating an off-screen inside the screen.

107. Bazin, *What is Cinema?* I:107. Both Bazin and Benjamin invoke the revolver, the former to write on the screen as the center of the universe (this is not accidental, since the moment of proscribed montage, the moment when the screen-as-center-of-the-universe becomes the clearest for Bazin is when death is close by, Chaplin and the lion having both to be within the frame-as-cage), the latter, invoking the bullet and ballistics, to write about the decentering effect of place and shot changes in film.

108. *Hitchcock*, François Truffaut, with the collaboration of Helen G. Scott, revised edition (New York: Simon and Schuster, 1984), 200-201.

109. Ibid., 256 (see also pp. 252-254: for *North By Northwest*, an exact copy was made of the United Nation's lobby; in *The Birds*, the restaurant is an exact copy of a restaurant in Bodega Bay, and the house of the farmer who's killed by the birds is an exact replica of an existing farm there—the same entrance, halls, rooms, kitchen; even the scenery seen from the window is accurate, etc.).

110. Bazin, *What is Cinema?* I:105 and 107.

111. Carl Theodor Dreyer, *Dreyer in Double Reflection*, trans. and ed. Donald Skoller (New York: Dutton, 1973), 141.

112. There are few other instances when music in cinema becomes legitimate: in films like Syberberg's *Parsifal*, with its *coincidence* between the voice and the body (foregrounded by the fact that two actors, one male and one female, claim the voice) but also with the floating of the background, which has lost its materiality (a frontal projection), and has become fluid, changeable, like music; when over-heard telepathically by someone in the diegesis—saving him from the diegetic silence-over.

113. Ernest R. Hilgard, *Divided Consciousness*, 79.

114. Frazer quoted in Sigmund Freud, *Totem and Taboo*, trans. James Strachey (New York: W.W. Norton & Company, 1950), 55.

115. Ibid.

116. Freud, *Totem and Taboo*, 60.

117. Frieda Schaechter, "The language of the voices," in *Language Behavior in Schizophrenia: Selected Readings in Research and Theory*, comp. and ed. Harold J. Vetter (Springfield, Ill.: Thomas, 1968), 151.

118. Hence there is no need to try to validate the latter by the former through the following device found in many vampire films and books: one of the first stages of the journey toward the vampire's castle is the stop at the inn of the villagers and/or the encounter with the Gypsies (Murnau's and Herzog's *Nosferatus*, Browning's *Dracula*, Fisher's *The Horror of Dracula*, etc.). This to make it seem the villagers are giving credit to the distortion by the fiction films of the figure of vampire as it originally appears, for instance in the legends of the Slavic peasants.

119. In many cases the blurriness of a Richter photopainting is rather due to a frozen *presence* that has to be inferred from the blurriness it brings about in the visible, present elements.

120. Friedrich Nietzsche, letter to Jacob Burckhardt, January 5, 1889, in *Selected Letters of Friedrich Nietzsche*, trans. Christopher Middleton (Chicago: University of Chicago Press, 1969), 347.

121. *Gerhard Richter* (London: Tate Gallery, 1991), 110.

122. Hence *Erna (Akf auf einer Treppe)*, 1966, this other Nude Descending a Staircase, implies by means of the blurriness that each of the decomposed stages of Duchamp's *Nude Descending a Staircase* is still a composition.

123. It is not the same Nietzsche in the two positions, and, of course, this is not merely because in one he is the subject of the enunciation and in the other the *I* of the statement. *All the names of history are I* is there to remind us that the preceding enumeration includes *I am Nietzsche*, which is the most uncanny.

124. Nancy Burson, Richard Carling and David Kramlich, *Composites: computer-generated portraits* (New York: Beech Tree Books, 1986).

125. In Syberberg's cinema it is space itself that imagines and remembers by means of the frontal projection.

126. Mavromatis, *Hypnagogia*, 73.

127. *Life*, February 1989, 62.

128. Tzvetan Todorov, *The Fantastic: A Structural Approach to a Literary Genre*, trans. Richard Howard (Ithaca: Cornell University Press, 1975), 40.

129. Eisenstein, *Film Form*, 106.

130. M. Bouvier & J.L. Leutrat, *Nosferatu* (Paris: Gallimard, 1981), 210-211.

131. *Dreyer in Double Reflection*, 159.

132. Mircea Eliade, *Yoga: Immortality and Freedom*, **trans.** Willard R. Trask, 2nd ed. (Princeton, N.J.: Princeton University Press, 1969). 53.

133. Mircea Eliade, *Rites and Symbols of Initiation: The Mysteries of Birth and Rebirth*, trans. Willard R. Trask (Harper Torchbooks, 1975), 90.

134. Sergei Eisenstein, *Film Form*, 42 (my underlining).

135. Except in the case of tunneling.

136. In Bacon's *Double Portrait of Lucien Freud and Frank Auerbach*, 1964, part of the right leg and arm of the person in the right panel are hidden by a chair: this is not merely due to the point of view from which the painting is rendered, but to the fact that what is not seen in this instance is withdrawn from metamorphosis, with the consequence that the telepath, who is not limited by the angle of view, will still see the view from only that angle.

137. Raymond T. McNally and Radu Florescu, *In Search of Dracula: A True History of Dracula and Vampire Legends* (Greenwich, Connecticut: New York Graphic Society, 1972), 43.

138. Stoker, *Dracula*, 43.

139. Ernest Jones, *The Life and Work of Sigmund Freud, v.3: The Last Phase 1919-1939* (New York: Basic Books, 1957), chapter 14.

140. Ilya Prigogine & Isabelle Stengers, *Entre le temps et l'éternité* (Librairie Artheme Fayard, 1988), 60.

141. Jorge Luis Borges, *The Book of Sand*, trans. Norman Thomas Di Giovanni (New York: E.P.Dutton, 1977).

142. In Robert Zemeckis' *Back to the Future 2* (1989), when the two versions of the doctor are in the same frame, one of them having come from the future, instead of witnessing a convincing simulation of a natural interaction between the two during their brief conversation—and we know from *Who Framed Roger Rabbit* that Zemeckis is quite adroit at making the matted and non-matted characters interact convincingly, even in the limit case of an interaction between human and animation characters—the spectator sees one of them at times look aside while speaking to the other, at other times have his back to him, so that the eye-directions of the two do not match. It is due to the taboo on encountering one's double that the spectator witnesses this non-convincing matting. Some artists/writers try to find situations where the awkwardness and sloppiness that plagued their earlier writings/filmmaking is now necessitated by the subject matter itself and is this time executed soberly and in control (that some of the anxiety induced in the version of the doctor that has come from the future for the split second when he glimpses himself before he swish pans his gaze is displaced to the film director makes of this remake not some school exercise, but still a challenge): a *back to the future*.

143. David Thouless, "Condensed matter physics in less than three dimensions," in *The New Physics*, ed. Paul Davies (Cambridge: Cambridge University Press, 1989), 209.

144. Gail Kligman, *The Wedding of the Dead* (Berkeley: University of California Press, 1988).

145. The unknown young woman he met in Barcelona accompanies him to an appointment set for Robertson with a woman named Marina, whom he, Locke, has never met before. No one shows up. Though he later remarks that he is encountering more and more coincidences, strangely enough it never occurs to him that the young woman who was with him in the car may have been Marina.

146. In the future an abyss will grow between the utilitarian direction of technology and scientific-religious depth.

147. Peter Handke, *Nonsense and Happiness*, trans. Michael Roloff (New York: Urizen Books, 1976).

148. Robbe-Grillet, *La Maison de Rendez-vous*, 143.

149. Duras has her own solution: in order to remember, one must not go back to see the same film (*India Song*) an n+1 time, but see another film either with the same image track but a different sound track, or with the same sound track but a different image track (*Son Nom de Venise*). A memory haunted by amnesia (since the appearance of the double often signals demise), rather than, as in *Hiroshima Mon Amour*, fated to forgetfulness.

150. Mavromatis, *Hypnagogia*, 30.

151. Stanislavski, *An Actor Prepares*, 54.

152. Ibid., 55.

153. Akira Kurosawa, *Something Like an Autobiography* (New York: Alfred A. Knoff, 1982), 197.

154. David Pirie, *The Vampire Cinema* (Leicester, England: Galley Press, 1977), 54.

155. Jahn & Dunne, 295.

156. See for instance figure 14 in Jahn & Dunne, 286-289.

157. T. S. Eliot, *The Waste Land and other poems* (New York: Harcourt, Brace and World, 1934), 43.

158. Hilgard, *Divided Consciousness*, 258.

159. Le Fanu, *In a Glass Darkly*, 459.

160. Gerald S. Wilkinson, "Food Sharing in Vampire Bats," *Scientific American*, February 1990, 76.

161. This in part explains the excessive weariness of the people in the book, as if only a fire could wake them from their sleep, and indeed the first section of the book consists of photographs of fires.

162. Mavromatis, *Hypnagogia*, 163.

163. In the case of Dreyer's *Vampyr*, where the vampire in the diegesis is not an aristocrat, the film's producer and main actor is an aristocrat: Baron Nicolas de Gunzburg.

164. quoted in Mavromatis, *Hypnagogia*, 175.

165. quoted in Brooks Riley, "I am like the jungle at the creation," *Film Comment* (November-December), 1979, 45.

166. One notices an intriguing similarity between reports of the transportation of an item of extended death (undeath) and those of extended life (cryonics): compare the *Nosferatu* intertitle to «The first embryos were sent from Oldham to David Whitting *for freezing* in London—by courtesy of British Railways *and the guards on the Manchester-London expresses can have had no idea of the moments contents of the packages they handled for us so efficiently!*» (my italics).

167. Lotte Eisner, *Murnau* (Berkeley: University of California Press, 1973), 224.

168. An observer on the outside of a black hole's event horizon is not affected by the breakdown of predictability at the singularity, for no signal can reach him from it. Are black holes' singularities the universe's hallucinations? What goes on in the mind of the schizophrenic and of those on LSD is as objective as what goes on inside a black hole, where time, space and the laws of physics no longer function.

169. Schizophrenia being an altered state of the mind, a far from equilibrium state of consciousness, it is not surprising that the schizophrenic sometimes feels that a specific, rather mundane change, for example whether or not one falls asleep before a specific hour, whether or not one goes through a door, will radically alter the state of the universe—a phenomenon similar to the *butterfly*

effect encountered in the case of the weather, that paradigm for chaotic, far from equilibrium states.

170. Ariès, *Western Attitudes toward Death*, 34-37.

171. Franz Kafka, *The Complete Stories*, ed. Nahum N. Glatzer (New York: Schocken Books, 1971), 254-6.

172. See Toufic, *Distracted*, 114. There is no excuse for Wenders' betrayal of Nicholas Ray in *Lightning Over Water*, since around the same period that he was betraying Ray, he made a film, *Reverse Angle*, critical of Coppola's betrayal of him during *Hammett*.

173. Dreyer, *Dreyer in Double Reflection*, 163 (my italics).

174. Lawrence O'Toole, "I feel that I'm close to the center of things," interview with Werner Herzog, *Film Comment* (November-December), 1979.

175. Werner Herzog, *Fitzcarraldo: The Original Story*, trans. Martje Herzog & Alan Greenberg (San Francisco: Fjord Press, 1982), 157.

176. Bruce Lamb quoted in Stanislav Grof, *The Adventure of Self-Discovery* (Albany: State University of New York Press, 1988), 54-55.

177. "I feel that I'm close to the center of things," 41.

178. Carlos Castaneda, *Tales of Power* (New York: Washington Square Press, 1974), 72.

179. In 1972, Anne Rice's 5-year-old daughter, Michelle, died of Leukemia. While writing her first vampire book, and «unaware of the significance of what she was doing, she added a beautiful little girl with Golden curls (like Michelle), whom the vampires save from mortal death by making her a vampire... The first version ended with the child, Claudia, and Louis happily joining other vampires in Paris. In the revision, «I felt that Claudia had really been meant to die at the end of "Interview" the way Michelle had died...

««In cheating»—that is, in allowing Claudia to live,—Rice says she did herself psychic damage: «I almost died myself and went kind of crazy. I saw germs on everything and washed my hands 50 times and really cracked up... If somebody is meant to die and you don't do it, you're really risking your well-being at the end of the book.»» in "Novels You Can Sink Your Teeth Into," Susan Ferraro, *The New York Times Magazine*, October 14, 1990, pp. 74 and 76.

180. H. Strangerup transposing the reaction of the critics to *Gertrud*: «Dreyer aurait du mourir dix ans plus tôt, après *Ordet*... Oui, c'était vrai: Dreyer était un homme mort. Le bruit se répandait qu'il s'agissait du film sénile d'un metteur en scène sénile,» in "L'accueil de Gertrud à Paris," *Cahiers du Cinéma* 207, December 1968, 73-74.

181. Some use themselves as the experimental sample, their writing as the control sample.

182. Vladimir Nabokov, *Despair* (New York: Vintage International, 1989), 15-16.

183. Or we could view the three shots that immediately precede the aforementioned sequence as the index that his mind has changed: in the first shot he is standing on an escalator looking around; in the second shot, someone

standing on the escalator, a few feet in front of him, falls at the ramp; the third shot is a close-up of Jonathan looking. The shot showing the man falling on the escalator in front of Jonathan parallels the shot, later in the film, when the man he shoots in the back falls on the escalator (it functions as a kind of extra-diegetic presentiment). In both cases, one should abstain from looking for, postulating a psychological decision (not even in the form of: "not deciding is a decision, by default").

184. Philip K. Dick, *Eye in the Sky* (New York: Collier Books, 1957), 195-197.

185. Louis Althusser, "Ideology and Ideological State Apparatuses (Notes Towards an Investigation)," in *Video Culture*, ed. John Hanhardt (Rochester, New York: Visual Studies Workshop Press, 1986), 86.

186. We have an implicit *reconnaissance* for those we recognize, including ourselves.

187. Pencil on paper, 23x30.7 cm. Oslo, Oslo Community Art Collection, Munch Museum.

188. Crayon on plate. 75x57. Munch Museum.

189. Whether the oil, pastel and casein on cardboard. 91x73.5 cm. Oslo, National Gallery; or the tempera on plate. 83.5x66 cm. Munch Museum.

190. Oil on canvas, 93x72 cm. Munch Museum.

191. Pastel and oil on canvas. Oslo, private collection. Formerly Collection Arthur von Franquet, Braunschweig.

192. The bad temptation is to short-circuit the coming out short of words, the scream, instead of enduring it until music begins («It is Heinrich Heine who said that where the words come out short there music begins»), superimposing a music-over: «when they [the paintings] were brought together, suddenly a single musical note went through them and they became completely different from what they had been.»

193. Oil on canvas, 67x100 cm. Rasmus Meyers Samlinger.

194. Lithograph, 46.5x56.5 cm. Oslo Kommunes Kunstsamlinger.

195. Oil on canvas. 89x82 cm. Munch Museum.

196. Oil on canvas. 78x114 cm. Munch Museum.

197. Nicholas Abraham and Maria Torok, *The Wolf Man's Magic Word*, trans. Nicholas Rand, foreword by Jacques Derrida (Minneapolis: University of Minnesota Press, 1986).

198. The presence in many of Hitchcock's films of characters who have to copy someone else—in *Rebecca*, the new wife, who has to copy Rebecca; in *Vertigo*, Judy, who has to copy Madeleine Elster, who is supposedly copying Carlotta Valdes—echoes Hitchcock's placing the utmost importance on the story-board (which has to be copied by the cinematographer, Hitchcock never looking into the viewfinder).

199. The same way that in Islam and Jewish religion man is in the image of a God who has no image, in many of the films that deal with the failure of mourning we have the case of someone asked or who himself/herself tries to be in the image of the dead, who has no image.

200. What happens when one always opts for history in the alternative history/forgery? There is an extra body (the other instance of the multiplication of bodies is produced by freezing/immobilization: Bokanowski's *L'Ange*, Munch's *The Sphinx*, etc.): the buried body of a woman who is mistaken for Rebecca in *Rebecca*; the scene with the two Madeleines in the tower in *Vertigo*—this extra body shows that the alternative forgery/history is/hides an objective non-psychological undecidability between the two terms of the alternative. One could therefore say that within the economy of Hitchcock's films, a corpse should never be buried in secret (*The Trouble with Harry*), wasted, for it will be needed. Superimposed on this reason for the failure to successfully bury the corpse incognito are two more reasons. 1) The taboo on unfinished business: the dead person has to be recognized by the authorities as dead, his death has to be inscribed, accounted for in the public register. The insufficiency of four or more people knowing of his death in their role as private citizens is compounded by the fact that they manifest symptoms of obsessional neurosis. 2) Which leads us to the second additional reason for the recurrent failure of the burial: *The Trouble with Harry* (1954) is a sort of case study of obsessional neurosis: the understatement that characterizes the characters' reactions to events is an instance of *isolation*, the depriving of an event of the affect; the erasure of the event of the discovery of the corpse by six people, indeed of all the events between the double discovery of the corpse by a child for whom the day after today is yesterday (were we, as in Godard's *Bande à part* (1964), to have a voice-over recapitulation of what had already occurred in the film for the benefit of those spectators who arrived late, in this case at the point at the very end of the film when the boy sees the corpse, it would say: "nothing has been missed")—which is the other way of reacting to unfinished business: magically erase what is asking for the deployment of its consequences. The recurrent burying of the corpse and digging it up is therefore an example of a *diaphasic symptom* (see Chapter VI in Sigmund Freud's *Inhibitions, Symptoms and Anxiety*); it also can be viewed from the perspective of the obsessive's doubt as to whether he has performed a certain act, in this case, whether he has buried the corpse, so that he has to repeatedly dig up the corpse to check that he did actually bury it.

201. Though he seems to have sensed the proximity of the alternative he is oblivious about, hence his further highlighting of history through making the characters involved in the forgery explicitly interested in history: the husband's genuine historical interest in the San Francisco of bygone years; Scottie's visit to the bookstore to get historical information about Carlotta.

202. An episode that seems to have been modeled on Freud's uncanny encounter with the double on a train (going to Tara?), related in "The Uncanny," in *Standard Edition of the Complete Psychological Works of Sigmund Freud XVII*, ed. James Strachey (London: Hogarth Press, 1958), 248.

203. "The aftereffects of Hypnosis" in *Hypnotic Susceptibility*, Ernest R. Hilgard, with a chapter by Josephine R. Hilgard (New York: Harcourt, Brace & World, 1965), 58.

204. The more wide-ranging the observation the more universal is the interaction, but the very limit of observation, total observation, has already instituted freezing (Henri Bergson is right in writing that the photograph is taken in things). What is imperceptible is the passage from universal interaction, which occurs as we asymptotically approach *omnipresence* (continuous observation), to the freezing. Indeed, the asymptotic nature of this omnipresence is not experienced within the universal interaction realm, as a failure in it (hence one should not enclose "*omnipresence*" within quotation marks), but tangentially, as the inferred imperceptibility of the switch from universal interaction to freezing. For all practical purposes—a joke, since universal interaction and freezing are reached only when the practical has been suspended—universal interaction and freezing coexist.

205. R.L. Pfleegor & L.Mandel, "Interference of Independent Photon Beams", *Physical Review* 159, no.5, 25 July 1967.

206. One of the hypotheses concerning the cause for hypnosis in animals (it has been observed in insects, crustaceans, fish, amphibians, reptiles, chicken (Herzog's *Every Man for Himself and God Against All*), lower mammals...) is that it is a *death feigning* mechanism. It is also *death feigning* in the case of human beings: unless one reaches very deep trance (and even then?), the unconscious attained in hypnosis is not the unconscious of death. The former unconscious remains open to chronology (for instance the hypnotist may, when faced during ideomotor signaling with the raising of the finger that signals an unwillingness to answer, address the subject's unconscious and suggest that it work on the issue in question till the next meeting, when it is to be ready and willing to answer), and to implication ("you will fall asleep" given in the tricky form of an implied implication: "you may fall asleep very soon, or in five minutes").

207. Werner Herzog, *Of Walking in Ice*, trans. Martje Herzog & Alan Greenberg (New York: Tanam Press, 1980), 5. Eisner died on November 25, 1983.

208. Monday, 12/14/92. Will I ever read the last entry of *Of Walking in Ice* without crying?

209. The fact that in mystery stories that do not resort to twins or biological doubles the person in one location is revealed not to really look like the one in the other location does not prove that the alibi was not a valid alibi, for, due to the absence of mirror-image in many instances of dissociation/doubling, even were the same person simultaneously in two places, s/he would most probably look very different in the two locations. Hence the *false* in *false alibi* does not necessarily indicate an alibi that turns out not to be one, it having been demonstrated that we were really dealing with two different persons at the two different locations; it may rather indicate that the alibi is, because of the absence of mirror-image, most often intrinsically false and hence that the predicate *false* rather than undoing the alibi, on the contrary often confirms it (in which case the incredulity about an alibi such as the one in Christie's *Thirteen at Dinner* is not only due to the purported impossibility for a person to be simultaneously in two different locations but is also due to the looking alike of the person in

the two different locations despite the absence of mirror-image). It is most probably the case that this facet of false alibi and dissociation/doubling was unconsciously taken into account by *Despair*'s Hermann while devising his crime. It is thus disappointing that those who apprehend Hermann do not recognize the perfection of his crime: they do not acknowledge that a crime where the criminal is caught can still be the perfect crime (the possible change of the name of the one who died and/or of those who continue to live after the former's death can occasion another variant where the criminal is caught *and* we have a perfect crime).

210. Alan Greenberg, *Heart of Glass* (Munchen, Skellig, 1976), 21.

211. With the concomitant implied blankness, suggested absence of any elements in the section that will function as a matte: there are no Palestinians («In Israel today it is the custom officially to refer to the Palestinians as "so-called Palestinians," which is a somewhat gentler phrase than Golda Meir's flat assertion in 1969 that the Palestinians did not exist» (Edward Said, *The Question of Palestine*, 2nd ed. (New York: Vintage Books, 1992), pp. 4-5); «The Zionists made it their claim that Britain was blocking their greater penetration of Palestine. Between 1922 and 1947 the great issue witnessed by the world in Palestine was not, as a Palestinian would like to imagine, the struggle between natives and colonists, but a struggle presented as being between Britain and the Zionists. The full irony of this remarkable epistemological achievement—... the sheer blotting out from knowledge of almost a million natives—is enhanced when we remember that in 1948, at the moment that Israel declared itself a state, it legally owned a little more than 6 percent of the land of Palestine and its population of Jews consisted of a fraction of the total Palestinian population» (ibid., 23)). Jean Genet relates in his *Prisoner of Love* (page 24) a game of cards he witnessed in which the participants, Palestinian fighters, played, gambled without having any cards in their hands.

212. 780,000 Arab Palestinians were dispossessed and displaced in 1948.

213. *American Cinematographer*, July 1988, 48.

214. When, near the end of the film, Marnie and her husband return to her mother's house, it is raining. The water makes the ship as well as the painted bricks of the houses look glossy. When the film's director of photography, Robert Burks, and the production designer, Robert Boyle, remarked to Hitchcock how phony the set looked, Hitchcock's response was: «I don't see anything wrong with it Bob. I think it looks fine.»

215. The shot of Marnie and her husband coming to visit Marnie's mother foreshadowed the penetration of the trauma/painted-backdrop since it showed lightning *behind* the ship in the background.

216. Just as Marnie leaves the house in the company of her husband, she looks in the direction of the children playing on the street. Shot of the children, with two boys, their baseball gloves on, giving her their back, but with nobody in the direction in which the latter are facing, that of the ship. It almost looks like a typical Hitchcock blot/anomaly (such as the revolving of one windmill

in the opposite direction to the wind in *Foreign Correspondent*). A shot that has a psychotic tonality, does not get totalized in the happy ending, mars it, maintains things in suspension. Following the character's reenactment of the traumatic event, the spectator has to himself/herself repeat, by rewinding in order to look closely at the shot, until s/he can discern what actually occurred: for the interval of a few frames at the beginning of the shot a third boy is shown running off-frame to fetch the ball, so that the two boys standing still in the rest of the shot are waiting for him.

217. It is difficult to miss the irony in the subtitle to Coppola's *Dracula*: "Love Never Dies". Love never accompanies us over the threshold of death, for beyond death is not eternity but the labyrinthine absence of time. Indeed, that is probably why Dracula cannot meet his wife despite the fact that as someone who committed suicide, and as a consequence was witheld burial in consecrated ground, she is herself an undead. Hence the appropriateness of the lyrics we hear at one point in *Buffy, the Vampire Slayer*: "Lovers... enjoy your time while you can".

218. While the U. S. forces were returning Iraq back to the pre-industrial age.

219. Nor, as Saddam would like to believe, Nabuchodonosor. Nor is Baghdad (illuminated by the fireworks of ineffective ground-air defense on the first day of the Gulf War), as in one shot in Herzog's otherwise sublime *Lessons of Darkness* (1991), Kuwait City (on the initial day of the Iraqi invasion). It is praiseworthy to consider flying to Mars or Saturn to find «images that are still pure and clean and transparent» (from an interview with Herzog in *Tokyo Ga*); unfortunately the danger then is that from such a distance one might easily mistake Baghdad for mere Kuwait City. Blair's Jacob Maker, more sober, visited many planets without incurring such mistakes.

220. "Iis" is the present third singular of "bee".

221. Nabokov, *Despair*, 27.

222. Nigel Andrews, "Dracula in Delft," *American Film* 4 (1), 1978, 33.

223. Jan-Christopher Horak, "W.H. or the mysteries of walking in ice," in *The Films of Werner Herzog: Between Mirage and History*, ed. Timothy Corrigan (New York: Methuen, 1986), 26.

224. Ibid.

225. Andre Bazin, *What is Cinema?* I:9.

226. Until 1951 the film base was made of cellulose nitrate, which is explosive and chemically unstable and even under the best storage conditions does not last more than fifty years. More than half the films made in the United States are destroyed. Only seventy-five of Méliès' over five hundred films still exist. In 1941, in Sweden, the negative of all the films produced by the film production company Svenska—which produced all the films of Mauritz Stiller and Victor Sjostrom—from 1907 till then were burned in an explosion: «the negatives of 95 percent of all films produced in Sweden in the preceding thirty-four years were destroyed in a few minutes» ("Filmic Evidence," in *Film History: Theory and Practice*, Robert C. Allen & Douglas Gomery (New York: Newbery Award Records, 1985), 32). An effort has been made to transfer as much as possible of the nitrate

stock to acetate stock, the latter, used in films made past 1951, being stable. But as of 1985, the Library of Congress still had 80 million feet of nitrate film. This is not all: most color films made past 1950 (the year Eastman Kodak introduced its multi-layer film that replaced the much more stable Technicolor system) are subject to color fading; Nestor Almendros: "In ten years, the films I've made I'm sure will have vanished. The museums of the future will have lots of well preserved black and white films and nothing of our time" ("Colour Problem," *Sight & Sound* 30, no. 1 (Winter 1980-81), 12-3).

227. M.-L. Potrel-Dorget, "Dialectique du surhomme et du sous-homme dans quelques film d'Herzog," *Revue du cinema* 342.

228. Eliane Escoubas, "L'Œil (du) teinturier," *Critique* 418 (Mars, 1982), 231.

229. Michel Foucault, *Discipline and Punish: Birth of the Prison*, trans. A. Sheridan (New York: Pantheon, 1977), 196-7.

230. Antonin Artaud, *The Theater and its Double*, trans. Mary Caroline Richards (New York: Grove Press, 1958), 24.

231. René Girard, "The Plague in Literature and Myth," in *To Double Business Bound: Essays on Literature, Mimesis, and Anthropology* (Baltimore: The John Hopkins University Press, 1978).

232. Dreyer, *Dreyer in Double Reflection*, 144.

233. Serge Daney, *Ciné Journal, 1981-1986*, preface by Gilles Deleuze (Paris: Cahiers du cinema, 1986), 125.

234. Paul Virilio's *Esthètique de la disparition* (Editions Balland, 1980) on petit mal and the editing the latter makes possible. This confirmed what one *discovered* after reading it through taking LSD and in relation to schizophrenics.

235. Not to be included in this extendible list are instances where an external similarity between film and the world occurs: both Chaplin's *The Gold Rush* (1925) and John Ford's *The Iron Horse* (1924) deal among other things with the frontier, show small towns that were built so to speak overnight (one of the intertitles of *The Gold Rush* states: «One of the many cities of the far north, built overnight during the great gold rush») and then disassembled when the train workers had to move on to the next stage of the construction of the train tracks or when the gold diggers having exhausted the gold in a certain area or having found none there moved on. We are the closest here to film sets, which are either disassembled or left behind, deserted, once the shoot is over. This similarity must have given some filmmakers an intuitive affinity for the subject of the frontier, for instance for Westerns.

236. Bazin, *What is Cinema?* I:107.

237. In Coppola's *Dracula* (1992), the first time we see Dracula walking in the streets of London (1897), we both hear the sound of a film projector and see the passers-by move in the manner we have come to associate with people filmed at 18 frames per second and projected at 24 frames per second.

238. Mavromatis, *Hypnagogia*, 25.

239. Heinrich von Kleist had already beautifully written about the grace of what is either marionette or god in "Sur le théâtre de marionnettes".

240. One can imagine buildings being from the advent of Wodiczko's projections build from materials that absorb the light that he projects on them, *Stealth buildings*.

241. To an unexpected gesture the other can link by changing his/her behavior, with the latter alteration the effect of the gesture; or one can be sensitive to the manner of linking, in this case to the unexpectedness, so that the absence of connection occasions another absence of connection with his/her past.

242. The historical figure Dracula practiced impalement; in Stoker's novel we have an inversion and Dracula, now a vampire, has to be killed by impaling.

243. We are far removed from archaic societies among other things because of the breech of the aura (reproduction; detail of reproduction) but also because when we do a close-up of part of the carving or sculpture from such societies we call it a detail, when for archaic societies *pars pro toto*: «the part *is* at one and the same time also the whole... if you receive an ornament made of a bear's tooth, it signifies the whole bear has been given to you...» (Sergei Eisenstein, *Film Form*, 132). In this respect, we come closest to their way of thinking when we are dealing with situations of self-similarity, for instance holograms or fractal objects.

244. Though to the film spectator the mysterious figure does not look overexposed, an undead would speak about the excess of light when referring to such a figure. Film, this art of "light and shadows", rarely achieves true figures of light. Another instance of figures of light, figures that manifest characteristics we associate with light, are the immobile man and woman sitting around the table under an overexposed lamp in Ernie Gehr's *Wait*: their immobility is due to the fact that in the case of light time stops (the same way the spectator, by a visual illusion, sees colors and Gehr's black and white *History*, on two or three occasions s/he sees the two figures briefly move).

245. Oil on canvas, 84.5 x 121 cm.

246. Daniel Paul Schreber, *Memoirs of My Nervous Illness*, trans. and ed. Ida Macalpine & Richard A. Hunter, introduction by Samuel M. Weber (Cambridge: Harvard University Press, 1988), 126.

247. See also *Distracted*, 158-163.

248. The movement was technically produced by moving very quickly the Hi-8 video camera, with shutter speed of 100,000.